WOO

WOODWORK

G. W. BRAZIER
B.E.M., D.L.C. (HONS.)
Principal Lecturer, Handicraft,
Dudley College of Education

N. A. HARRIS
M.C.C. Ed
Head of Technical Department,
King Edward VI Grammar School, Stafford

METRIC
EDITION

1971

CHATTO & WINDUS
LONDON

Published by
Chatto & Windus (Educational) Ltd
42 William IV Street
London W.C.2

✳

Clarke, Irwin & Co Ltd
Toronto

First published 1958
Reprinted 1959, 1960, 1962, 1965
Second edition – revised and extended 1969
Third edition—metric 1971

ISBN 0 7010 0045 7 *Non-Net*
ISBN 0 7011 0565 8 *Net*

© G. W. Brazier and N. A. Harris 1958, 1969 and 1971

Printed in Great Britain by
Butler and Tanner Ltd
Frome and London

PREFACE
TO METRIC EDITION

In this new edition the sections devoted to construction, adhesives, mechanical principles and special tools have been considerably expanded. In addition to this, the section devoted to the history of furniture has been extended to the present day and includes the latest materials and techniques of construction. The new edition therefore covers up to the Advanced level of G.C.E. By suitable selection, students working for either O level of G.C.E. or for C.S.E. may be guided to discard those blocks of material which are surplus to their requirements. Student handicraft teachers in Colleges of Education will find the book to be a valuable source of reference, while those studying for National Certificate Examinations will be able to select the material appropriate to their particular course of study.

All dimensions are given in millimetres and metres and all other units conform to the Système International d'Unités (SI) including multiples and sub-multiples. It is recommended that the bracketed units be dropped from common usage.

Multiplication Factor		*Prefix*	*Symbol*
1 000 000 000	(10^9)	giga	G
1 000 000	(10^6)	mega	M
1 000	(10^3)	kilo	k
100	(10^2)	hecto	h
10	(10^1)	deca	da
0·1	(10^{-1})	deci	d
0·01	(10^{-2})	centi	c
0·001	(10^{-3})	milli	m
0·000 001	(10^{-6})	micro	μ
0·000 000 001	(10^{-9})	nano	n
0·000 000 000 001	(10^{-12})	pica	p

To a woodworker it is fairly easy to reduce existing imperial sizes of timber to metric sizes, particularly since the vast majority of sectional sizes used in furniture making are only nominal, depending upon strength, proportional considerations and aesthetics. A natural tendency to translate the usually accepted imperial size of timber into the numerical metric equivalent should be avoided. Thus, where 1 inch thick material was previously used, 25 mm thickness should be considered, not 25·4 mm. Similarly:

Instead of 2 inch thickness, use 50 mm

$1\frac{1}{2}$,,	,,	,,	38 mm
$1\frac{1}{4}$,,	,,	,,	32 mm
$\frac{7}{8}$,,	,,	,,	22 mm
$\frac{3}{4}$,,	,,	,,	18 mm*
$\frac{5}{8}$,,	,,	,,	16 mm
$\frac{1}{2}$,,	,,	,,	12 mm
$\frac{3}{8}$,,	,,	,,	9 mm
$\frac{1}{4}$,,	,,	,,	6 mm
$\frac{1}{8}$,,	,,	,,	3 mm

All temperatures are expressed in degrees Celsius (°C). This is identical to degrees Centigrade.

G.W.B.
N.A.H.

* 18 mm thickness is suggested instead of the nearer equivalent of 19 mm because of the frequency of use of this size in situations where it must be divided into 3 equal parts, for example, rails which end in a mortice and tenon joint where a 6 mm chisel will be used.

ACKNOWLEDGEMENTS

FOR the completion of this book the authors are indebted to the pupils they have taught, for their suggestions, criticisms and problems. Without their help we could not have stood aside and looked at the teaching of our craft through their eyes, rather than our own. In particular, thanks must be given to R. A. Evans for the preparation of many of the furniture drawings in the history section, and to Heal & Son and Gordon Russell Ltd for the loan of photographs and permission to reproduce the drawings of their furniture. We are also indebted to Evode Ltd, Stafford, for technical information concerning modern adhesives.

As an aid to the teacher, the diagrams in this book are obtainable in the form of film strips from V.I.S. Ltd, 12 Bridge Street, Hungerford, Berks.

CONTENTS

PART I · WOOD TECHNOLOGY

PART II · DESIGN AND CONSTRUCTION

CONTENTS

PART III · TOOLS

CONTENTS

PART IV
THE HISTORY OF PERIOD FURNITURE
1100–1971

PART I
WOOD TECHNOLOGY

Chapter 1

TREE GROWTH AND STRUCTURE

World Timbers—Composition of Timber

THE roots of a tree extract chemicals in solution from the soil and carry these foods to the leaves of the tree by way of the sapwood (Fig. 1). The leaves, activated by air and sun, convert these chemicals into starches and sugars, passing them to the cambium layer by means of the bast, where they form the new sapwood and bast each year. In autumn the fruit of the tree forms from the flower, providing seeds for new trees (e.g. conkers—horse chestnut; acorn—oak; pine cone—pine tree; etc.).

When a tree is cut across the trunk, the picture seen is very similar to that shown in Fig. 2, with the various parts clearly discernible. Each and every part has a purpose to play in the life cycle of the growing tree.

The Pith is the soft, thin centre of the tree and marks the original sapling from which the tree grew.

The Heartwood is the "inactive" wood which comprises the greater part of the tree and which acts as a pillar supporting the living wood. It is the part most valued for use since it contains little food for feeding wood pests and thus is less liable to attack. It is also much stronger and denser than the sapwood, since the cell walls have become harder with age.

The Sapwood is the "living" wood, consisting of the last ten years or so of growth and containing starches and sugars which attract woodworm and beetle since they provide a food supply. It is also more liable to twist and warp than the heartwood since it contains more moisture. It should never be used for cabinet construction or structural work and can often be identified by its light colour compared with the heartwood.

The Cambium Layer is the microscopically thin layer of cells which lie between the sapwood and the bast. Each year the cambium layer fulfils two vital functions, firstly, to build a

3

new layer of sapwood which is seen as an annual ring, and secondly, to build a new layer of bast. If both the cambium

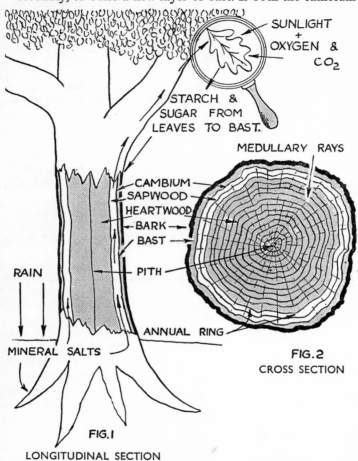

SUNLIGHT
+
OXYGEN &
CO_2

STARCH & SUGAR FROM LEAVES TO BAST.

MEDULLARY RAYS

CAMBIUM
SAPWOOD
HEARTWOOD
←BARK→
BAST

PITH

RAIN

ANNUAL RING

MINERAL SALTS

FIG.2
CROSS SECTION

FIG.1
LONGITUDINAL SECTION

layer and the sapwood are cut through, right round the tree, the tree will die.

The Bast is the inner part of the bark, usually lighter in colour than the outer bark. It carries the starches and sugars from the leaves to feed the cambium layer.

The Bark is the outer skin of the tree which serves as protection to the cambium layer against damage by animals and humans. It is sometimes used by man. (The American Indian made birch bark canoes; corks are obtained from the bark of the Spanish cork oak.)

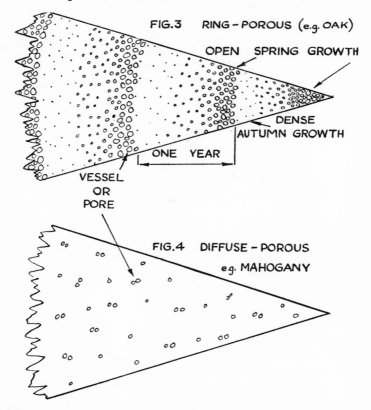

FIG.3   RING – POROUS (e.g. OAK)

OPEN   SPRING GROWTH

DENSE AUTUMN GROWTH

ONE YEAR

VESSEL OR PORE

FIG.4   DIFFUSE – POROUS e.g. MAHOGANY

The Medullary Rays are the layers of cells radiating approximately from the centre of the tree to the cambium layer. The term medullary rays is now being superseded by "Primary and Secondary rays", but these will take some time to become generally used. These cells are used as food reserve stores in case of drought or damage to the tree. They are present in all timbers but may only be seen in certain hardwoods. (The figure seen in quartered oak is caused by the medullary rays being cut along their length.)

The Annual Rings, sometimes termed "growth rings", can be seen in most timbers which come from areas where there is a marked seasonal growth in the standing trees.

In hardwoods the appearance of rings is caused by the open vessels or pores of the spring growth lying adjacent to the denser autumn growth. Timber with clearly defined annual rings is termed "ring-porous" (Fig. 3). If there is no clearly defined annual ring, the timber is termed "diffuse-porous" (Fig. 4).

In softwoods the appearance of rings is caused by the denser autumn growth and resin ducts lying adjacent to the larger, open cells of the spring growth.

WORLD TIMBER DISTRIBUTION

World timbers may be divided into three main classes (Fig. 5), but there will be considerable variations in those areas where high land causes lower temperatures throughout the year.

1. *The Evergreen Softwoods (conifers).* These trees grow thin, needle-like leaves which do not all fall at a certain time in the autumn, as do the leaves of the deciduous trees. The coniferous or evergreen softwoods are found in the forest belts which stretch across northern Canada, Scandinavia and northern Russia, where a very cold winter climate is experienced. Conifers may also be found, however, in regions with much warmer climates, but only where the land is so high above sea-level that the climate becomes similar to that of the colder regions (e.g. the Rocky Mountains, Andes and Himalayas).

The softwoods obtained from the coniferous trees are mainly used for carpentry and joinery, building, roofs, floors, doors, sheds and many other general purposes, since softwoods are much cheaper to buy than hardwoods. The latter fact becomes more understandable when it is realized that a coniferous tree matures in about a quarter of the time taken by a hardwood tree. The use of the terms softwood and hardwood can be very misleading since it is possible for some softwoods (e.g. pitch

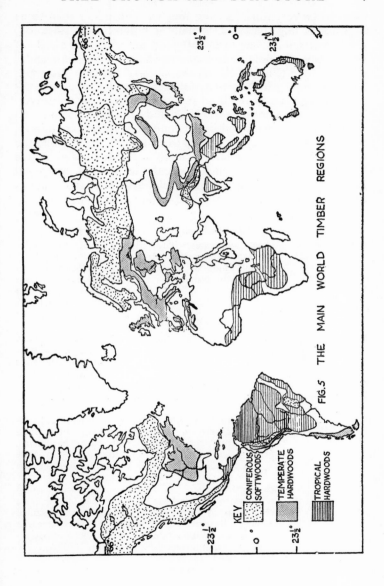

FIG. 5   THE MAIN WORLD TIMBER REGIONS

KEY
CONIFEROUS SOFTWOODS
TEMPERATE HARDWOODS
TROPICAL HARDWOODS

pine) to be very much denser, tougher and harder than some hardwoods (e.g. balsa). Originally a botanical classification, not a craftsman's, the term softwood means that the cells of such a tree are hollow and spindle-shaped when seen under a microscope (Fig. 6). Along the sides of the cells are small holes or "pits" which serve as connecting passages between the cells through which the food passes on its way to the leaves. These cells are known as tracheids and are about 3 mm long.

The types of tree found in the coniferous forests are numerous and include all types of pine trees, spruce, fir, yew and the giant redwood or sequoia. The larch is also a coniferous tree but is an exception in that it is deciduous and not evergreen. Below will be found listed the main characteristics and qualities of two softwoods commonly used in Great Britain.

	Scots Pine or Baltic Redwood	*Spruce*
Characteristics	Strong, moderately hard, but sapwood is attacked by all kinds of wood-borers. Very resinous.	Strong and light in weight, not resistant to decay and is difficult to treat with preservatives since the sapwood is not very permeable. Contains little resin, is elastic and resonant.
Working qualities	Works easily, takes glue and nails well. Easy to paint.	Works easily, takes glue, nails and screws well. Easy to paint and stain but difficult to preserve.
Colour	Creamy white to yellow.	Almost white
Locale	Scotland and Baltic countries.	Canada and Norway
Uses	Good quality structural work, carpentry, pit props, crates and telegraph poles.	Joinery, all types of building construction, wood pulp, paper, hardboard, food boxes (has little smell), ladders, Christmas trees.
Notes	This wood is often called red deal but it has been recommended by the Timber Research and Development Association (TRADA) that this name be dropped in favour of the names given above.	This wood is often called white deal, but the name spruce is recommended by the Timber Research and Development Association (TRADA).

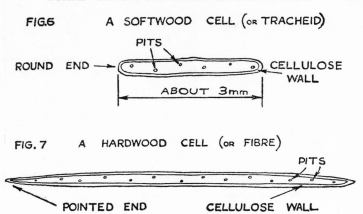

FIG.6   A SOFTWOOD CELL (or TRACHEID)

PITS

ROUND END →   CELLULOSE WALL

ABOUT 3mm

FIG. 7   A HARDWOOD CELL (or FIBRE)

PITS

POINTED END   CELLULOSE WALL

2. *The Temperate Hardwoods* (*deciduous*). These timbers come from the broad-leafed, deciduous trees of the temperate climates and are found in the British Isles, Europe, Japan, New Zealand, Chile and central U.S.A.

The temperate hardwoods are used for many forms of strong constructional work such as church timbers, cabinet making, decorative veneering, turnery and, many years ago, for "England's wooden walls". These hardwoods, which take a long time to grow to maturity, are more expensive than the softwoods and more difficult to replace as timber becomes more scarce. The cells or fibres of the hardwoods are very long, fibrous and needle-shaped (Fig. 7) and tend to make the hardwood timbers more elastic than the softwood timbers.

The types of tree found in the temperate, deciduous forests are oak, ash, elm, chestnut, lime, sycamore, walnut, apple, pear and many others. Very often conifers will be found growing in the same forests. The main characteristics of two widely used temperate hardwoods are listed on page 10.

	Oak	*Beech*
Characteristics	Heartwood very durable, sapwood attacked by Lyctus beetle. Very hard, tough, strong and decorative, open-grained. Quartered timber shows silver grain or figuring.	Very strong and tough, very close-grained, able to stand hard wear and shocks. Not attacked by Lyctus beetle owing to the small pores.
Working qualities	Polishes very well, easy to plane if tools are sharp. Takes screws well but nailing is difficult. Must be well seasoned.	Polishes well, needs sharp tools, turns well but is liable to warp unless carefully seasoned. Screws well, nailing is difficult. Bends well when steamed.
Colour	Light brown. Sometimes a dark brown colour due to the presence of a fungoid growth called "beefsteak fungus".	Either white or pale pinky brown
Locale	Great Britain, Austria, Japan, Yugoslavia, U.S.A.	Great Britain, Austria, Yugoslavia
Uses	Furniture, interior decoration, panelling, church building and furniture, gates, veneers. Is rather too open grained for general turnery.	Domestic woodware, tool handles, planes, mallets, benches, flooring, kitchen furniture, windsor chairs, Austrian bentwood chairs.

3. *The Tropical Hardwoods* (*evergreen*). These timbers come from the broad-leafed, evergreen trees of the tropical and sub-tropical forests of Africa, Burma, India, the Amazon Basin and other parts of South America, the East and West Indies.

The tropical hardwoods are extensively used in the furniture industry, all forms of decorative woodwork, shipbuilding (teak and mahogany), speedboats, veneers and turnery. The timber, when quartered, often shows a marked stripe and is difficult to plane unless dealt with in a special way. This stripe, or interlocked grain, is caused by the cells growing in a spiral fashion throughout the length of the trunk and although difficult to plane, the wood has a most attractive appearance.

The types of tree found in the tropical and sub-tropical forest are ebony, mahogany, ironwood, obeche, gaboon, teak, rosewood and African golden walnut. Some of these timbers present an attractive proposition to the timber merchant since it is possible to have a trunk up to 60 metres in length before coming to the first branch. This means economy in cutting, little wastage and a low price to the consumer.

	Mahogany	*African golden walnut*
Characteristics	Close-grained and strong, resistant to decay but attacked by wood-boring insects. Marked stripe when quartered.	Belongs to the mahogany family, open grain, wide boards obtainable. Strong and light in weight but splits fairly easily. Shows stripe when quartered.
Working qualities	Works well with sharp tools, tears if plane is blunt. Seasons well with the minimum of splitting and distortion. Very decorative, stains, polishes and takes glue well.	Works well with sharp tools. Splits easily, so nailing is difficult. Seasons fairly well, polishes and takes glue well.
Colour	Red. Cuban mahogany has a white deposit in the cells. Honduras mahogany has a black deposit.	Lustrous yellow colour which quickly darkens to a rich, golden brown. Has a black streak from mineral deposit.
Locale	Africa, Cuba, Honduras.	West Africa.
Uses	Furniture, pianos, shipbuilding, pattern-making, veneers, speedboat shells, straightedges and winding strips in the workshop.	Cabinet making, billiard tables, panelling, veneers. Often used to give simulated "teak finish".

THE COMPOSITION OF TIMBER

It has been seen that timber is composed of numerous cells of which the substance cellulose comprises the greater part. The cells are held together by a natural form of cement called lignin. In addition to these substances, wood also contains many natural oils, resins and acids which help to give to timber its characteristic smell and colour. Many of these substances are extracted from pulped wood by chemical means and used in industry. This increases the value of wood to man far beyond its obvious use for constructional purposes. Some of the uses of wood are listed on page 12.

Detailed chemical analysis of the substances in a tree shows that it possesses the following chemical make-up. (The percentages listed are of the DRY weight of the tree.)

1. Celluloses from 60% to 85% of the tree's dry weight.
2. Lignin from 15% to 25% of the tree's dry weight.
3. Resins, oils, tannin, sugar, starch, acid and colourmg matter are present in varying quantities.

In addition to these substances, another is also found in very large quantities when a tree is freshly felled. This is water, which may, in total weight, be up to twice the weight of all the other substances added together. Generally speaking, the moisture content may vary from 50% to 200% of the tree's dry weight, according to the type of tree and to what time in the year felling takes place.

The presence of this water causes major problems for the craftsman, since any change in the moisture content of a board of timber means that expansion or contraction will take place. This movement of the timber must always be allowed for in constructional work where solid wood is used.

USES OF TIMBER

Building	All softwoods and hardwoods
Cabinet making	Almost all hardwoods
Pit props	Pine
Tannin (tanning leather)	Oak
Pure turpentine	Bark and leaves of silver fir
Cellulose (paint and clothes)	Softwoods
Cork	Bark of cork oak (Spain)
Paper and pulp	Spruce, fir, pine
Resin	Pitch pine
Syrup	Sugar maple
Chewing gum	Sapodilla tree
Rubber	Rubber tree
All kinds of fruit	Apple, pear, plum, peach

Chapter 2

THE EFFECTS OF MOISTURE
LOSS ON TIMBER

AFTER a tree has been felled, the water begins to evaporate until, after a period of time, the tree has the same moisture content as the surrounding air. If the tree is cut into boards, the drying-out period is accelerated since evaporation will take place over a far greater area than it will in a solid trunk.

From the point of view of the craftsman, two important facts must be remembered. First, as moisture leaves the tree or board it will shrink, and conversely, if the tree or board is saturated with moisture after having been dried out, it will expand. In order to understand just how the timber will move, two simple rules must be remembered.

1. Whenever moisture leaves the timber, maximum shrinkage takes place in the direction of the annual rings (Fig. 8).
2. Under the same conditions minimum shrinkage takes place in the direction of the medullary rays, since they resist shrinkage along their length (Fig. 9).

By applying these rules to various sections of timber it becomes simple to understand how they change their shape when the moisture content of the timber changes. Reference to Fig. 10 shows a cross-section of a tree, the black area representing the original wet or "green" section of the board. As moisture leaves the "green" timber the shapes will change—

Square timber will become of rectangular or diamond section, depending upon where the timber was originally situated in the tree.

Round timber will become oval, no matter from where it is taken.

Plain-sawn timber will warp away from the heart of the tree and the edges of the board will become thinner than the centre. This is sometimes called "cupping".

Quarter-sawn timber will not usually cup or warp but

becomes thinner. The edge of the board to the outside of the tree will become thinner than the inner edge.

In the length of the board there is little shrinkage or expansion for all practical purposes, but some distortion may take

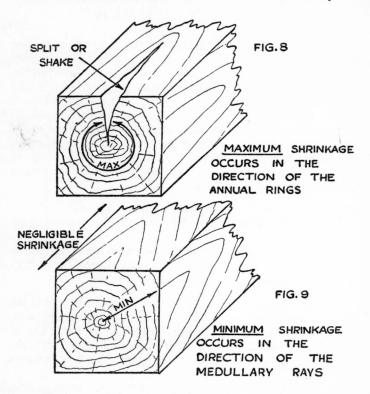

SPLIT OR
SHAKE

FIG. 8

MAXIMUM SHRINKAGE
OCCURS IN THE
DIRECTION OF THE
ANNUAL RINGS

NEGLIGIBLE
SHRINKAGE

FIG. 9

MINIMUM SHRINKAGE
OCCURS IN THE
DIRECTION OF THE
MEDULLARY RAYS

place. This may be due to bad seasoning (insufficient support), twisted grain or stresses set up by machining. The distortion appears in various forms:—

        Bowing (Fig. 11)
        Springing (Fig. 12)
        Winding or casting (Fig. 13)

Another class of faults seen in drying timber is not so easily

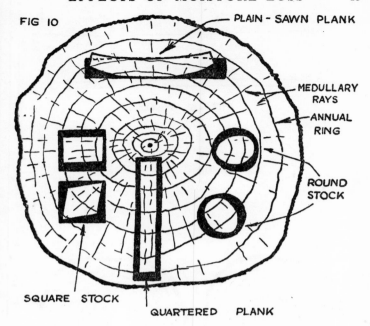

FIG 10

PLAIN - SAWN PLANK

MEDULLARY RAYS

ANNUAL RING

ROUND STOCK

SQUARE STOCK

QUARTERED PLANK

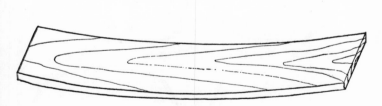

FIG. 11 BOWING (ENDS LIFT)

FIG. 12 SPRINGING (STAYS FLAT)

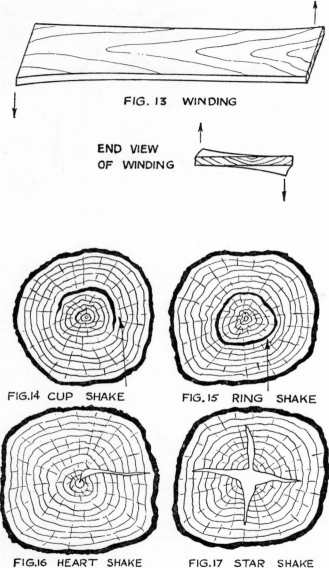

FIG. 13   WINDING

END VIEW
OF WINDING

FIG.14 CUP SHAKE   FIG.15 RING SHAKE

FIG.16 HEART SHAKE   FIG.17 STAR SHAKE

dealt with. These are known as shakes and are usually the result of a combination of circumstances.

Shakes arise partly because the moisture is able to leave the open end-grain more rapidly than the sides of the board or tree. Thus, drying out of the ends, and subsequent shrinkage, tends to become too rapid and splits of various kinds appear.

The Cup Shake (Fig. 14). An incomplete ring shake, sometimes due to bad felling of the tree, or high winds.

The Ring Shake (Fig. 15). A complete ring lying on one of the annual rings. Cases have been known where the whole of the inner wood can be pulled out of the trunk after cross-cutting, leaving the trunk in the form of a hollow pipe. Ring shakes are caused by bad felling and high winds.

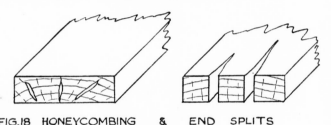

FIG.18   HONEYCOMBING   &   END   SPLITS

The Heart Shake (Fig. 16). Caused by bad felling, gale damage or simple shrinkage.

The Star Shake (Fig. 17). May be a combination of several heart shakes, from the same causes.

Honeycombing (Fig. 18). Usually seen in kiln-dried timber, resulting from a too rapid drying rate. The splits appear when the medullary rays split along their length.

End Splits (Fig. 18). May be advanced honeycombing or normal shrinkage on wide boards.

Thunder Shakes. Seen as a thin crack *across* the grain of a board. Believed to be due to bad felling or high winds; usually found in tropical timbers.

It is obvious that timber can undergo great changes as it dries out and it is equally obvious that "green" timber should never be used for constructional purposes. Under ideal conditions, the timber used for making anything should have the same moisture content as the air surrounding the place where the completed object is to stand. For practical purposes, however, certain safe limits may be laid down:—

For outdoor use moisture content may be up to 18% of the timber's dry weight.

For indoor use, up to 14% moisture content.

For indoor use where there is central heating, up to 10% moisture content.

Chapter 3

CONVERSION AND SEASONING

Natural Seasoning—Kiln Drying—Calculation of
Moisture Content—Market Forms

AFTER the tree has been felled it is often left in the timber
yards for some time so that some of the surplus moisture
is drawn out. If squares are required the first stage in the conversion is to remove four slabs (Fig. 19), leaving a waney-edge
baulk. (Wane is merely a trade term for bark.) This conversion
is carried out on either a band saw or a circular saw.

Plain-sawn timber comes from the most economical method
of conversion since there is very little loss of timber in the sawing. Timber sawn this way is generally cheaper than that sawn
by other methods which may be more wasteful. No slabs are
removed and each board bears the wane on the edge, although
this may be removed before the timber leaves the sawmill.
Boards cut in this way, also known as "slash-cut", "tangent-
cut" or "through and through", do not show any "flash" or
"figure" on their surfaces since in most cases the medullary
rays are cut *across* their length (Fig. 20). There will, however,
be two or three boards from the centre where the surfaces lie in
line with the medullary rays. These boards will not only show
"figuring" if the tree has a pronounced medullary ray, but will
also be less prone to distortion.

Quarter-sawing. The first stage in this method of conversion
is to cut the trunk or butt into four quarters as shown in Fig. 21.
The second stage in the sawing varies although the principle
behind the sawing remains the same. This principle is to cut the
boards so that their surfaces lie in the same direction as the
medullary rays, thus reducing the likelihood of distortion in
the boards and exploiting the beauty of the medullary rays
(e.g. quartered oak and, to a lesser extent, beech). From the
diagram it can be seen that there is some wastage of timber in
quartering. This is instrumental in increasing the price for
quartered timber although, in the long run, the consumer may

19

find it more economical owing to the fact that he has little wastage due to warping.

When conversion is completed, the timber is ready for seasoning to reduce the moisture content to a safe working level. The

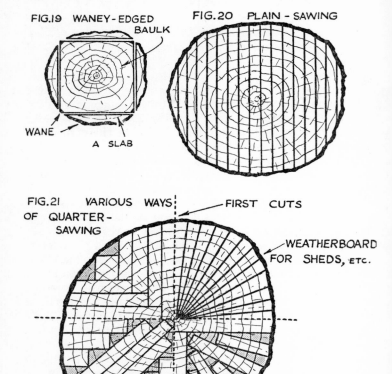

FIG.19   WANEY-EDGED BAULK

FIG.20   PLAIN-SAWING

WANE

A SLAB

FIG.21   VARIOUS WAYS OF QUARTER-SAWING

FIRST CUTS

WEATHERBOARD FOR SHEDS, ETC.

SHADED AREAS DENOTE WASTAGE

purpose of conversion is to allow free air circulation around the boards, thereby reducing the moisture content, while they are weighted to reduce distortion to the minimum.

Natural Seasoning (*the stack method*). Natural seasoning is

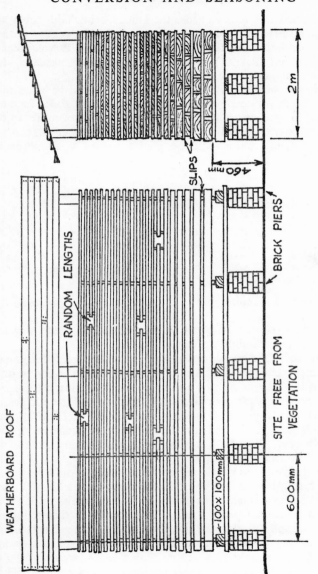

2 m

460 mm

SLIPS

BRICK PIERS

WEATHERBOARD ROOF

RANDOM LENGTHS

SITE FREE FROM VEGETATION

100 × 100mm

600mm

FIG. 22 THE STACK METHOD OF NATURAL SEASONING

B

best carried out under sheds, the stacks being laid down as shown in Fig. 22. The stack shown embodies many of the recommendations of the Timber Research and Development Association (TRADA), which has done much research to improve methods of seasoning.

The stacking strips, sticks or skids are placed between the boards to facilitate air circulation and should be about 25 mm square in section. They should be placed no more than 600 mm apart, to reduce sag in the board between the supporting points and should be placed vertically above each

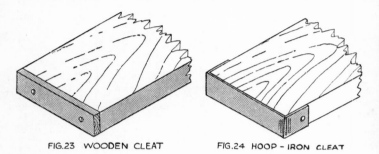

FIG.23 WOODEN CLEAT   FIG.24 HOOP - IRON CLEAT

other. They should be clean to prevent staining, and dry to minimize the possibility of rot and decay.

The ends of the boards on the stack should be treated in some way to prevent too rapid loss of moisture from the end grain. One of the best methods is a thick coat of oil paint, but sometimes wooden cleats are nailed on instead, to seal the end grain from the air (Fig. 23). Hoop-iron cleats nailed on (Fig. 24) are less satisfactory. Not only do the nails help to cause end splits in both cases, but the hoop iron may start stain patches on timbers of an acidic nature.

The brick piers which support the stack should be high enough to raise the first board in the stack to at least 460 mm above ground level. This helps to reduce reabsorption of ground moisture by the boards. This can be further reduced by choosing a well-drained site, if outdoors, with ashes to help keep down grass and weeds. The outside brick piers seen in the end view should be no more than 2 metres apart to limit the width of the stack and give maximum air circulation. The length of the stack will vary according to the length of the timber being seasoned.

If the stack must be raised out of doors an adequate roof should be provided with sufficient overhang to prevent the excessive heat from the sun and the rain from falling on to the stack. Weatherboard with a fall to one side is quite suitable.

The time taken to season boards using this method varies according to the thickness of the board. As a general rule it may be said to take approximately one year for each 25 mm of thickness.

Thus 25 mm thick boards take about 1 year.
      50 mm thick boards take about 2 years.

From this fact it can be seen that the thickest boards should be placed at the bottom of the stack since they will be moved last. In addition to this, the extra weight on top is necessary to reduce the possibility of distortion in the thicker boards. Any short boards should be placed as shown in Fig. 22 to reduce the possibility of distortion and sag.

Natural Seasoning (*the rack method*). This is not a controlled method since the boards are free to twist and warp (Fig. 25). It is, however, a quick method and is used to season light coloured woods such as holly and sycamore, which quickly discolour if left for long periods in a sooty atmosphere. The rack should be under cover, but if built out of doors should have some form of simple roof.

Advantages of natural seasoning:—

1. Timber is harder than artificially dried timber.
2. It is sweeter to work with hand tools and takes a better finish.
3. It is cheap and there are no running costs.

Disadvantages of natural seasoning:—

1. Wood is liable to be stained by soot and other chemicals in the air.
2. Danger of fungoid attack.
3. Danger of woodworm attack. (This can be reduced if the sapwood is removed during conversion.)
4. The long time taken, since the merchant's capital lies idle.

5. The varying humidity of the air. (The stacks will be drier in the summer months.)

6. Moisture content cannot be reduced below about 15%. (Average m.c. of the air in the British Isles.)

7. Danger of fire.

Kiln Drying. This is an artificial method of seasoning. The timber is stacked on movable trolleys and placed inside brick

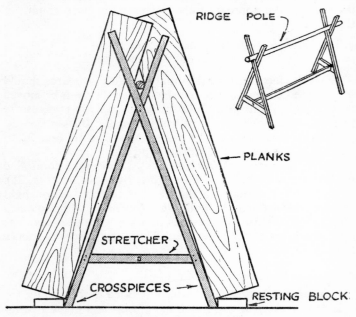

RIDGE POLE

PLANKS

STRETCHER

CROSSPIECES

RESTING BLOCK

FIG. 25   THE   RACK   METHOD

buildings which are then closed. The temperature inside the building or kiln is then raised, thus reducing the moisture content of the timber. Heat alone, however, would drive out the moisture too rapidly and cause severe honeycombing and splitting. To prevent this, steam is introduced into the kiln, thus preventing too rapid loss of moisture to the surrounding air. Air circulation is aided by means of electric fans and gradually the amount of steam is reduced. As this is done, the timber begins to give up its excess moisture until gradually it has the same moisture content as the surrounding warm air. The humidity inside the kiln is registered on dials in the control room and thus the absolute moisture content of the boards is known.

With this method, the drying time is considerably shorter than that with seasoning by natural methods. A board of 50 mm thick softwood which would normally take two years to

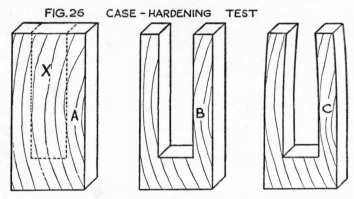

FIG.26   CASE - HARDENING   TEST

PLANK A - WOOD   AT X MARKED FOR SAWING
PLANK B - SOUND PLANK, WELL SEASONED
PLANK C - POOR KILN DRYING, CASE - HARDENED.
          SURFACE   STRESSES   MAKE   PRONGS
          BEND EITHER INWARDS OR OUTWARDS

bring down to a 15% moisture content using the natural method, can be brought down to 10% m.c. in about two weeks. Hardwoods, with their denser grain, take about four to five times longer.

Advantages of kiln drying:—

1. Reduced possibility of soot and chemical staining.
2. Timber does not lie exposed for a very long period, thus reducing the danger of fungoid attack.
3. Less chance of worm attack and any eggs already present are killed.
4. The exact moisture content is constantly registered.

5. There is a rapid turnover of the merchant's capital and he thus increases his profits.

Disadvantages of kiln drying:—

1. The initial cost of the kiln and its equipment is rather high (but bear in mind Note 5 above).
2. The timber is often "carroty" to work and tends to crumble, especially end grain.
3. There is a danger of honeycombing.
4. Case-hardening will result from too rapid drying. This will cause stresses in the timber which result in distortion when it is worked (Fig. 26).
5. Splitting and warping are certain to occur if the stack is not carefully built and controlled.

CALCULATION OF MOISTURE CONTENT

Saw a test piece from a board as shown in Fig. 27, and weigh this sample accurately. This is the weight of the wood plus any moisture which is present, and is known as the "wet weight".

FIG.27   SAMPLE   FOR   MOISTURE   CONTENT   TEST

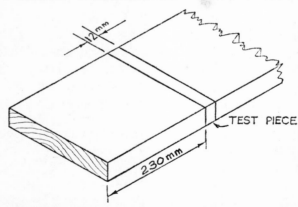

Take the sample and dry it in the oven without scorching it. After about half an hour take out the sample and re-weigh it, making a note of the weight. Continue to dry the sample again and re-weigh about every half-hour until eventually the weight remains constant. When this happens the sample is free from moisture and the weight is again noted. This is called the "dry weight".

The following formula may now be applied to find the proportion of water to dry wood in the original board.

$$\text{Moisture content:} = \frac{\text{Wet weight} - \text{Dry weight}}{\text{Dry weight}} \times 100\%$$

Example: Wet weight = 120 g
         Dry weight = 80 g

$$\text{Moisture content} = \frac{120-80}{80} \times 100\%$$

$$= \frac{40}{80} \times 100\% = 50\%$$

Thus, all timber in the stack of the same width and thickness has a moisture content of 50%.

A much quicker method of determining the m.c. of a board is by using an electric meter which shows the moisture content on a graduated scale. A current of electricity is passed through the board from two electrodes situated on the meter. If the board has a large moisture content it will offer an easy passage to the electric current and the dial will register a large reading. A fairly dry board will offer greater resistance to the passage of electricity and thus only a small reading will be noticed on the dial.

MARKET FORMS

The building industry began conversion to SI units in April 1970 and has already discovered many advantages to the system. Architects are designing new buildings with modules based on metric units (e.g. a 100 mm module for joinery production), thus aiding designers of contract furniture who may now be able to design with similar basic modules for built-in furniture. Timber-producing countries are still supplying timber in both imperial and metric units owing to the fact that one of the world's largest consumers, the U.S.A., is still continuing to use imperial units. There has, however, been a large measure of agreement on the standard sizes which will be available under metrication.

Softwoods. The cubic metre replaces the "Standard", previously used as the unit of measurement of large volumes of timber (1 standard contained 165 cu ft of timber). Since the cubic metre (m^3) is not a convenient unit for the small user of timber, he will be able to purchase by the square metre (m^2). He will be wise, however, to consider the table shown below before committing himself to specific lengths, widths and thicknesses since there has been much rationalization in the sizes agreed by the standardizing body. Softwoods are available in the sawn sizes shown in the table, and any departure from these standard lengths and sections will result in wastage or increased costs.

		Softwood sizes available—from the saw								
Length in metres	Thickness in millimetres	Widths available in millimetres								
		75	100	125	150	175	200	225	250	300
1·8	16	X	X	X	X					
2·1	19	X	X	X	X					
2·4	22	X	X	X	X					
2·7	25	X	X	X	X	X	X	X	X	X
3·0	32	X	X	X	X	X	X		X	X
3·3	38	X	X	X	X	X	X	X		
3·6	44	X	X	X	X	X	X	X	X	X
3·9	50	X	X	X	X	X	X	X	X	X
4·2	63		X	X	X	X	X			
4·5	75		X	X	X	X	X	X	X	X
4·8	100		X		X		X		X	X
5·1	150				X		X			X
5·4	200						X			
5·7	250								X	
6·0	300									X

An X in the column indicates that this size is available.

Having decided on the size and quantity of timber which he requires the large purchaser might be quoted a price of £63 per cubic metre for timber 50 mm thick. From this he would be able to calculate the price per square metre:

$$\text{Cost} = \text{£63 per m}^3 \text{ for 50 mm in thickness}$$

$$= \frac{\text{£63} \times 50}{1000} \text{ for one square metre (m}^2)$$

$$= \frac{\text{£63} \times 1}{20} \quad ,, \quad ,, \quad ,, \quad ,,$$

$$= \text{£3·15 per sq m.}$$

Since 50-mm boards are available in standard widths as shown above, he can now calculate the number of metres of board which he will be able to buy for a given sum of money, provided that he knows the best standard width to suit his requirements.

Example: The purchaser has decided to buy boards which are 250 mm wide, 50 mm thick, at the quoted price of £3·15 per square metre. Thus for a cost of £3·15 per m² he knows that he would obtain a board 1000 mm wide and 1000 mm long, or a board of equivalent area in the width that he needs. If he decides that he needs boards which are 250 mm wide, a standard width, he can now calculate:

For £3·15, board area = 1000 mm × 1000 mm

The boards required are 250 mm wide, so,

For £3·15, the same area gives $\frac{1000}{250} \times 1000$ mm in length

$$= 4000 \text{ mm or 4 m in length.}$$

Thus, for an expenditure of £3·15 the purchaser would receive, in boards 250 mm × 50 mm, a total length of 4 metres. Since the standard board length in this section size is 3·9 m he can now calculate how many boards he will require for the work in hand, also the cost per 3·9 m board:

Cost for 4 m of board = £3·15

,, ,, 3·9 m of board = £3·15 × $\frac{3·9}{4}$ = $\frac{\text{£12·285}}{4}$

$$= \text{£3·07.}$$

This board section, bought by the metre run, would be

$$\frac{\text{£3·15}}{4} = \text{79p per metre.}$$

It must be emphasized that both the designer and user of timber will find it much more economical to work with the standard sizes obtainable, rather than design and purchase outside of this range.

Hardwoods. The basic unit for buying hardwoods is the cubic metre but the purchaser will probably find it more convenient to calculate his prices by the square metre as shown in the example above. For hardwoods, the following standard sizes have been agreed.

Lengths—Start at 1·8 m and rise in 100 mm steps.
Widths—Start at 150 mm and rise in 10 mm or 25 mm steps.
Thicknesses—19 mm—25 mm—32 mm—38 mm—50 mm
63 mm—75 mm—100 mm—125 mm—From
125 mm, rising in 25 mm steps.

Some hardwood suppliers quote prices by the square metre but a purchaser may be quoted, for example, £168 per cubic metre for a particular hardwood and, if he wishes to convert this to the more understandable square metre, he will have to calculate as shown below.

Example: Quoted price is £168 per cubic metre and the buyer wishes to obtain timber 25 mm in thickness.

1 m³ = 1000 mm × 1000 mm × 1000 mm and costs £168

$$1000 \text{ mm} \times 1000 \text{ mm} \times 25 \text{ mm costs } \frac{£168 \times 25}{1000}$$

$$= \frac{£4200}{1000}$$

$$= £4·20.$$

Thus 1 square metre of 25 mm thick hardwood would cost £4·20. If the buyer wishes to obtain his 25 mm thick boards in a width of 150 mm he knows that for an outlay of £4·20 he will obtain

$$1000 \times \frac{1000}{150} \text{ mm in length} = 1000 \times \frac{20}{3} \text{ mm}$$

$$= \frac{20000}{3} \text{ mm} = 6666 \text{ mm}$$

$$= 6·66 \text{ m.}$$

Thus, for an outlay of £4·20 the buyer would obtain one board 6·66 m in length, 150 mm in width and 25 mm in thickness.

In the case of both hardwood and softwoods, the price quoted will be for the material as it comes from the saw. If a planed surface is required by the purchaser he must be prepared to pay a surcharge of between 5% and 10% on top of the quoted sawn price to cover the machining costs involved. It must also be realized that to plane both sides of a board reduces the original thickness by about 3 mm to 4 mm. The purchaser relies on the supplier to convert his stock material in the most economical way possible, with the minimum of wasted shavings and sawdust, for which the purchaser pays.

Built-up materials. Plywoods, blockboards, compo-boards and similar built-up materials are supplied in standard lengths and widths for each given thickness. The most popular standard length is 2440 mm with a width of 1220 mm, and whole sheets in this size tend to be cheaper. The buyer will be quoted by the standard sheet size of 3 square metres (2·44 m × 1·22 m). For small quantities the price may be quoted by the square metre, but this price will reflect the wastage involved when large sheets of material are cut up. Larger quantities will be quoted in 10 square metre units. Standard sizes are:

Lengths and widths— 915 mm—1220 mm—1525 mm
1830 mm—2135 mm—2440 mm
2745 mm—3050 mm—3660 mm

Thicknesses in mm— 3·2— 5·0— 6·5— 8·0
9·5—12·5—16·0—19·0
22·0—25·5—32·0—35·0
38·0—41·0—44·5—47·5

It should be noted that, when ordering, the first dimension given indicates the direction in which the grain of the surface lamin must lie. In a sheet of blockboard 2440 mm × 1220 mm × 9·5 mm, the grain lies in a direction parallel with the longer side. This is most important when ordering built-up materials with veneered faces.

The price of built-up materials will vary according to a number of factors:

1. Type of materials involved, e.g., blockboard, plywood, hardboard, etc.

2. Thickness of material.
3. Number of lamins and their quality.
4. Quality of face lamins, whether good one side (A/BB) or good on both sides (B/B).
5. Whether there are expensive facing veneers.
6. Type of adhesive used in bonding.

Grading of built-up materials. The code letters shown below have been widely adopted by the suppliers and producers of built-up materials both in this country and overseas.

Face quality A—Almost knot free (up to 5 mm maximum diameter), a few brown streaks, swirls and slight discoloration permitted.

B—Allowing a few knots (up to 8 mm diameter), some brown streaks and slight discoloration. Joints to be glued and adjacent strips matched for colour.

BB—Knots are plugged except such small ones as are permitted in B quality, joints and discoloration allowed.

S—Good paintable quality (knots up to 10 mm in diameter), discoloration permitted, joints are glued.

C—Should be of one or more pieces of veneer and may contain knotholes no larger than 25 mm diameter, open pitch pockets not wider than 25 mm, splits not wider than 5 mm which taper to a point, worm holes not more than 16 mm wide, 38 mm long.

WG—Only guaranteed to be well glued, admits knots, plugs and joints and some manufacturing defects.

B.S.S. 1088 indicates Marine Grade quality.

B.S.S. 1455 or WBP indicates Weather and Boil Proof quality.

Round Logs. Timber is rarely bought in this form by the small user, more often by the timber merchant. The prices quoted will be by the cubic metre or, more rarely, in the case of very rare and expensive timbers such as rosewood, by weight. The calculation of the volume of the log in cubic metres is carried out in the following way (Fig.27a). The length of the log is multiplied by the area of the log, taken at a point halfway along the length. The calculation of area is simplified by substituting the area of a square for the area of a circle at the mid-point.

Example: To calculate the cubic content of a log which is 8 metres long and has a mean girth (circumference at the mid-point) of 1·6 m. A circle with a circumference of 1·6 m is

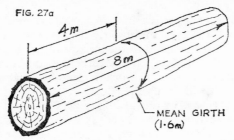

FIG. 27a

MEAN GIRTH (1·6m)

approximated in area to a square with a side of $\frac{1\cdot6}{4}$ m.

Thus,   cubic content = Length × Area at Midpoint

$$= \text{length} \times \left(\frac{\text{Mean Girth}}{4}\right)^2$$

$$= 8 \times \frac{1\cdot6}{4} \times \frac{1\cdot6}{4} \text{ cubic metres}$$

$$= 8 \times 0\cdot4 \times 0\cdot4 \text{ cubic metres}$$

$$= 1\cdot28 \text{ cubic metres.}$$

Whichever form of timber the buyer wishes to obtain, it is important to be aware of the marketing methods shown above and to pay attention to the following points:

1. The timber should be free from excessive knots, shakes, splits and distortion. If these are present, ask for an allowance to make up for the wastage.

2. The timber should be well seasoned, depending upon the use to which it is to be put, free from disease, fungus and woodworm. The sapwood should either be removed or an allowance made for it.

3. Know before ordering what is a reasonable price to pay and do not pay more unless for special quality or for specially selected timber.

Chapter 4

DEFECTS IN TIMBER

Fungi—Woodboring Insects

SOME defects or peculiarities of growth in timber are sought after for the interest and beauty they give to the wood surface. Even knots may add to the interest of the grain. Some of these desirable "defects" are listed below, and although they may sometimes cause extra work in cleaning up and polishing, the final result will justify the effort.

Figuring is caused by the medullary rays being cut along their length. The surface of the timber is enriched by "flashes" of various sizes which follow no set pattern on the grain. For figuring to be seen, the timber must have a large number of cells in the medullary rays (e.g. oak and beech).

Stripe is an effect seen on many tropical timbers and is caused when straight boards are cut along the spirally grown trunk. This exotic appearance means difficulty in working, since each stripe indicates interlocking grains which tear easily. A sharp scraper plane, however, will deal adequately with the most difficult board.

Colour in timber may be merely a combination of chemical colouring matter natural to the timber, or induced by a parasitic growth. English oak in its normal condition has a light golden colour, but if infected by a certain non-malignant fungus, may become a deep rich brown shade. There is no danger of decay from this particular fungus and, in fact, the timber is specially selected and sold as "brown oak".

Ripple or flash is caused by uneven growth of the tree and produces a satin-like surface on the plank. Sycamore is often affected in this way and is in demand for making violin backs. Such timber is often referred to as "fiddleback" sycamore.

Burr or bird's eye, sometimes seen in walnut and maple, is caused by small twigs and growths on the lower butt and roots of the tree. Because of the extreme difficulty encountered in planing this timber, it is often used in the form of veneer.

Not all defects, however, are as attractive to the woodworker as those above. The majority of fungoid growths and wood-borers may cause untold damage to both growing trees and finished articles.

FUNGI

Fungi are parasitic organic growths which live on the foods provided in timber and in doing so may completely break down its cell structure. For a fungus to live on timber the moisture content must be at least 20%, oxygen must be available and the temperature from 0–37° C. If these conditions are present, a seed or spore which may settle on the timber at any time will germinate.

When the seed has germinated it sends out roots or hyphae which spread through the cells of the timber by means of the pits and vessels. The roots then extract food, including the cellulose, to feed the flower or fruit body and, in doing so, initiate the breakdown of the timber. This breakdown may be so complete that the wood can be crumbled by the pressure of thumb and finger. The fruit body, in the meantime, is producing more spores which may be carried by animals, man or the wind to carry on the cycle elsewhere.

Dry rot is one of the most common fungoid growths but is not well named since it is caused by dampness. It is sometimes referred to as brown rot and is usually associated with both indoor and outdoor decay. Wood attacked by this fungus loses its strength, becomes light in weight and eventually splits into small cubes as if charred, taking a deep brown colour. The flower looks like a soft white spongy cushion. There is no cure for dry rot. All infected timber must be cut out and burned, including timber for at least 300 mm beyond the signs of damage.

When the damaged timber has been removed, bricks or steel girders should be sterilized with a blow-lamp flame or a 4% solution of sodium fluoride (37g to 1 litre of water) and the fruit body burned. The source of dampness which enabled the fungus to grow should be located and removed by checking for ventilation and rubbish. If this is not done it is quite possible that the trouble will recur. Before leaving the site it is advisable to wipe all tools used and the shoes with the sodium fluoride solution; brush the clothes and wash thoroughly so that no spores are carried away.

To avoid the ravages of dry rot is much easier than to attempt to cure it. Only the simple precautions shown below are necessary:—

1. Use timber with a moisture content below 20%, then the fungus cannot live.
2. Ensure adequate ventilation round the timber by removing rubbish under floorboards and clearing ventilator bricks of debris.
3. While the wood is dry, use preservatives such as creosote, tar, paint, varnish or polish.
4. Use timbers which are immune from attack by virtue of their chemical constituents (e.g. Western red cedar or teak).

Superficial moulds appear as fluffy green or grey outgrowths of a form of moss. They are sometimes seen on timber in seasoning stacks and stores. They do not destroy the timber but do indicate a source of dampness which must be located and removed.

Staining fungi change the colour of the timber but do not destroy it, since the fungi feed only on the starches and sugars but not on the cellulose walls of the cells. Both staining fungi and superficial moulds may be avoided by taking the following precautions:—

1. Convert quickly after felling and stack as soon as possible.
2. Use clean stacking strips.
3. Ensure good air circulation between boards.
4. Use an antiseptic dressing on the boards.
5. If possible, convert during the winter months.
6. Remove all sapwood.
7. Keep the timber dry.

Chemical stains such as those caused by soot, or iron cleats on the ends of boards, do no harm to the timber other than spoiling its appearance. Conversely, some chemical stains, such as the black mineral streaks in African walnut, may actually enhance the appearance of the timber.

WOODBORING INSECTS

The damage caused to timber by insects is equal to, if not greater than that caused by fungi. It is quite possible to confuse the symptoms of damage caused by some boring insects with those of the early stages of dry rot. There are, however, several distinguishing features of woodworm damage, which become apparent on close examination of the timber. These symptoms are:—

1. In most cases dust may be observed coming from the damaged timber through the boreholes.
2. The presence of boreholes where the adult beetle has emerged from the wood.
3. The galleries which the worms have bored will become apparent if the top surface of the timber is removed.

The life cycle of woodboring insects is common to all varieties. The egg is laid by the adult female beetle on, or in, the timber and after an incubation period the egg hatches. The larva or grub penetrates the timber and is responsible for most of the damage, which consists of long galleries usually bored in the direction of the grain. After a certain period of time the larva becomes a pupa, dormant and inactive, until eventually it emerges from the chrysalis as an adult beetle. It then leaves the timber, by boring an exit hole, to search for other places to continue its ravages. The exit hole may often be the first evidence of woodworm attack. By the time this happens of course, the damage has been done.

There are several common varieties of woodborers active in Great Britain and timber from other countries may be imported with eggs and larvae already inside. Several of the more common species are detailed below, together with suggested remedial action.

The lyctus or powder-post beetle is the most common variety. It is a reddish brown colour and about 5 mm in length. The larva is a yellowish white colour with brown jaws and is also about 5 mm in length. The female beetle lays about 30 to 50 eggs in the sapwood of open-grained timber during June but rarely, if ever, pays attention to close-grained timbers such as beech.

Oak is one of the favourite timbers of the lyctus beetle larva and during a life cycle of less than one year it may completely destroy the sapwood. The heartwood, which is denser and of little food value, is rarely attacked. This woodborer is very difficult to detect until it emerges from its exit hole, since the unwanted dust from the galleries is not expelled, but packed tightly behind the larva as it travels through the timber.

When an exit hole about 1·5 mm in diameter is seen, immediate action should be taken. If the hole is seen in stacked timber, remove the damaged boards and cut off the sapwood. This should then be burned. Other boards in the vicinity should also be stripped of sapwood and sprayed with an insecticide to kill any eggs which may already have been laid by adult beetles. The beetles, it must be remembered, can fly and the pest can therefore spread very rapidly. If a large quantity of timber is suspected of infestation, it can be sterilized in a drying kiln by raising the temperature to 55° C for a period of $2\frac{1}{2}$ hours under conditions of 100% humidity.

A recent method of controlling larvae and beetles in antique furniture has proved effective. The furniture is subjected to X-rays for a short period of time. This means that on approaching the adult stage, the beetles are sterile and unable to produce young. Thus, at the end of their life cycle, they leave no successors to carry on damaging timber. For more local damage to furniture there are many proprietary brands of worm killer which must be injected into the boreholes. To be fully effective, however, the wood must be well saturated with the preparation. The most effective prevention against the lyctus beetle is to remove sapwood from timber before using it.

The furniture beetle attacks hardwoods and softwoods of practically every variety. The adult beetle is about 5 mm long and is reddish brown in colour. The eggs are usually laid on the surface of the timber in varnish cracks, crevices or open shoulders on joints. When the larva hatches it bores into the surface of the timber for a short distance and then cuts a pupal chamber. The dust, unlike that caused by the lyctus beetle, is fine grained and falls easily from the entrance holes in the timber, thus advertising the presence of the larva.

The damage done is very severe. There are numerous boreholes and complete loss of strength in the timber, so much so that stools and chairs will collapse when used. For slight damage it is possible to inject benzene, turpentine or paraffin into the boreholes but severe damage calls for use of X-rays or fumigation with hydrocyanic acid gas. (This gas is poisonous to human beings and should only be used by experts.)

It is far better to prevent attack by furniture beetle than have the difficult job of curing it. If the following precautions are taken there is little risk of damage:—

1. Polish furniture regularly with turpentine-based wax polishes, including the under-surfaces and backs which are not seen. This fills crevices where eggs may be laid.
2. When making furniture, ensure tight joints with no gaps in the shoulders.

The death watch beetle, about 6 mm long, is a chocolate brown colour with yellow hairs on the wing covers. It generally favours hardwoods for attack, especially in old buildings where the timbers may be damp or decayed. This beetle, in fact, rarely attacks sound timber and this point should be remembered in control operations. The eggs, laid on the surface of the timber, hatch in about two to eight weeks and the larva then searches for decayed timber before penetrating. Once inside the timber, the larva, if left alone, continues to bore a maze of galleries for a period which may be up to 10 years. The adult beetle eventually emerges from an exit hole about 3 mm in diameter.

Control of the death watch beetle is very difficult. Damaged timber must be removed and burned if this is possible. (In the training ship *Conway* this was not possible and X-rays were used to good effect.) Once the beetles have been destroyed, steps must be taken to remove the source of dampness which, in most cases, initially decayed the timber and encouraged the presence of the death watch beetle.

The pinhole borer, about 3 to 6 mm long and brown in colour, is a native of tropical countries. It attacks both the heartwood and sapwood of unseasoned timber only, usually when the trees are newly felled.

The adult female lays the eggs and deposits a black slimy food for their early feeding. This stains the boreholes and makes identification of this beetle comparatively easy. The boreholes too are rather unusual, in that they tend to lie across the grain of the wood instead of in line with it. The galleries usually consist of isolated holes up to 1·5 mm in diameter.

Control of the pinhole borer is largely limited to the forest and sawmill. In the tropical regions, where the beetle abounds, the timber should be felled, debarked, converted and kiln dried as soon as possible, thus killing both beetles and larvae.

The longhorn beetle varies in length from 6 to 75 mm and is brown in colour. It mainly attacks unseasoned timber, dying trees and newly felled logs, especially when the bark is left on the trunk. The longhorn beetle rarely attacks seasoned timber and is hardly ever seen in properly conducted timber yards.

Control of the longhorn beetle begins with good forestry inspection, so that decayed or dying trees are felled and removed. In the timber yards the trees should be debarked, converted and seasoned as quickly as possible after having been felled. The sapwood should be removed before the timber is stacked.

Chapter 5

BUILT-UP MATERIALS

Manufacture of Plywood
Construction Problems with Solid Wood

BUILT-UP materials are sheets of wood, up to 3660 mm by 1830 mm in size, made by gluing together several thin sheets of wood called lamins or veneers. The grains of successive sheets are laid at right angles to each other, giving maximum strength and rigidity. Even more important than this, the alternating sandwich construction ensures that any tendency of one lamin to shrink or expand across the grain is prevented by the adjacent sheets, which oppose any movement of themselves in

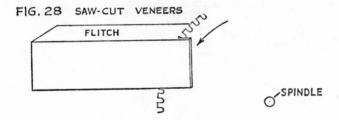

FIG. 28   SAW-CUT   VENEERS

FLITCH

SPINDLE

the direction of the grain. Thus, in built-up materials, any tendency to warp or distort is minimized.

The lamins used to build up the large sheets which are available, may be obtained in various ways after the log or flitch has first been steamed to render it less brittle.

Saw-cut veneer shown in Fig. 28 is rather thicker than knife-cut veneer and is not widely used today because of wastage. The finely set saw has deep gullets so that the sawdust clears easily and does not cause overheating of the blade.

Flat knife-cut veneer is thinner than if saw-cut but may vary in thickness from 0·5 mm to 1·5 mm (Fig. 29). Veneers obtained using this method, like saw-cut veneers, are often used for facings on a groundwork of less expensive timber.

Rotary knife-cut lamins are used to build up the main body of plywoods. It is a cheap method of production entailing very little wastage and is most widely used today. After debarking, any knots are bored out and closely fitting wooden pegs are glued into the trunk to fill up the holes. (These plugs may often be seen on the face of plywood as thin circular or elliptical

FIG 29 FLAT KNIFE-CUT VENEERS

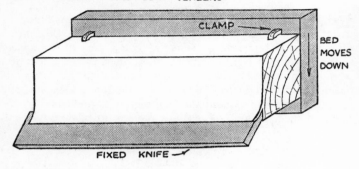

FIG 30 ROTARY KNIFE-CUT

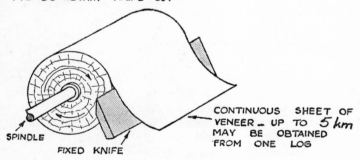

discs.) The log is then steamed and centred on a large rotary spindle (Fig. 30). A large flat knife, geared to the required depth of cut, automatically approaches the rotating log and removes a continuous layer of timber which is fed on to a cranked roller. From this roll of veneer is cut the required size of sheet for the particular requirements of the manufacturer or consumer.

Half-rotary cut veneers are produced as shown in Fig. 31.

This method is used to produce veneer on the quarter which, if there is a pronounced medullary ray, shows as figuring on the veneer surface. These veneers are often used as facings on

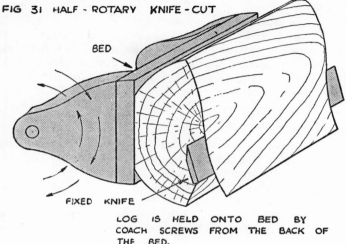

FIG 31 HALF - ROTARY KNIFE - CUT

BED

FIXED KNIFE

LOG IS HELD ONTO BED BY COACH SCREWS FROM THE BACK OF THE BED.

cabinet work and are cut in such timbers as oak, walnut and mahogany. The groundwork, of plywood or laminboard, is usually a cheaper timber such as pine or gaboon.

THE MANUFACTURE OF PLYWOOD

After the lamins have been cut to the required size they are passed through rollers which coat the surface with glue. This glue may be of the animal variety, casein, blood albumin or, best of all, synthetic resin. The sheets are then put together, with grains alternating, between large, hollow steel shelves in a press. When the shelves or plattens have been filled, the press is closed and the layers of plywood are pressed closely together. Steam is then introduced to the hollow plattens to speed the setting of the glue and increase production.

When the glue is dry the sheets are removed from the plattens and the edges are trimmed to the exact size required. Finally the sheets are passed between the rollers of a sanding machine which smooths away any blemishes on the surface and gives the required thickness. This thickness is expressed in terms of millimetres.

Advantages of built-up materials:—

1. Large sizes are obtainable.
2. There is negligible shrinkage, twist and distortion.
3. They are cheaper than using expensive solid hardwoods, since a thin veneer can be laid on a cheaper groundwork.
4. Rare woods, such as burr walnut, go much further.
5. They are easily bent and moulded to shape under steam and pressure (see Fig. 307).

Disadvantages of built-up materials:—

1. Outdoor use is limited since the lamins will separate if a reversible glue is used, i.e. one which returns to its gelatinous form when exposed to excessive humidity. Exterior grade plywood, glued with synthetic resin glue, does not suffer from this defect.
2. The edges present an untidy appearance but this may be remedied by using solid lippings or moulded edges (Fig. 32).

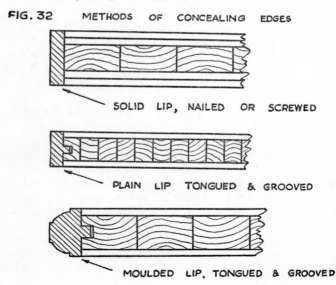

FIG. 32   METHODS   OF   CONCEALING   EDGES

SOLID LIP, NAILED OR SCREWED

PLAIN LIP TONGUED & GROOVED

MOULDED LIP, TONGUED & GROOVED

FORMS OF BUILT-UP MATERIAL

Plywood, the most widely used of the built-up materials, is made into all forms of modern furniture and panelling. It is made up of 3, 5, 7, 9 or more layers to give even stresses. Ply with five or more layers is called multiply. Each layer is of the same thickness and successive layers are laid with the grains alternating at right angles to each other. Plywood is sometimes

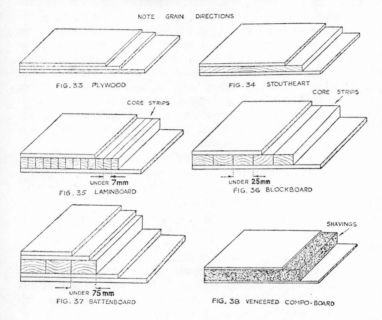

NOTE GRAIN DIRECTIONS

FIG. 33 PLYWOOD

FIG. 34 STOUTHEART

CORE STRIPS

FIG. 35 LAMINBOARD
UNDER 7mm

CORE STRIPS

FIG. 36 BLOCKBOARD
UNDER 25mm

FIG. 37 BATTENBOARD
UNDER 75 mm

SHAVINGS

FIG. 38 VENEERED COMPO-BOARD

given a top and bottom face of oak, then called "oak-faced plywood" (Fig. 33).

Stoutheart is a similar material to plywood but the centre layer is much thicker than the two outer plies. It is made in 3-ply only (Fig. 34).

Laminated wood is a rather expensive material but is very strong and stable. It is also called "laminboard". Note that the grains of the "core strips" are laid in such a manner as to give minimum warpage and that the core strips are always less than

7 mm in width. Laminboard is obtainable in large sheets, from 12 to 50 mm in thickness (Fig. 35).

Block board. The core strips are from 7 to 25 mm in width and are again laid in such a way as to give minimum warpage (Fig. 36). It is less favoured than laminboard but is obtainable in the same sizes. One advantage of block board is that a whole door can be made from one sheet with no jointing at all.

Battenboard. The core strips are up to 75 mm wide but are made from lower grade materials. Warpage is more likely with the wider core strips. Instead of one lamin on each side of the core, there are two lamins (Fig. 37) with their grains laid in one direction only, to resist the increased tendency towards warping.

Veneered compo board. This is a poor quality board, made from compressed shavings bonded with a synthetic resin glue. It does use up sawmill waste, however, and can be used where the finished job is liable to come into contact with a fairly high temperature (e.g. radiator surrounds) (Fig. 38). Screws do not hold well in this material. It is becoming widely used for carcases and radio cabinets and speakers.

Hardboard. This is a strong form of cardboard, very much compressed. It is used for cheap carcase backs, drawer bottoms, painted wall panels, etc. It is made from highly compressed wood pulp with a bonding adhesive.

CONSTRUCTION PROBLEMS WITH SOLID WOOD

It has been seen that with built-up materials there is no need for allowances for movement, owing to the stable nature of the material. In items of furniture made from solid wood, allowances must be made for the wood to shrink *and* expand with changes in temperature and humidity.

Reference to Fig. 39 shows how wood shrinks and expands. Note that the shrinkage or expansion with the grain is so small that it can be ignored for all practical purposes. Across the grain, however, wood does shrink and expand, even from day to day. This must be allowed for and not prevented, otherwise the wood will split or buckle.

For practical purposes, under normal conditions, the allowance required for this shrinkage or expansion is 3 mm for each 300 mm of width, or 1%.

FIG. 39 MOVEMENT ALLOWANCE (SOLID TIMBER)

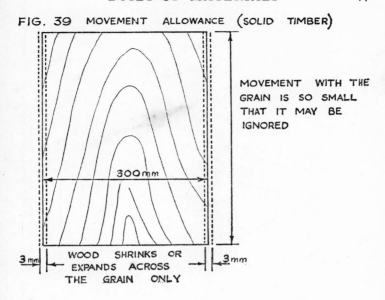

MOVEMENT WITH THE GRAIN IS SO SMALL THAT IT MAY BE IGNORED

300mm

3 mm

WOOD SHRINKS OR EXPANDS ACROSS THE GRAIN ONLY

3 mm

FIG. 40 BATTENING A DRAWING-BOARD

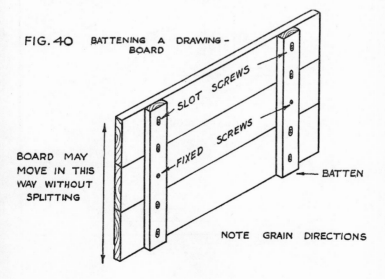

SLOT SCREWS

FIXED SCREWS

BATTEN

BOARD MAY MOVE IN THIS WAY WITHOUT SPLITTING

NOTE GRAIN DIRECTIONS

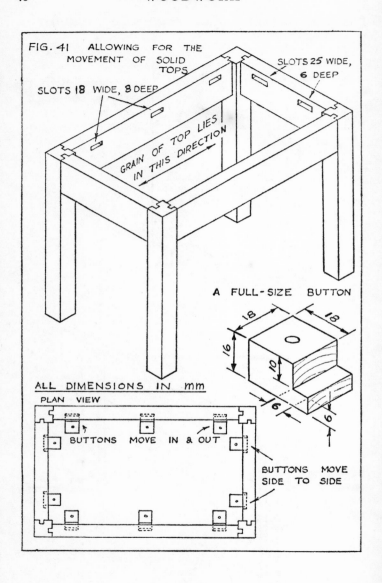

FIG. 41 ALLOWING FOR THE MOVEMENT OF SOLID TOPS

SLOTS 25 WIDE, 6 DEEP

SLOTS 18 WIDE, 8 DEEP

GRAIN OF TOP LIES IN THIS DIRECTION

A FULL-SIZE BUTTON

18

18

16

10

6

6

ALL DIMENSIONS IN mm

PLAN VIEW

BUTTONS MOVE IN & OUT

BUTTONS MOVE SIDE TO SIDE

Battening a drawing board. Good quality drawing boards are made from several boards of even-grained timber, free from knots, such as parana pine. Since the board must not twist or warp, two stout battens are fixed to the back of the board as shown in the diagram. The centre screw is a fixed one but the screws on either side are run through slots in the batten, thus

FIG. 42 EXPANSION IN SOLID DOOR - PANELS

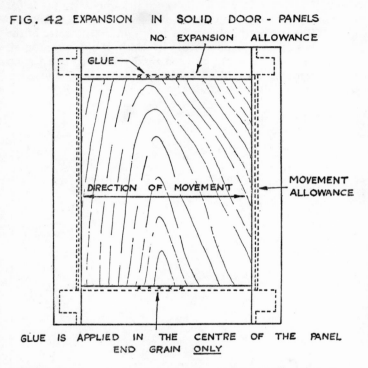

GLUE IS APPLIED IN THE CENTRE OF THE PANEL
END GRAIN ONLY

allowing the board to shrink or expand. This method of allowing movement is known as "slot-screwing" (Fig. 40).

Buttoning a stool or table top. When a stool or table top is made from solid timber, the top must not be prevented from moving, otherwise it will split or buckle. To allow this movement we use buttons of the shape and size shown (Fig. 41). It will be seen that it is unnecessary to allow for any movement in the length of the top. Allowance has been made, however, for movement *across* the grain. The number of buttons used will vary according to the size of the top and the quality of the timber used; whether it is quarter-sawn or plain-sawn.

A solid panel in a framed-up door (Fig. 42). In a door or carcase back, the panel may be either solid or plywood. If a solid panel is used, allowance must again be made for movement. It will be noted that allowance has only been made for shrinkage *and* expansion across the grain but not along the grain. Glue is placed only on the end grain in the centre of the panel, thus allowing it to move in its width. If glue were run all round the panel it would be fixed rigidly and prevented from moving. In time it would split or buckle, depending on whether the timber shrank or expanded.

Chapter 6

SURFACE TREATMENT OF TIMBER

Preservation

THE surface treatment given to a wood surface will vary according to a number of factors:—

The use to which the job is to be put.
Indoor or outdoor use since appearance may be important.
The type of timber used.
The degree of preservation required.

It is emphasized that the main purpose of painting, polishing or creosoting is not for decorative purposes but to preserve the timber from decay, fungi and worms.

Burning. Some protection is given to posts below ground level by burning the ends. The charcoal or carbon gives some protection but does not seal the timber. It does, however, repel insects and fungi.

Tar. Tar provides complete protection against dampness by completely sealing the wood. It is mainly used on posts below ground level and once done rarely needs re-doing. The tar is applied while hot, using a long-handled brush. Care should be exercised in heating the tar since it is very inflammable. It is a fairly cheap method of preservation, since tar is a by-product of coal when coal gas is extracted.

Creosote. Creosote provides temporary protection to wood above ground level but little protection underground. It is toxic to insects, worms and plant life but does not completely seal the timber. It is therefore necessary to repeat the treatment at about three-year intervals. It is again a by-product of coal and, being cheap, is used on sheds and fences.

Copper-chrome-arsenate. The use of creosote as a timber preservative has many limitations, in addition to those mentioned above. Creosoted timber cannot be painted or glued and there is an increased fire risk. In the building industry, much use is now being made of vacuum/pressure impregnation of timber by solutions of copper-chrome-arsenates. This gives complete protection above and below ground against all known forms of timber decay; all insect attack, including termites and marine borers, but at the same time it is harmless to human, animal and plant life. The timber may also be painted or glued with synthetic resin glues, it is clean, odourless, non-oily and non-volatile and it is impossible to wash out more than a trace of the preservative. If treated boards are sawn into shorter lengths it is important to treat the sawn ends with the solution.

Light coloured timbers which have undergone this treatment may be identified by the pale green colouring or by the use of the trade name "Tanalised". The company responsible for this trade name also incorporates flameproofing with the preservative treatment, under the trade name of "Pyrolith".

Oil Paint and Varnish. Oil paints and varnishes are used both indoors and outdoors but special grades should be used if the wood is exposed to the elements. They act by sealing the timber from dampness but are also toxic to insects, animals and humans if lead-based. The tops and bottoms of windows and doors should not be neglected because they are not seen.

Both paint and varnish must be used sparingly, but at the same time sufficient must be applied to give a complete coating to the wood or metal. Always finish the brush strokes in the direction of the grain of the wood, for the sake of appearance. A good paint job usually consists of two under coats of a matt surface paint and one high-gloss top coat. Painting should be repeated at regular periods, since paint deteriorates with age. Old paint should be burned off before new is applied. A second coat must not be applied before the previous coat has dried out thoroughly, and a good surface is obtained if the paint is rubbed down with a wet pumice block before the next coat is applied. Glasspapering of successive coats may be dangerous to the health if lead paints are used and the dust is inhaled.

The base or vehicle is made from linseed oil, turpentine and drying agents, plus a pigment or coloured powder to give the required colour of paint. Turpentine is used to thin down paint which is too thick.

Cellulose Paints. These paints are used for similar purposes to oil paints but are more expensive, quicker drying and more permanent. They also give a finer surface. The base of these paints is cellulose and special "thinners" must be used to thin down a paint which is too thick.

Staining. Staining does little to enhance the appearance of timber, in fact, it is often considered that it reduces the lustre obtained by later polishing. This is due to the opaque pigments blocking the passage of light which would otherwise be reflected back through the top milli-fraction of the wood surface. It is this light reflection which gives the "glow" in natural wood finishes.

If stains are used, the spirit-based varieties are less inclined to raise the grain surface than those with water as their base. Both varieties must be applied quickly to preserve a wet edge and careful examination is required so that "tears" and double runs are rapidly removed before the stain has time to dry. If a spirit-based stain is to be used, it is necessary to damp down the wood surface with clear methylated spirit before applying the stain. When the surface is dry it should be rubbed down with No. 0 glasspaper. The cutting action of the glasspaper re-levels the surface after the grain has been raised and thereby reduces the need for heavy glasspapering after the stain has been applied. If water-based stains are to be used, then apply clean water in the same way.

Polishing of the stained surfaces should not be undertaken until the surface of the timber is completely dry.

Wax Polish. Used as a polish to give a smooth glossy finish to furniture and is seen to its best advantage on open-grain timbers such as oak. It can, of course, also be used on close-grain timbers such as walnut. It seals the timber and is repellent to woodboring insects but it is of no use for outdoor work.

The secret of obtaining a good wax finish is to apply "one part wax to 99 parts elbow-grease". Wax put on thickly collects dust and becomes very dirty. The surface should first be given a thin coat of a mixture of equal parts of white shellac polish and methylated spirit. When dry this should be lightly rubbed down with a No. 0 glasspaper since the grain surface will be raised. Wax is now rubbed well into the grain with a lintless cloth, until the surface is completely covered with a fine film of wax. After about an hour this should then be burnished with another lintless cloth. The process may then be repeated if necessary.

The best wax polish is made from equal parts of wax and turpentine. The wax is shredded and dissolved in the turpentine, best American turps giving a better polish than synthetic turps. The mixing process may be accelerated by heating up the mixture in a water container similar to the glue pot. The mixture, which is highly inflammable, should never be heated over an open flame. When the mixture is completely melted down it should be set aside to form a stiff paste.

French Polish. This polish is used to give a high gloss surface to close-grain, exotic or decorative timbers. It seals the grain of the timber effectively but is only usually done on surfaces which are seen. Thus, under-surfaces may be attacked by wood-boring insects. It is not a suitable finish for oak since the high gloss is incompatible with the robust grain of the timber.

It is a difficult method of polishing, needing expert treatment and great care. The polish, a mixture of shellac and methylated spirit, is charged into a rubber and occasionally given a dot of raw linseed oil to ease the movement of the rubber. If wood such as mahogany is being polished, the open pores of the grain must first be filled with a grain filler. Sometimes plaster of paris is used but if so, the wood surface must then be stained. Afterwards it is glasspapered down (No. 0 glasspaper).

The lightly charged polish rubber is now lightly moved over the wood surface, using a circular motion and moving from one edge of the surface to the other. Gradually a thin layer of polish is deposited on the surface. Certain points must be watched while rubbing on the polish:—

1. Too heavy pressure will lift off the layers of polish already deposited.
2. A sticking rubber should be given a dot of raw linseed oil, or
3. The polish surface must be left for a while to harden up.
4. Periodically the surface should be smoothed down with pumice powder in a paste form, thus aiding the production of a mirror-like finish.

When a sufficient surface has been built up, the circular

motion is changed to a long stroke with the grain to finish off. The use of linseed oil tends to cause oily patches or "mistiness" on the final surface. This can be removed by very lightly dusting the surface with a clean rubber, very lightly charged with methylated spirit.

The best French polishes are made from pale shellac and wood naphtha or white methylated spirit, but it is best, for the amateur, to buy a ready-made French polish of a recognized brand, thus ensuring the correct consistency.

Polyurethane is, in effect, a liquid plastic which looks like a varnish before application but has very different structure and properties. Some polyurethanes harden on exposure to air, others to the water vapour in the air, the time varying according to conditions of temperature and air movement. Usually, they will be touch dry in 30 minutes, sanding dry in 2 to 3 hours, and fully hardened in about 12 hours. After this, the surface is extremely hard and durable against knocks and abrasions, chemicals and water, including hot drinks.

Such a finish has obvious advantages for furniture but the high gloss can be objectionable if used in the normal way. If the polyurethane is thinned to a ratio of 1 : 4 with one part of white spirit (turps sub.), a much more acceptable furniture finish will be obtained. Two or three coats will be required, according to choice, but the coats must be allowed to harden and then be "cut down" with fine steel wool between applications. If the final coat is "cut down" very gently with fine steel wool and then given a single coat of wax polish it will be difficult to distinguish from the traditional wax polishing of wood. The difference will be noted, however, in the far superior lasting quality of the surface.

Drying time may be extended to several days in the case of some very oily timbers. In such cases the surfaces should be wiped over with a de-greasing agent just prior to brushing on the polyurethane.

PART II

DESIGN AND CONSTRUCTION

Chapter 7

DESIGN OR PLANNING

TO decide whether an article is of good or bad design is a very difficult matter. We all decide for ourselves, this decision being based on the things we have lived with and seen during our lives. Those who have paid close attention to what is good and bad in design from an objective point of view, agree that there are certain common factors to be found in articles of good design whether they be hand-made or machine-made, wooden, steel, fabric or pottery. These factors are:—

Fitness for purpose
Right use of material
Sound construction
Harmonious appearance

Fitness for purpose. This means that the thing made must do the job it is intended to do, in the best possible manner. Thus, a medicine chest must be capable of holding medicine bottles; a book-rack must not allow the books to fall out; a teapot should pour without drips and without allowing the lid to fall off. A chair should be at the correct height for comfort and good posture.

Right use of material. The material should be treated in a manner natural to it. Wood should not be made to imitate steel and vice versa. A few years ago chairs were made from pressed steel and then painted to imitate the grain of wood. At the very least this amounts to dishonesty and the results are rarely pleasing to the eye. Each material has its own characteristics and should be worked accordingly. Thus, solid timber constructions are mainly composed of combinations of straight lines; built-up timbers have a more plastic nature when steamed and therefore can take on more curved and flowing forms. Reference to Figs. 305, 306 and 307 will illustrate how the form and construction of a chair varies according to the material used.

Sound construction. The quality of the craftsmanship must be of the best. In woodwork the joints must be strong and well made, of the right sort for the job and close fitting.

Harmonious appearance. This may often be found to follow as a matter of course, if the previous criteria have been fulfilled. It is the most difficult factor to deal with but certain guides may be suggested:—

1. The article must be of good proportions. These proportions may be effected as follows:—

   (a) The more pleasant shape offered by the rectangle compared with the square.

   (b) The greater stability in appearance when the bottom rail of a door is wider than the top rail. If these rails were made equal in width, foreshortening would make the bottom one look narrower and make the door appear top heavy. For the same reasons, in a chest of drawers, the drawers at the bottom should be deeper than those at the top.

   (c) Asymmetry in shape is often less monotonous than symmetry. The curves in a moulding are more pleasant if based on parts of an ellipse rather than parts of a circle. The rectangular shapes in a bookcase are more interesting if they are unequal rather than repetitions of the same rectangle.

2. Decoration (do not confuse this word with design) should arise naturally in the construction of the article and never be "put on" as an afterthought. The points to note here are:—

   (a) The value of simple mouldings such as the chamfer and ovolo which, by means of light reflection, soften the harsh outline of a square corner.

   (b) The natural beauty of the grain of timber, often spoiled by staining which robs the surface of lustre.

   (c) The value of the run-off or stopped chamfer in uniting a stile and rail which run at right angles to each other. The chamfer may also be used to good effect to reduce dust-collecting surfaces.

   (d) Simplicity in decoration is far better than over-lavish treatment. Follow the general rules above and—"If in doubt, leave it out".

   (e) Much furniture contains opposing horizontal and vertical lines. Greater unity of the whole may be ob-

tained by carrying the eye smoothly from the vertical
to the horizontal. Note how this is achieved on the
part view of the sideboard shown in Fig. 42a. The eye
follows the curve of the vertical leg into the horizontal

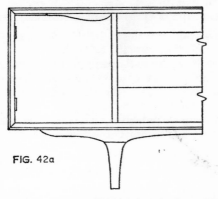

FIG. 42a

rail without jarring. Note the similar effect resulting
from the deep chamfer running around the inside edge
of the main carcase.

In order to assist those who are unskilled in designing, or
planning an article of furniture, the step-by-step build-up of a
design is illustrated below.

TO DESIGN A FIRESCREEN IN OAK

Before beginning to draw out the firescreen, first decide on
the purpose of the object. Is it to cover the fireplace when there
is no fire, or is it literally a screen to keep off the heat?

1. Having decided that the screen's purpose is to cover the
empty fireplace opening, we have the first clue to the design.
Measure the fireplace opening so that the screen will give
coverage. (In most modern houses the average size is 600 mm
high, 400 mm wide.)

2. To meet our main purpose then, we could therefore prop
a polished piece of wood against the fireplace, thereby covering
the rather ugly fireplace opening. We should not be doing the
job in the best possible way, however, since the board may

blow over or slip and fall down. Furthermore, if solid timber is used, it would certainly warp.

3. This means that we must enclose the wood in a solid frame and thus prevent warping and make it heavier and less likely to blow over.

4. This immediately presents new problems:—

> (a) How wide and thick should the stiles (verticals) and the rails (horizontals) be?
>
> (b) How thick should the panel be, since it must rest in either a groove or a rebate on the inside edge of the frame? This will influence the size and kind of mortice and tenon joint used.
>
> (c) How can we reduce top heaviness, especially if feet are to be made to prevent falling over?

5. We have now reached the stage when drawing may begin, so draw to a suitable scale the panel as seen in the front view, i.e. 600 mm × 400 mm.

6. Round this panel we must draw the frame. It will be found by practice that about 50 mm in width will look about right, neither too heavy nor too light.

7. From the side view we must now decide the thickness of the frame. Assuming that the panel will be either 6 mm thick plywood or solid wood with a 6 mm thick edge, we know that we must have a 6 mm groove inside the frame. Reference to Fig. 97 shows us that this means a 6 mm thick tenon for the frame joints. Since the mortice which takes the tenon needs adequately thick sides, add 6 mm each side of the tenon and we arrive at the answer—The stiles and rails need to be 18 mm thick.

8. To reduce the effects of foreshortening, make the bottom rail 25 mm wider, by reducing the panel size. This also means that we shall have a longer shoulder on the rails, making for surer squareness of the frame, and bigger tenons meaning greater strength. For similar reasons, increase the width of the top rail to 65 mm.

9. Draw in the feet as solid blocks, large enough to prevent the screen from tipping. About 200 mm × 75 mm × 40 mm will be found sufficient. The feet will have to be placed on the bottom rails, not the stiles, since the jointing might interfere with the M. and T. joints in the frame.

10. To prevent top heaviness the following suggestions should be considered (Fig. 43):—

   (a) Reduce the top weight by curving the top rail (about 12 mm drop at each side).
   (b) In the front view, taper the stiles towards the top. (Try about 12 mm taper.)
   (c) In the side view, taper the stiles and top rail. (Try a finished thickness of about 14 mm.)

11. The joint sizes must now be decided. From the information shown on Figs. 56 and 97, show the haunched mortice and tenon joints between the stiles and rails. The joints must be haunched to fill in the grooves at the top of the stiles caused by the plough plane. The haunch also helps to prevent wind in the frame. The feet will be joined to the bottom rails by means of a cross-halving joint (Fig. 104) or, better still, a stopped bridle joint (Fig. 103).

12. So far there has been only *functional* decoration in our planning of the firescreen. (The shaping was carried out to reduce top weight only.) The following decorative details should now be considered:—

   (a) Would a run-off or stopped chamfer on the inner edge of the frame aid unity, by blending together the stiles and rails? It would certainly reduce the dust-collecting surface.
   (b) The rectangular blocks of the feet look very clumsy. Their appearance would be helped with some simple form of rounding or shaping. This would also improve the unity of the design and give a greater appearance of stability.
   (c) Would rounding of the bottom corners of the frame aid in unifying the stile and rail and also remove a rather ugly corner?
   (d) Is the panel too big? Would it not be better to insert a vertical member in the centre of the frame, thus giving two long panels? (Such a vertical member is known as a muntin.) If a plywood panel is used, would a "herring-bone" facing veneer achieve a similar effect?

These problems are largely a matter of personal taste. Experience and observation of the things around us help to decide these factors.

13. Having designed or, to use a better word, planned our

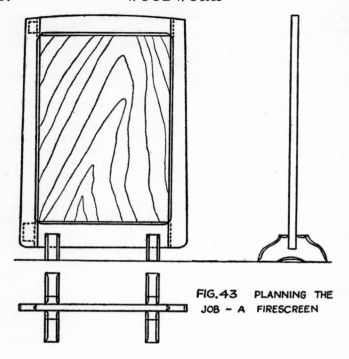

FIG. 43 PLANNING THE
JOB - A FIRESCREEN

| 35mm | 40mm | 35mm |

CUTTING LIST				
PART	Nº	L	W	T	REMARKS
STILES					
RAILS					
FEET					
PANEL					
FIRESCREEN					
NAME		FORM			
SCALE:		DATE			

6mm

110mm

FIG. 44

firescreen, the proportions should be viewed critically and if satisfactory, the drawing should be dimensioned. To complete the drawing, a cutting list as shown in Fig. 44 should be added; usually in the bottom right corner of the drawing sheet. This cutting list contains all the relevant information concerning the drawing, in a tidy manner. The sizes given in the small boxes are the sizes of timber required to make the object, not the finished sizes which are shown on the drawing itself. The extra allowances shown on the cutting list include the timber required for planing face side, face edge, width and thickness. To work out the cutting list sizes, the following allowances are advised:—

    (a) Measure the length of the wood, including the joints, and add 12 mm normally. (Where mortices come close to end grain a horn may be needed and an extra allowance should be included.)

    (b) To the finished width add 6 mm.

    (c) To the finished thickness add 3 mm.

Chapter 8

BOX OR CARCASE
CONSTRUCTIONS

*The Dovetail Slope—Carcase Backs—Panel Shapes
Carcase Doors—Hinging—Ball Catches—Handles—Box
Constructions—Box Handles—Lapped and Secret
Dovetails—Drawer Construction*

THE basic joint in box or carcase constructions is either the
simple box joint shown in Fig. 45 or the through dovetail
joint shown in Fig. 46. Of the two, the dovetail joint is superior
since the tails and pins may be arranged in such a way as to
reduce the tendency for the joint to be pulled apart. (If a hang-
ing cupboard is to be made, the tails should be placed on the
sides, not the bottom.) If this consideration does not apply, it
is normal to put the tails on the long sides of the carcase and
the pins on the short sides.

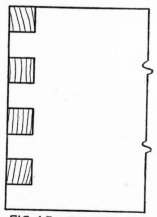

FIG. 45   THE BOX JOINT

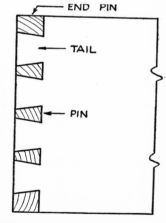

FIG. 46 THE   DOVETAIL JOINT

The dovetail slope. This will vary according to the timber
which is to be used:—

66

For hardwoods—slope 1 in 8 (Fig. 47).
For softwoods—slope 1 in 6 (Fig. 47).

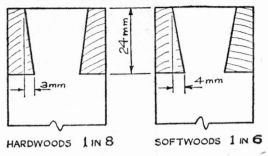

HARDWOODS **1** IN **8**   SOFTWOODS **1** IN **6**

FIG.47   THE   DOVETAIL   SLOPE

Incorrect slopes cause poor joints as shown in Fig. 48. To save time in setting out, a dovetail template is very useful (Fig. 49).

When presented with the problem of setting out a series of dovetail joints, guesswork is a tedious and lengthy procedure. By use of the simple method shown below, there is a saving in time and well-proportioned joints result.

Example. A box has been designed which has sides 90 mm deep and 9 mm thick. To set out the dovetails, follow this procedure:

1. Mark the shoulder line of the dovetails, 9 mm from the squared end of the wood.
2. The end pins (Fig. 50), which are unsupported on one side, must be about 3 mm or so wider than the enclosed pins. Mark this 3 mm in from each side of the wood (*a–a'*).
3. In the remaining 84 mm must go the tails and pins in which:
   (a) The wider ends of the pins must be *about* the same thickness as the wood (9 mm).
   (b) The tails should be about three times as long across the ends as the pins. (This is simply a matter of good proportions and appearance. For maximum strength the pins and tails should be equal in size.) ˙
4. Since the wood is 90 mm wide we will try setting out 3 tails. (1 tail for each 25 to 30 mm of width.)

5. Divide the distance between the lines *a–a'* into as many equal parts as there are tails, using the ruler as shown in Fig. 50. (3 equal parts in this example since there are 3 tails.)

6. Transfer these equal divisions to the shoulder line.

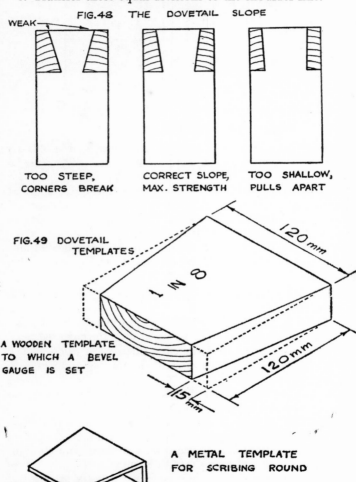

FIG. 48 THE DOVETAIL SLOPE

WEAK

TOO STEEP, CORNERS BREAK

CORRECT SLOPE, MAX. STRENGTH

TOO SHALLOW, PULLS APART

FIG. 49 DOVETAIL TEMPLATES

1 IN 8

120 mm

120 mm

15 mm

A WOODEN TEMPLATE TO WHICH A BEVEL GAUGE IS SET

A METAL TEMPLATE FOR SCRIBING ROUND

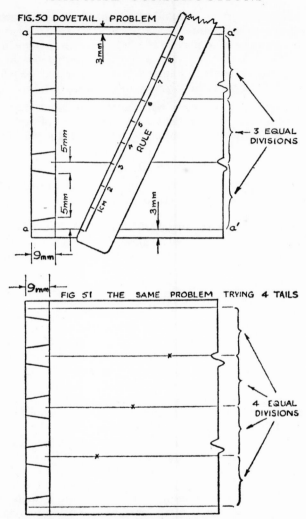

FIG.50 DOVETAIL PROBLEM

3 EQUAL DIVISIONS

FIG 51 THE SAME PROBLEM TRYING 4 TAILS

4 EQUAL DIVISIONS

7. These divisions mark the centres of the wide end of the pins, so mark 5 mm (about half of the wood's thickness) on each side of the divisions. For the end pins, mark in 5 mm from the a–a' line.

8. Using the correct dovetail slope, draw in the dovetail angles to these points.
9. The same problem may be tried using 4 tails, as shown in Fig. 51. Whichever joints look most suitable should be used. Adjustments to improve proportions may be made by reducing either pin sizes or the number of tails.

In box constructions it is well to bear in mind that the strength of the box is dependent upon the number of dovetails there are; for the greater the number, the greater the glue area.

CARCASE BACKS

In carcase constructions there is usually a back fitted, or in the case of a box, a bottom. The back may be fitted in various ways:—

Screwed on as shown in Fig. 52. This method should only be used with plywood backs since no allowance is made for shrinkage or expansion of the panel. It is not a suitable method with polished cabinets, since the end grain of the plywood presents an ugly appearance. It can, however, be used for painted jobs such as bathroom cabinets.

Rabbeted as shown in Fig. 53. The small flat cog is made to fill the gap caused by running the rebate plane along the full length of the top, bottom and sides. The depth of the rabbet must be at least 12 mm to allow for pinning or screwing a 6 mm holding fillet. This method may be used with plywood, glass or solid panels. With solid panels an allowance must be made for shrinkage or expansion across the grain.

Grooved as shown in Fig. 54. This is the best method but is more difficult to achieve. It is mainly used with solid panels, box tops and bottoms, and the necessary shrinkage and expansion allowances must be made. The end pin and tail carry a mitre which runs flush with the groove on its inner edge. The mitred portion completely covers the groove and conceals its presence. Since the end grain gluing of the mitre is weak, the glue area at the corner is often increased by using two small tails instead of one large one.

Having considered the methods of fitting a panel, we must now decide on the shaping of the panel itself. The shaping illustrated on p. 73 is suitable for both carcase backs and doors.

CARCASE BACKS

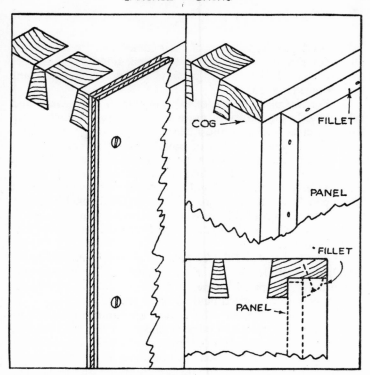

FIG.52 SCREWED ON   FIG.53 RABBETED

COG

FILLET

PANEL

FILLET

PANEL

FIG. 54 GROOVED CARCASE BACKS

END TAIL HAS NO SLOPE HERE

MITRE

PANEL GROOVE

THE SECTION HOLDING THE PINS HAS BEEN TURNED UPSIDE DOWN TO SHOW THE DETAIL

PANEL SHAPES

Plywood panels, because of their method of build, do not allow for shaping. If solid wood is used, however, the panel may be shaped in a variety of ways to give a more pleasant appearance (Fig. 55).

(a) *The flat panel* is one of the simplest in appearance and relies mainly on beauty of grain for effect. It is usually from 6 to 9 mm in thickness and mainly used for box bottoms.

(b) *The bevelled panel* is of more pleasant appearance but care must be taken that the angle of the bevel is not too steep. If this is not done and shrinkage occurs, a large gap will be exposed between the panel and carcase side. This will cause the loose panel to rattle in its groove. The bevelled panel is usually from 9 to 12 mm in thickness and fits into a 6 mm groove in the carcase. This method is also used for box bottoms as well as carcase backs.

(c) *The bevelled and fielded panel* is an improvement on the bevelled panel. It gives a more distinct light reflection and accentuates the panel shape. It is usually about 12 mm in thickness with the raised field no more than 2 mm high.

(d) *The overlaid panel* gives a flush appearance and, in conjunction with a moulded edge as shown in Fig. 55, makes a most attractive panel suitable for backs of carcases, door panels or box tops. The timber used must be about 12 mm in thickness with 4 mm grooves and should preferably be quartered. This applies particularly to box tops, where the panel may be strong enough to distort the box sides if warping were to take place. The same applies to door panels, since quartered timber is less likely to twist the door framing.

(e)*The flush, beaded panel* is mainly used for carcase backs and presents an attractive appearance. The expansion allowance is rather a dust trap, however. The panel thickness is from 9 to 12 mm, with a 6 mm tongue. The expansion allowance is made only on the side grain of course. The bead may be made with either a scratch stock or the head of a countersunk screw set in a wooden block.

(f) *The cavetto moulding* makes a most attractive panel shape. It has the advantage that no gap is exposed if the panel should shrink, because the last 12 mm of the panel has parallel sides.

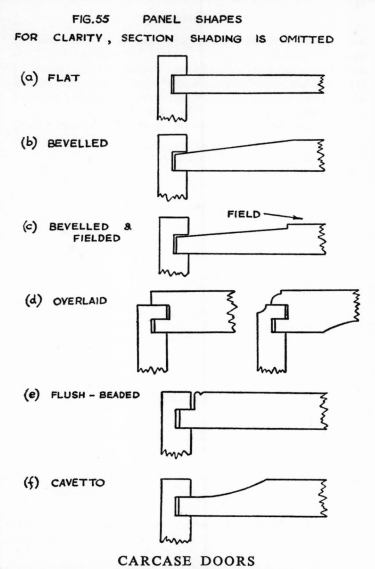

FIG.55   PANEL   SHAPES
FOR   CLARITY , SECTION   SHADING   IS   OMITTED

(a) FLAT

(b) BEVELLED

(c) BEVELLED &
    FIELDED

FIELD

(d) OVERLAID

(e) FLUSH – BEADED

(f) CAVETTO

CARCASE DOORS

For door constructions the traditional method is to use a
framed-up panel or panels. Solid, unframed timber would be

impracticable owing to warping and distortion. Built-up materials such as laminboard or block board may be used unframed, but on solid wood carcase constructions a framed-up door looks more in keeping with the traditional construction. (This consideration does not apply with veneered carcases, where built-up materials may be preferable for the doors.)

In the door construction shown in Fig. 56, the frame holds

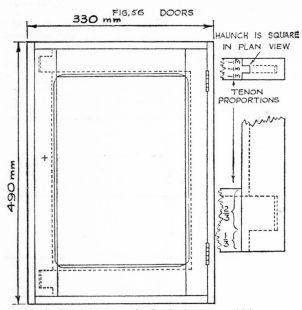

FIG. 56 DOORS

330 mm

490 mm

HAUNCH IS SQUARE
IN PLAN VIEW

TENON
PROPORTIONS

In a small cabinet of this size, the finished sizes would be:—

Carcase	150 mm × 12 mm	Top Rail	50 mm × 15 or 18 mm
Back	6 mm plywood or 9 mm solid	Bottom Rail	55 mm × 15 or 18 mm
Stiles	40 mm × 15 or 18 mm	Door Panel	6 mm plywood or 9 mm quartered timber in the solid

the solid panel loosely at the sides but is glued at the centre of the end grain. This allows the panel to shrink and expand without distorting the frame (see Fig. 42 also). To reduce the total weight on the door hinges, the panel may be bevelled and fielded but the taper must be fairly shallow. If this is not done the door panel will rattle if shrinkage takes place. On the inner edges of the door frame, a chamfer or bevel will reduce the dust-collecting surface.

The door itself should not be made until the carcase is completed and glued up. The frame is then made 3 mm over size in length and breadth and planed to fit the carcase opening, starting at the hinging edge. An alternative method sometimes favoured is to scribe the size of the carcase opening directly on to the stiles and rails. The top rail should be made slightly wider than the stiles, the bottom rail wider still. This gives improved appearance and stronger joints, for wider tenons are possible. With wider tenons there is less risk of wind in the door frame and the longer shoulders are an aid to squareness. The tenon proportions are shown on Fig. 56 and ensure maximum strength in the joints. The haunch fills the gap caused by grooving with a plough plane, and helps to prevent wind in the frame. The tenons should be stopped or stubbed so that any shrinkage of the stile will not leave the tenon protruding. A contraction gap should be allowed between the bottom of the stopped tenon and the mortice.

After the completed door frame has been glued, it should be fitted to the carcase one side at a time, starting at the hinging edge. The top and bottom should then be fitted in that order and finally, the locking stile. The locking stile should bear a slight taper towards its inner edge to allow for the curve of the arc made as the door closes. This will ensure minimum gap between the door locking stile and the inside of the carcase.

FLUSH DOORS

Modern furniture often calls for the use of a flush door, not only from the point of view of appearance, with clean unbroken lines, but also to remove dust collecting ledges. Doors of this type may be made with plywood, laminboard or block board as the base material which is then lipped, to hide the core end grain, and veneered. If the lipping is done before the veneering, the edges of the veneer are prone to chipping and other accidental damage (Fig. 56a). If the veneering is done before the lipping, the veneer is protected from damage but the line of the lipping will be seen around the door edges. A suitable compromise in this dilemma is to use heavy quality 1·5 mm constructional veneer for the lipping and apply it with an impact adhesive. Note that both sides of the door are veneered to balance the stresses caused by veneering. If this is not done the door will probably distort.

FIG.56a

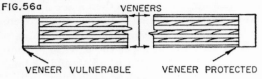

VENEERS

VENEER VULNERABLE   VENEER PROTECTED

HINGING

When the door has been accurately fitted to the carcase it must be hinged. The number of hinges used, and their size, depends upon the size of the door. Two hinges will usually be found sufficient in doors up to about 500 mm in height, whereas three might be required for 750 mm. The hinges must clear the tenons to prevent screwing into the end grain, which is never a secure method. Generally it is safe to fit the hinge in line with the rail inner edge.

The hinge may be let half into the door and half into the carcase as shown in Fig. 57, method A. The depth should be set on a marking or cutting gauge, using the actual hinge which is being used, as shown in Fig. 57. The same is done to mark the width of the flap. The length of the hinge should be scribed first on to the door frame and from the frame to the carcase while the door is in position. An alternative method of fitting the hinge is shown in method B, Fig. 57. Using this method, the hinge is let wholly into the door edge and there is therefore no break on the inside line of the carcase to mar appearance. In addition, a slightly longer screw may be used to fit the hinge to the carcase side, giving greater rigidity.

Hinging faults will arise if the gauge settings are not accurately made and carefully worked to. The most common faults are:—

Hingebound (Fig. 58). The remedy for this is to pack up the housing with thin card, thus throwing the hinge into the correct position.

Housings too shallow (Fig. 59). This is easily remedied by cutting the housing more deeply.

Screwbound (Fig. 60). Either countersink the hinges more deeply or use smaller screws.

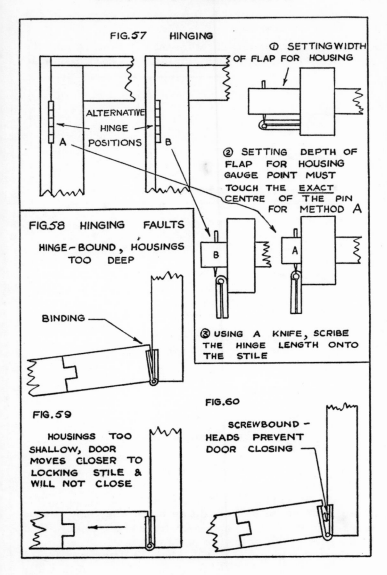

FIG. 57   HINGING

① SETTING WIDTH OF FLAP FOR HOUSING

ALTERNATIVE HINGE POSITIONS

A   B

② SETTING DEPTH OF FLAP FOR HOUSING GAUGE POINT MUST TOUCH THE <u>EXACT</u> CENTRE OF THE PIN FOR METHOD A

B   A

③ USING A KNIFE, SCRIBE THE HINGE LENGTH ONTO THE STILE

FIG. 58 HINGING FAULTS

HINGE-BOUND, HOUSINGS TOO DEEP

BINDING

FIG. 59

HOUSINGS TOO SHALLOW, DOOR MOVES CLOSER TO LOCKING STILE & WILL NOT CLOSE

FIG. 60

SCREWBOUND - HEADS PREVENT DOOR CLOSING

Hinge recesses are not flat. This will cause hinge strain and
pulling of the screws.

When screwing on the hinges for the first time, fix only the
centre screw in the flaps. If any adjustment is needed, this can

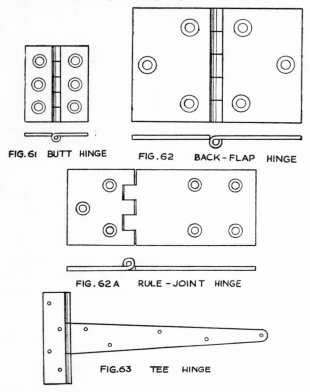

FIG. 61   BUTT   HINGE   FIG. 62   BACK - FLAP   HINGE

FIG. 62 A   RULE - JOINT   HINGE

FIG. 63   TEE   HINGE

be done on the outer screws. The most common hinges encountered are:—

1. Butt hinges (Fig. 61). The best hinges for use in cabinet
construction are made from drawn brass. They may also be
obtained in folded brass and mild steel and are distinguished
by the equal width of the two narrow flaps.

2. Back-flap hinges (Fig. 62). Made in drawn and folded
brass, also mild steel. They are distinguished by their wider

flaps and the fact that they will move through more than three-quarters of a full turn. One special variety of back-flap hinge (Fig. 62A) is made for use on tables such as the Pembroke table of the Regency period, where there is a hinged top and a rule-joint edge (See Fig. 235m). This hinge, known as the rule-joint hinge, is made with one flap wider than the other since the screws have to be placed a long way from the knuckle on the one side. The holes are countersunk on the opposite side to the knuckle, unlike the butt and back-flap hinge.

3. The tee hinge (Fig. 63). Made from mild steel and often black japanned to prevent rust. Used for such work as shed doors and light gates; sometimes they are called cross-garnet hinges.

BALL CATCHES

The ball catch and striking plate offer a good method of securing a small carcase door (Fig. 64). They are concealed, tidy and positive in their action. To fit the ball catch, the following procedure should be adopted:—

(1) Make a slight cut with a twist bit spur, to take the flange of the ball catch and remove the waste wood with a very narrow chisel to a sufficient depth for the flap to be flush with the edge of the door.

(2) Select a second twist bit of the same width as the barrel of the ball catch and, using the hole made by the first twist bit for centre, bore out sufficiently deep for the barrel of the catch. Tap in the ball catch, using a small tube and hammer to prevent damage to the ball and its spring.

(3) Screw the door on to the carcase, close it, and mark where the ball strikes the carcase.

(4) Measure the distance from the outer edge of the door to the centre of the ball in the door edge. The hole in the catch plate must be this distance in from the edge of the carcase. Measure this distance in from the edge of the carcase and drill a shallow hole, big enough to allow the ball to drop in. (A twist bit should not be used since the point might go right through the side.)

(5) Locate the catch plate in position and scribe round it with a sharp penknife.

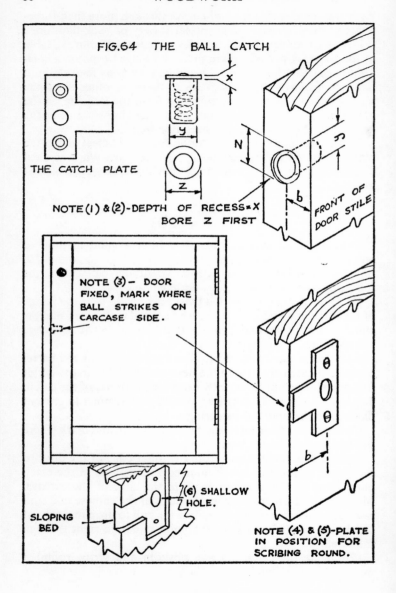

FIG.64 THE BALL CATCH

THE CATCH PLATE

NOTE (1) & (2) — DEPTH OF RECESS = X
BORE Z FIRST

FRONT OF DOOR STILE

NOTE (3) — DOOR FIXED, MARK WHERE BALL STRIKES ON CARCASE SIDE.

NOTE (4) & (5) — PLATE IN POSITION FOR SCRIBING ROUND.

SLOPING BED

(6) SHALLOW HOLE.

(6) Remove the waste to the depth required to sink the plate and cut a little deeper for the sloping lead to the hole.

(7) Bend the catch plate slightly, to match the lead in and screw the plate into position.

With this method, the door should, if properly made and free from wind, remain flush with the carcase. On large doors it is more usual to use two ball catches to ensure this; one placed on the top and one on the bottom of the locking stile. If the door is not flush, but is intended to be either set-in or protruding, an allowance should be made when measuring (4) above. Nylon roller catches and magnetic catches are also available for securing doors and are often used in preference, owing to the comparative ease of fitting.

HANDLES

The size, shape and position of a handle should be governed by how it is to be used. The most common fault is that handles are made far too big for the way in which they are gripped. The handles shown in Fig. 65 have been based on the two most important factors:—

1. How they are gripped.
2. The average size of the fingers.

From these factors we can determine the overall size of the handle. If the handle is to be jointed to the door it should be done by means of a mortice and tenon joint, using a piece of end grain timber. The joint should be wedged as shown in the diagram (Fig. 65). Both jointing and cutting for the wedges must be completed before shaping begins, otherwise holding the wood becomes a problem.

Various handle shapes are illustrated but it should be remembered that simplicity of shape may often be more successful than over-lavish treatment and decoration. (This applies particularly to handles which are turned on the lathe (Fig. 66).) In shaping, avoid sharp corners which are easily knocked off, and in order to ensure a comfortable grip, recess the underside of the handle to fit the finger grip (Fig. 65), using a firmer gouge.

In a door on a small cabinet, set the handle on the stile, slightly above the half-way line. (This slight asymmetry is more pleasant in appearance.) In a drawer, the handle or handles should also be slightly above centre on the drawer front. From the point of view of appearance, handles should usually be in a dark coloured timber. Not only will the dark timber contrast

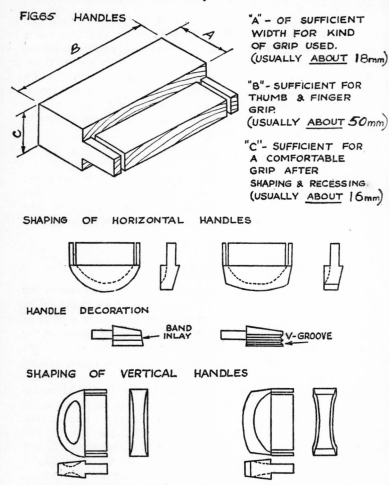

FIG.65   HANDLES

"A" - OF SUFFICIENT WIDTH FOR KIND OF GRIP USED. (USUALLY ABOUT 18mm)

"B" - SUFFICIENT FOR THUMB & FINGER GRIP. (USUALLY ABOUT 50mm)

"C" - SUFFICIENT FOR A COMFORTABLE GRIP AFTER SHAPING & RECESSING. (USUALLY ABOUT 16mm)

SHAPING OF HORIZONTAL HANDLES

HANDLE DECORATION

BAND INLAY

V-GROOVE

SHAPING OF VERTICAL HANDLES

well with a lighter background but there will be less tendency for finger marks to show. For final finishing the handle should not be wax polished but given three or four coats of clear cellulose or polyurethane. Between coats, they should be allowed to harden and then be cut down with No. 0 glasspaper or fine steel wool.

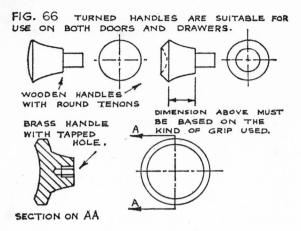

FIG. 66 TURNED HANDLES ARE SUITABLE FOR USE ON BOTH DOORS AND DRAWERS.

WOODEN HANDLES WITH ROUND TENONS

BRASS HANDLE WITH TAPPED HOLE.

DIMENSION ABOVE MUST BE BASED ON THE KIND OF GRIP USED.

SECTION ON AA

BOX CONSTRUCTIONS

The simplest form of box construction (Fig. 67) has a screwed-on base and a rabbeted lid. The overhang on the base may be given a simple moulding to match the lid. This method of fixing the base by screwing makes no allowance for expansion or contraction of the base; it can, therefore, only be used on small boxes where the movement will be small.

One-piece sides, sawn apart after gluing, ensure that the lid is identical in shape with the box (Fig. 68). The second method, shown in Fig. 69, is a further improvement since the two small dovetails give greater gluing area near the mitre and consequently a stronger lid. The lid portion of the sides is grooved and can then take an overlaid panel for the top. This means that the mitred end is essential to conceal the grooves and that the top dovetail has a slope on one side only, since it runs along the side of the groove (see Fig. 54). The box bottom may also run in a groove as shown in Fig. 69. This is, in fact, essential on large boxes where the amount of movement may be in the region of 1% of the width. Any attempt to prevent this movement in solid timber would probably result in splitting.

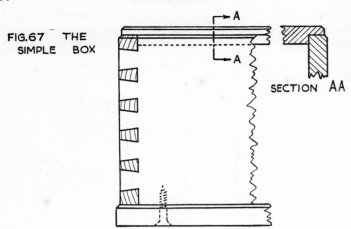

FIG.67 THE SIMPLE BOX

SECTION AA

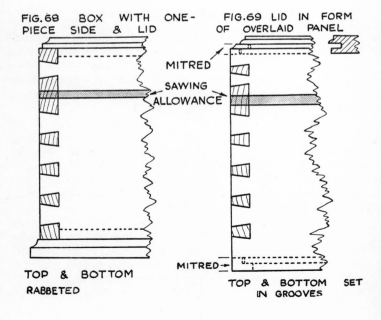

FIG.68 BOX WITH ONE-PIECE SIDE & LID

FIG.69 LID IN FORM OF OVERLAID PANEL

MITRED

SAWING ALLOWANCE

MITRED

TOP & BOTTOM RABBETED

TOP & BOTTOM SET IN GROOVES

BOX HANDLES

FIG. 70 SCREWED ON FROM BENEATH LID

FIG. 71 JOINTED INTO TOP OF LID

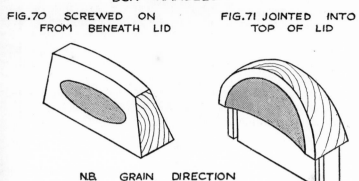

N.B. GRAIN DIRECTION

FIG. 72 A MORE SATISFACTORY METHOD FOR HINGED LIDS ON ONE-PIECE SIDES

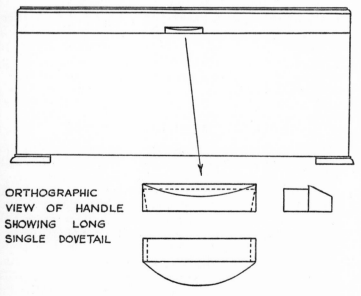

ORTHOGRAPHIC VIEW OF HANDLE SHOWING LONG SINGLE DOVETAIL

D

The overlaid panel shown in Fig. 69 calls for great accuracy in marking out and grooving. The overlaid portion of the top, and the edge of the box side, may be given a moulding suitable for the type of timber. Usually, strong mouldings such as the chamfer and cavetto are suitable for open-grain timbers such as oak. Walnut and mahogany, with their finer grain, call for a more delicate moulding such as the ovolo.

Whenever a solid panel fits into a groove it must be remembered that only end-grain gluing is permissible if the wood is to be allowed to move freely.

BOX HANDLES

The same considerations apply to the design of box handles as applied to door handles. Fitness for purpose is the keynote of sound design, so the shape and size must be determined by the way the handle is used. It may be questioned if handles on small boxes are necessary at all, for if the hand can comfortably span the lid, there is the method of opening.

There are three varieties of handle possible on box lids:—

1. Screwed on from below the lid, using side-grain timber (Fig. 70).
2. Jointed, on top of the lid, using end-grain timber (Fig. 71).
3. Dovetailed into the front edge of the lid, using end-grain timber (Fig. 72). This method is normally used on boxes with hinged lids.

SPECIAL DOVETAIL JOINTS

Lapped dovetails are used when it is necessary to conceal the end grain of the tails. This arises on such work as drawers and is helped by the fact that the drawer front is usually thicker than the sides (Fig. 73a). In large carcase work, such as book cases and bedside cabinets, it may be necessary to hide the dovetail joints to give clean, unbroken lines. This may entail the use of secret mitred or secret lapped dovetails at the top corners of the carcase, but the less laborious lapped dovetails at the bottom corners, with the open tails hidden underneath.

When making lapped dovetails, either the pins or the tails may be cut first, as with the common through dovetail. The use of a cutting gauge is strongly recommended for marking the joint shoulders of all special dovetail joints. Once the end grain of the material has been shot square the cutting gauge can be set to the thickness of the material which has to be jointed. This completely eliminates errors caused by faulty measurement.

Secret lapped dovetails are often used as the top corner joints on large carcases (Fig. 73b). The joints are completely concealed but the end grain of the lap does show. This may be

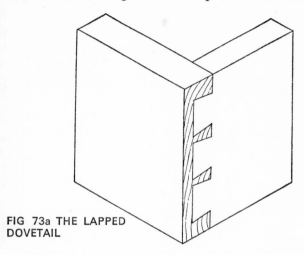

FIG 73a THE LAPPED
DOVETAIL

made less noticeable by incorporating a simple moulding such as an ovolo at c (Fig. 73c). The lap can also be given a shallow slope and be slightly recessed, as at b. If the front of the carcase is to carry a deep chamfer, as shown at a, the end pin may be mitred to prevent the awkward appearance of a mason's mitre. In this example the end grain of the lap has been left showing, in keeping with current furniture fashion. A mason's mitre may be seen in Fig. 242—2.

When making secret lapped dovetails extreme accuracy is necessary in both setting out and in cutting. It is usual to cut the pins first since it is almost impossible to scribe the shape of the closely linked tails on to the timber for the pins.

The secret mitred dovetail (Fig. 73d) is one of the most difficult joints to make well. It is used when the dovetails must be

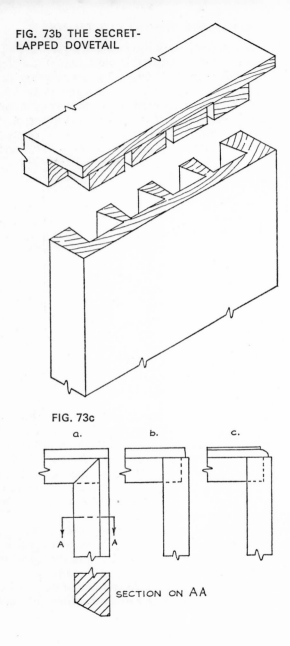

FIG. 73b THE SECRET-
LAPPED DOVETAIL

FIG. 73c

a.   b.   c.

A   A

SECTION ON AA

completely concealed and had a special use in furniture of the Georgian Period when it was required to construct furniture containing secret drawers. It is used today when a cabinet construction has to be veneered. If through dovetails are used,

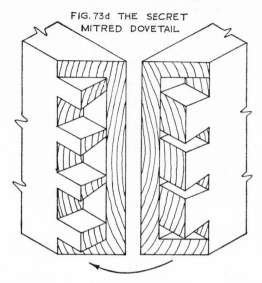

FIG. 73d THE SECRET MITRED DOVETAIL

subsequent shrinkage eventually leaves the end grain of the pins standing proud of the tails. The shape of the tails can then be seen quite clearly through the veneer.

When making secret mitred dovetails it is again usual to cut the pins before the tails and to use a cutting gauge for striking the joint shoulders and laps.

DRAWER CONSTRUCTION

It is often said that the quality of a craftsman is illustrated by his ability to make and fit a drawer to a table or cabinet. This may or may not be true but there is no doubt that to make a close fitting drawer is a true test of skill. Traditional methods are worthy of study, and examination of 18th-century furniture will be rewarding to the 20th-century craftsman.

One important fact must be remembered before considering

the drawer itself—that it is not possible to have a well fitted drawer in a poorly made table or cabinet. The drawer cannot, in fact, be put in as an afterthought. This will be more fully understood if the typical table arrangement shown in Fig. 73e is examined. It is essential that the drawer bearer and kicker lie absolutely parallel to each other and "out of wind" on both sides of the table. The drawer-bearing surfaces of the bearers

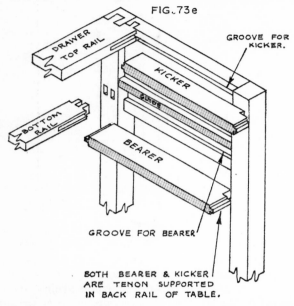

FIG. 73e

DRAWER TOP RAIL

GROOVE FOR KICKER.

KICKER

GUIDE

BOTTOM RAIL

BEARER

GROOVE FOR BEARER

BOTH BEARER & KICKER ARE TENON SUPPORTED IN BACK RAIL OF TABLE.

and kickers must also lie "flush" with the surfaces of both the top and bottom drawer rails. The drawer guides must also lie "flush" with the inside faces of the table legs.

In carcase constructions, the underside of the carcase top serves as the kicker for the drawer while similar joint constructions to those shown in Fig. 73f are made for the bottom rail and bearers. Drawers guides are, of course, unnecessary since the inside faces of the carcase sides guide the running of the drawer. An additional bottom drawer rail must run across the back of the carcase, however, to serve as support for the rear ends of the bearers (Fig. 73f). If the carcase is to carry a row of drawers arranged vertically, the underside of each bearer acts as the kicker for the drawer below. When gluing the bearers in a carcase assembly it is well to consider the problems caused by shrinkage and expansion when grains run in opposite directions. For this reason the bearer is glued at the tenon in the front rail and for about one third of the length of the housing. The remainder of the housing and the rear tenon are left dry.

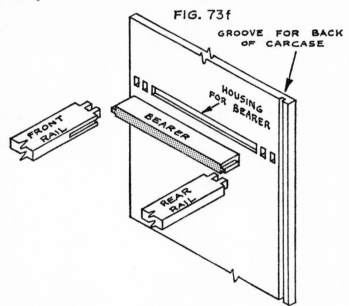

FIG. 73f

GROOVE FOR BACK OF CARCASE

HOUSING FOR BEARER

BEARER

FRONT RAIL

REAR RAIL

In a well-made assembly the drawer tightens very slightly as it is pulled fully open, thus preventing the drawer and its contents from shooting right out onto the floor. To achieve this, the space into which the drawer is to fit must be made slightly wider and deeper at the back than at the front. The amount is very small, about 0·5 mm for every 500 mm of depth in the drawer space. In framed table constructions this allowance is made by taking slightly more shavings off the bearers at the back than at the front when cleaning up. The same is done to the drawer guides (Fig. 73g).

In carcase constructions, the carcase should be made about 0·5 mm wider at the back than at the front. This means that the carcase is made very slightly out of square in the early stages of construction (Fig. 73h). The carcase drawer bearers also have a few extra shavings removed at the back, the same as in table constructions. In both carcase and table construc-

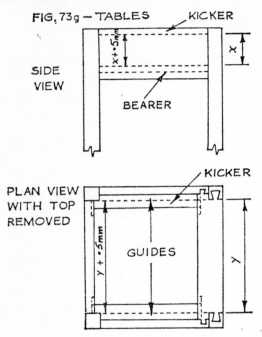

FIG. 73g – TABLES

tions it is essential that the drawer bearing surfaces are "out of wind" otherwise the drawer is bound to jam.

The procedure for making the drawer now follows the same pattern for both tables and carcases. First, plane the drawer front in the following order; face side, face edge, thickness. Do nothing at all to the width at this stage. Mark a large inverted V to indicate the front face of the drawer while the face side points inwards and the face edge points downwards (Fig. 73i). This means that the face side will eventually be on the inside of the drawer carcase. Refer now to Fig. 73i which shows the sequence of planing the drawer front to fit the opening into which it is to go. Edge (a), the face edge, is first planed (if necessary) to make an exact fit along the top of the bottom rail. When this has been done, edge (b) of the drawer front is planed to make a perfect fit to side (b) of the opening. This procedure is repeated for edges (c) and (d) until the edges of the drawer

FIG. 73h – CARCASES

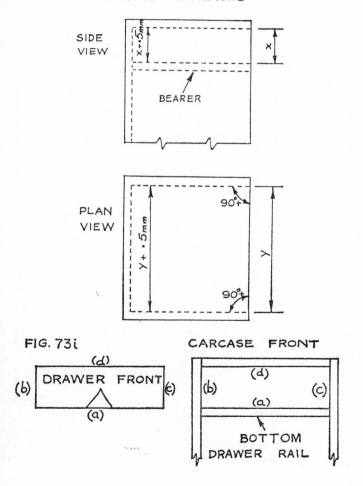

FIG. 73i   CARCASE FRONT

front make an exact fit in the drawer opening. If all of the
drawer front edges are planed very slightly out of square, so
that they taper towards the inside, it should just be possible
to push the drawer front into the opening space (Fig. 73j).

The drawer sides may now be fitted in a similar way but
first plane them both on face side, face edge and thickness.
Now plane both sides to the required width so that they will
just enter the drawer opening, on their respective sides, to a

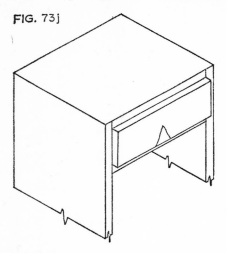

FIG. 73j

depth of about 50 mm. Mark the outside face of the side with
an L or R as shown in Fig. 73k so that they do not become
mixed up at a later stage in the fitting. The face sides of both
drawer sides should be on the inside of the drawer carcase,
face edges pointing downwards. At the same time it is a
distinct advantage if the grain directions can be arranged in
such a way that later cleaning up is facilitated (See Fig. 73v).
The end grain of the sides may now be shot so that both sides
are exactly the same length.

The drawer back is fitted in a similar way to the drawer
front except that side (d) is gauged to the required width (Fig.
73 l). The width, shown as x on the diagram, is equal to the
total depth of the drawer opening minus the space above the
drawer back (usually 6 mm) and the height of the drawer

bottom (usually 12 mm). The total reduction is therefore 18 mm. Note that the face side of the drawer back faces inwards to the drawer carcase and the face edge again points downwards.

Now arrange the lapped dovetails at the front end of the drawer side and the through dovetails at the rear end (Fig. 73m).

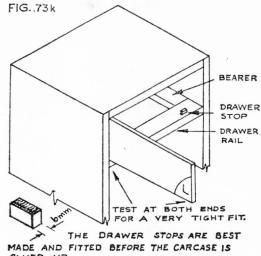

FIG..73k

BEARER

DRAWER STOP

DRAWER RAIL

TEST AT BOTH ENDS FOR A VERY TIGHT FIT.

THE DRAWER STOPS ARE BEST MADE AND FITTED BEFORE THE CARCASE IS GLUED UP.

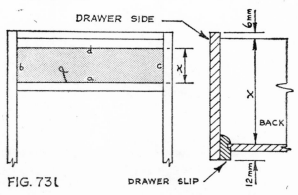

DRAWER SIDE

DRAWER SLIP

FIG. 73l

DRAWER SECTION
SHOWING WIDTH OF BACK.

Make sure that a tail will cover the place where the groove for the drawer bottom will eventually be cut on the inside face of the front. When the dovetails have been cut, scribe them onto the drawer front and back to the depth that they are to be set

FIG. 73 m

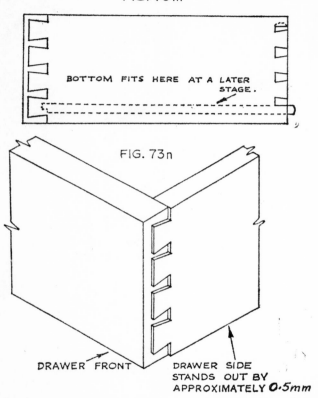

BOTTOM FITS HERE AT A LATER STAGE.

FIG. 73 n

DRAWER FRONT

DRAWER SIDE STANDS OUT BY APPROXIMATELY 0·5mm

in. This depth should be such that the sides stand out about 0·5 mm when fitted (Fig. 73n). This procedure facilitates cleaning up and also ensures a better fit of the drawer.

If the sides of the drawers have been made suitably light in thickness it will not be possible to groove them for the bottom without making them unduly weak and likely to split along the

groove. (From the point of view of proportion, a drawer
450 mm long × 300 mm × 100 mm deep, needs sides about
9 mm thick.) In order to maintain this light appearance it will
be necessary to make drawer slips (Fig. 73 1) which can by

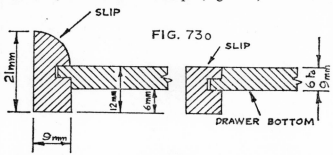

FIG. 73o

glued to the inside surface of the sides. Two types of slip are
illustrated in Fig. 73o. One will present a flush appearance
inside the drawer while the other gives a rounded fillet in the
corners of the drawer bottom. Difficulty is sometimes experi-

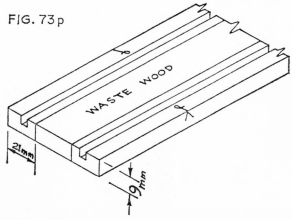

FIG. 73p

enced in ploughing the grooves in the slips, particularly if they
have been planed down to size and removed from the parent
board. This difficulty may be overcome by leaving the slip on
the parent board until after the groove has been ploughed, the
board being fixed to the bench by means of G cramps (Fig.

73p). An alternative method is shown in Fig. 73q but in this case the board is held in the vice while the groove is ploughed along the edge. After the grooving has been completed, the thickness of the slip can be gauged with the marking gauge and

FIG. 73q

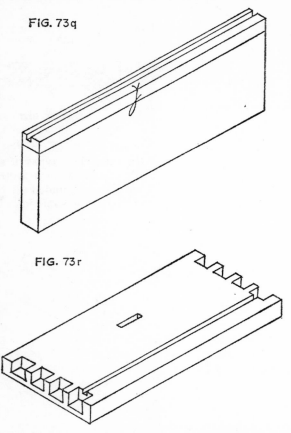

FIG. 73r

the slip may be sawn from the parent board. The edge can now be replaned and further slips prepared if required.

The drawer front should now have the groove ploughed to take the tongue on the drawer bottom (Fig. 73r). If the drawer is to have a tenoned handle, the mortice should now be cut.

This would be extremely difficult to do once the drawer carcase has been glued together. The handle should be set a little above the centre line of the drawer rather than on the exact centre, if this type of handle is preferred.

Following the normal cleaning up procedure and waxing on the inside surfaces only, the drawer carcase may now be glued. Great care must be taken to ensure that the carcase is both square and "out of wind". When the glue has dried, scribe off

FIG. 73s

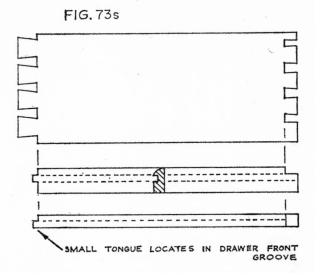

SMALL TONGUE LOCATES IN DRAWER FRONT GROOVE

the slips to the carcase sides as shown in Fig. 73s. After cutting the tongue and ledge at their respective ends of the slips, glue the slips into position on the drawer, after having cleaned up and waxed them.

Work may now begin on the drawer bottom. If solid wood is to be used, plane the face side, face edge and thickness but leave the surplus on the width and the length. Rabbet the face edge, thus leaving a tongue to locate in the groove in the drawer front, and then square the end grain at one end only. This end may now also be rabbeted, thus leaving a tongue to fit into the slip. This is shown on the left hand side of Fig. 73t. Note that the right hand end grain of the drawer bottom and the width are still oversize to the drawer carcase. Place the drawer bottom so that it lies upside down on the underside of the carcase, as shown in Fig. 73t and scribe the required length against the inside of the other slip. Add 3 mm for the other tongue, square off and remove the waste end grain and then rabbet for the tongue as done previously on the left hand side.

FIG. 73t

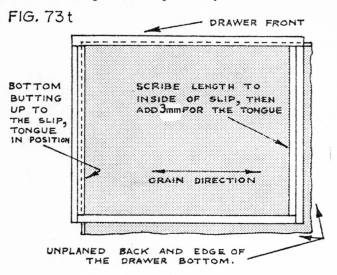

DRAWER FRONT

BOTTOM BUTTING UP TO THE SLIP, TONGUE IN POSITION

SCRIBE LENGTH TO INSIDE OF SLIP, THEN ADD 3mm FOR THE TONGUE

GRAIN DIRECTION

UNPLANED BACK AND EDGE OF THE DRAWER BOTTOM.

It should now be possible, perhaps aided by careful fitting, to slide the drawer bottom into position. Mark the required width allowing it to overlap the back by about 6 mm (Fig. 73u). This allows for any possible shrinkage of the bottom at a later date. The countersunk slots for the screws may now be marked out and cut and the projecting edge of the drawer bottom slightly rounded, as shown in the end elevation of Fig. 73u.

The bottom may now be cleaned up, wax polished and screwed into position. It is best not to glue it at this stage, since the carcase will be more easily held in the vice if the bottom is removed (Fig. 73v). The drawer should be fitted to the main carcase at the same time that cleaning up takes place. A very sharp, finely set smoothing plane should be used to remove the 0·5 mm left proud during the construction of the dovetail joints

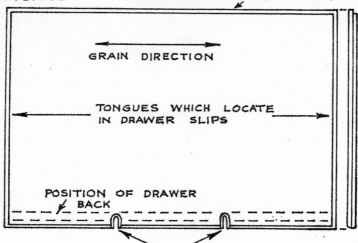

FIG. 73u

TONGUE FOR DRAWER FRONT

GRAIN DIRECTION

TONGUES WHICH LOCATE
IN DRAWER SLIPS

POSITION OF DRAWER
BACK

SCREW SLOTS TO ALLOW SOLID
BOTTOM TO SHRINK AND EXPAND

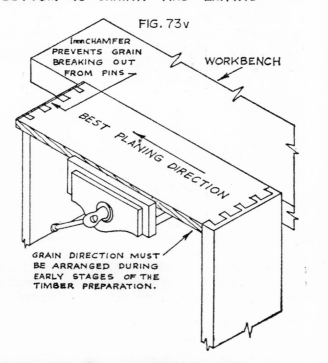

FIG. 73v

1mm CHAMFER
PREVENTS GRAIN
BREAKING OUT
FROM PINS

WORKBENCH

BEST PLANING DIRECTION

GRAIN DIRECTION MUST
BE ARRANGED DURING
EARLY STAGES OF THE
TIMBER PREPARATION.

and the top and bottom edges of the drawer must also be cleaned up. Great care is needed at this stage; a few shavings too many can completely spoil the fit of the drawer. Constant testing for fit is essential. When the drawer makes an easy, sliding fit the outer surfaces should be given a coating of non-gummy wax polish. Under no circumstances should glasspaper be used on the outer surfaces of a drawer. If this is done, the particles of glass embedded in the surface of the wood will cut the drawer bearing surfaces and make the drawer loose in a very short space of time.

When the drawer fit is considered satisfactory, clean up and polish the drawer front and secure the handle. Finally glue the drawer bottom in position, running the glue into the drawer front groove only. This will allow the drawer bottom to shrink or expand with changing humidity without imposing stresses and causing possible distortion to the drawer.

MACHINE-MADE DRAWER CONSTRUCTION

The traditional method of drawer construction is both laborious and highly skilled. In machine-made furniture the method has been rationalized to simplify construction and

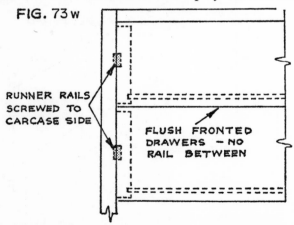

FIG. 73 w

RUNNER RAILS
SCREWED TO
CARCASE SIDE

FLUSH FRONTED
DRAWERS — NO
RAIL BETWEEN

reduce production time. Instead of the traditional bearers, kickers and drawer rails, a single runner is screwed to each side of the table or carcase. This runner engages in a groove cut in the side of the drawer (Fig. 73w). By adjusting the length of the runner so that it meets the drawer front when the drawer is fully closed, the need for separate drawer stops is also removed (Fig. 73x). Fitting such drawers to the carcase calls for much less skill than the traditional method.

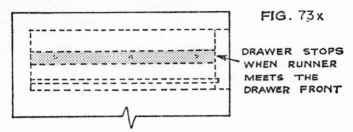

FIG. 73x

DRAWER STOPS
WHEN RUNNER
MEETS THE
DRAWER FRONT

The machine type of construction means that the drawer sides must be made rather thicker than those seen in traditional drawers. It is rare for a machine-made drawer to have sides less than 9 mm thick, even if the drawer is fairly small in

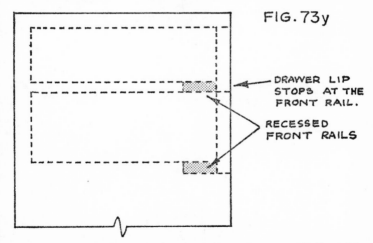

FIG. 73y

DRAWER LIP
STOPS AT THE
FRONT RAIL.

RECESSED
FRONT RAILS

size. This extra thickness is necessary because of the wide groove for the runner. It also means that the slips may be dispensed with since the sides are also strong enough to carry the groove for the bottom. The use of plywood for the drawer bottom removes the necessity for contraction and expansion allowances and the bottom is secured to the underside of the drawer back by means of fixed screws.

Removal of the front rail of the main carcase facilitates the construction of flush-fronted drawers and removes the break of line caused by the intervening rail. This is in keeping with the lines of modern furniture. This appearance may also be achieved in traditional hand constructions by setting the front rail back inside the carcase for a distance equal to the thickness of the drawer front. A lip on the underside of the drawer front serves as drawer stop and hides the front rail from view (Fig. 73y).

Chapter 9

STOOL AND FRAMED-UP CONSTRUCTIONS

Haunched Mortice and Tenon Joints—Stubbed M. & T.
Joints—Stretcher Arrangements—Twin M. & T. Joints
—Fitting Stool Stops—Stool Sizes—Top Rail Shaping
—Wedging of M. & T. Joints

THE basis of all stool, table and chair constructions is a frame, similar to the door frame shown earlier. The joints used are mortice and tenon joints of various kinds, as shown in Figs. 74A to 76 inclusive. A simple form of stool, shown in Fig. 74A, consists of 4 legs, 4 top rails, 4 stretchers and a solid top. The details of the joints used are:—

The haunched mortice and tenon (at A, Figs. 74A and 74). The top rails in the stool are fairly wide and are made from 18 mm stuff since they must support the seat top and give rigidity to the frame (60 mm is a reasonable width if the stool has stretchers). If a wider rail (e.g. 85 mm) is used, the stretchers may be omitted since the tenon is made wider, and is consequently stronger. The thickness of the top rail (18 mm) is necessary to give a strong tenon with shoulders on both sides of the joint. The proportions of the tenon are shown in Fig. 74.

Shoulders are necessary for the joint to resist leverage and, incidentally, to present a clean appearance in the joint. The shoulder below the tenon, usually about 6 mm long, is made for the same reason. (It also prevents any subsequent shrinkage of the rail from exposing gaps in the mortice.) The 20 mm of solid wood above the mortice is necessary to prevent weakness in the mortice, due to the closeness of the end grain. (An over-tight tenon would otherwise split the mortice.) During construction a 25 mm horn, extra to the haunch, is often left on the top of the leg to give added strength to the mortice. After the stool is glued up the mortice is safe and the horn may be sawn off. The haunch helps to prevent twist in the frame and prevents warping in the top third of the rail. In the plan view, the haunch appears as a square.

A 32 mm thick leg gives adequate strength in a stool. The

FIG. 74A STOOL CONSTRUCTION

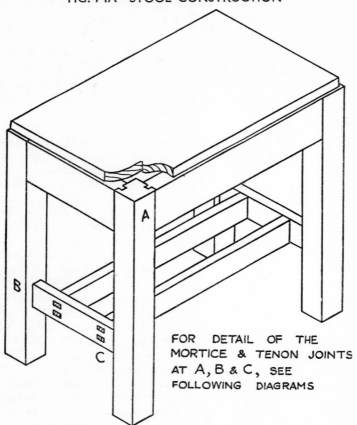

A

B

C

FOR DETAIL OF THE
MORTICE & TENON JOINTS
AT A, B & C, SEE
FOLLOWING DIAGRAMS

leg may be reduced to about 29 mm, however, if a more slender appearance is required. In the plan view of Fig. 74, it will be seen that the tenons meet in a mitre but there should be about 1 mm clearance between the ends of the two joints. This both allows for any possible shrinkage in the width of the leg and ensures that the gluing up of the second tenon does not push out the first one.

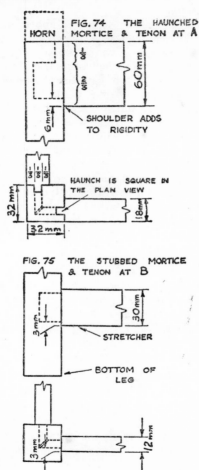

FIG. 74 THE HAUNCHED MORTICE & TENON AT A

HORN
60mm
6mm
SHOULDER ADDS TO RIGIDITY
HAUNCH IS SQUARE IN THE PLAN VIEW
32mm
32mm
18mm

FIG. 75 THE STUBBED MORTICE & TENON AT B

30mm
3mm
STRETCHER
BOTTOM OF LEG
3mm
12mm

The stubbed or stopped M. and T. joint (at B, Figs. 74A and 75). A stubbed mortice and tenon does not go right through the stile or leg. In the example shown, the stretcher rails would be about

30 mm × 12 mm to support the leg adequately and prevent splaying when the stool is used. If this splaying was not prevented, the constant leverage on the top joint would probably cause it to pull apart.

With the size of stretcher suggested above, the mortice need only be about 18 mm deep. If we are to get a sufficiently thick tenon (say about 6 mm), we cannot insist on the $\frac{1}{3}$, $\frac{1}{3}$, $\frac{1}{3}$ proportions suggested for the plan view of joint A. In the joint shown in Fig. 75, shoulders of 3 mm have been arranged all round the tenon, leaving the tenon 6 mm thick. This is only possible because the legs are so much thicker than the stretchers and would not be possible in a frame where the stiles and rails were of the same thickness. (If this were done on a 12 mm thick stile and rail the mortice cheeks would be very weak at 3 mm.)

It will be noted that there is no haunch on this mortice and tenon joint. It is, of course, quite unnecessary since there is no end-grain weakness in a mortice set high in the leg.

The arrangement of the stretchers between the legs may be carried out according to the skill and taste of the worker. Three methods are shown in Fig. 77, becoming progressively more difficult to make:—

(a) All stretchers tenoned into the legs.
(b) Two stretchers tenoned into the legs, the other two stretchers twin-tenoned into the first two. This arrangement is referred to as H stretchers.
(c) Crossed stretchers; a very difficult construction entailing an angle cross-halving and either tenons with V-cut shoulders or recessed mortices.

The twin M. and T. joint (at C, Figs. 74A and 76). This is the joint used when a stretcher is tenoned into a stretcher as in Figs. 74A and 77(*b*). It is also used on long housings as shown in Fig. 107. The tenon takes up the full width of the wood and on a 30 mm wide stretcher, as shown in Fig. 76, the joints and shoulders would be arranged as shown. This type of M. and T. joint is often wedged, thus making small, internal dovetail shapes which cannot be pulled apart. (See later notes on Wedging.) Note that the wedges are arranged so as to press on the end grain of the mortices. If placed the other way, the mortices would be split open.

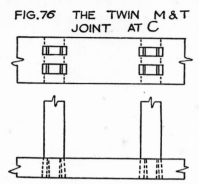

FIG.76 THE TWIN M&T JOINT AT C

THE WEDGED M & T JOINT IS, IN EFFECT, AN INTERNAL DOVETAIL WHICH CANNOT BE PULLED APART

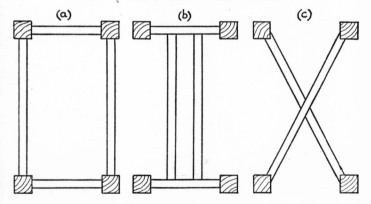

FIG.77 STRETCHER ARRANGEMENT

(a) (b) (c)

FITTING STOOL TOPS

Solid wood tops must always be allowed to move with changing temperatures and humidity. They must not, therefore, be screwed rigidly to the rails so that movement is prevented. The best method is buttoning (Fig. 41).

The buttons are most conveniently cut from a long piece of end-grain timber, prepared as shown in Fig. 78. The button sizes given match the mortices shown in Fig. 41. When the buttons have been parted they should be fitted to the mortices in the rails. The top of the button should be chiselled slightly, so that it is about 1 mm below the rail level. If this is done, the

FIG. 78   MAKING   BUTTONS

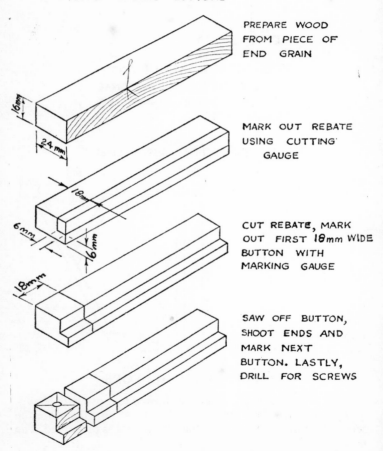

PREPARE WOOD
FROM PIECE OF
END GRAIN

MARK OUT REBATE
USING CUTTING
GAUGE

CUT REBATE, MARK
OUT FIRST 18mm WIDE
BUTTON WITH
MARKING GAUGE

SAW OFF BUTTON,
SHOOT ENDS AND
MARK NEXT
BUTTON. LASTLY,
DRILL FOR SCREWS

stool top will be pulled tightly down on to the top rails when the buttons are screwed home.

Laminboard tops need no allowances for shrinkage or expansion. The quickest method is to drill through the top of the rail, at an angle (Fig. 79). The inside of the rail is then recessed, using a gouge, to take the screw head. This method usually

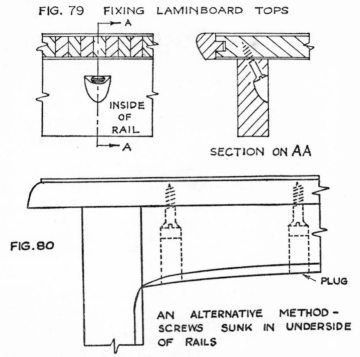

FIG. 79   FIXING LAMINBOARD TOPS

INSIDE
OF
RAIL

SECTION ON AA

FIG. 80

PLUG

AN   ALTERNATIVE   METHOD –
SCREWS SUNK IN UNDERSIDE
OF RAILS

calls for an overhanging top to the stool. If a flush or recessed top were to be used, the screw point would probably push out the grain at the edges. Even with an overhanging top, careful measurement is needed to calculate the amount of screw which will protrude above the rail. If this is not done, or if the gouge recess is made too deep, the screw point will come through the stool top.

An alternative method is shown in Fig. 80. Here the screws

are set in vertical holes, bored from the underside of the stool rails. This method is more suitable for use with tops which are slightly set in from the outside edge of the rails.

Seagrass tops call for a rather different arrangement in the top rail jointing (Fig. 81), since the rails are fairly narrow. The legs project about 12 mm above the top rails to give room for a small bevel, and to present a stop to the seagrass. If this were

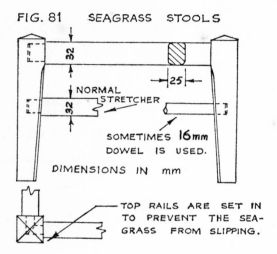

FIG. 81   SEAGRASS   STOOLS

32

25

NORMAL
STRETCHER

32

SOMETIMES 16mm
DOWEL IS USED.

DIMENSIONS IN mm

TOP RAILS ARE SET IN
TO PREVENT THE SEA-
GRASS FROM SLIPPING.

not done, the seagrass would slip sideways. For the same reason, the outside of the top rail is usually set in a little from the leg. Because the leg projects a sufficient distance above the top of the mortice, a haunch is not needed and a common, stopped mortice and tenon joint may be used. The top rails, usually about 32 mm × 25 mm, are best made from beech, which resists the strong inward pull when the seagrass is woven to form the top.

The seagrass may be arranged in a variety of attractive patterns, and simple chamfers on the legs, run-off or stopped, help to soften the outline of the stool. The top rails are slightly rounded in section (Fig. 81), not as a means of decoration but to prevent the otherwise sharp corners from cutting the seagrass.

STOOL SIZES

The size of a stool will vary according to the use to which it is to be put and the height of the user from behind the knee to the heel. As a general guide, however, the following sizes are suggested:—

Footstool or seagrass stool—top 350 mm × 250 mm, height about 250 mm.

Dressing-table stool—top 450 mm × 300 mm, height about 400 mm.

Kitchen stool—top 350 mm × 250 mm, height about 450 mm.

TOP RAIL SHAPING

The top rail of a stool or table may be left straight and given a chamfer running off into the leg, as shown in Fig. 82. This tends to give unity to the frame. The curved rail shown in

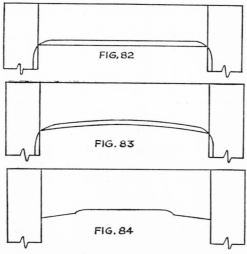

FIG. 82

FIG. 83

FIG. 84

Fig. 83 increases the unified look of the stool by carrying the eye naturally from the leg to the rail. The shaped and curved rail shown in Fig. 84 stops just short of being rather fussy. It would be most suitable for such articles as dressing-table stools or small side-tables.

WEDGING OF MORTICE AND TENON JOINTS

As mentioned previously, a wedged mortice and tenon joint is, in effect, an internal dovetail joint and resists being pulled apart.

In softwoods the wedges are driven down the sides of the tenons as shown in Fig. 85.

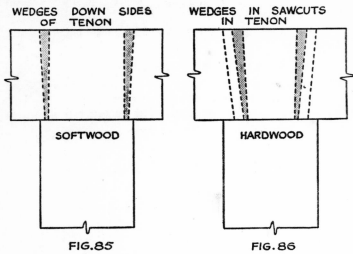

FIG.85   FIG.86

In hardwoods the wedges are driven into prepared saw-cuts about 3 mm from the edges of the tenon (Fig. 86). Preparation for wedging is carried out by widening the mortice from 1 to 1·5 mm on the outside edge, tapering to nothing on the inside edge (Fig. 87). The saw-cut in the tenon is carried almost to the shoulder of the joint (Fig. 88).

The wedges may be made in various ways. One method, economical of both labour and materials, is to use the waste wood cut from the tenon shoulders (Fig. 90). Another method is to use a long piece of end-grain timber, planed down to the correct size (Fig. 91).

The correct size of wedge to use is illustrated in Fig. 89 and should exactly fill the saw-cut in the tenon when driven home.

This wedge fits tightly against the sides of the saw-cut, leaving no weakness due to glue gaps (Fig. 93). If the wedge is made too thick, the tenon may split. Even if this does not happen, the

PREPARATION   FOR   HARDWOOD   WEDGING

FIG. 87

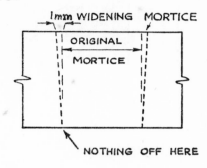

1mm WIDENING MORTICE

ORIGINAL MORTICE

NOTHING OFF HERE

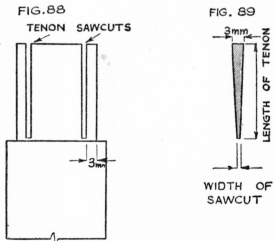

FIG. 88

TENON SAWCUTS

3mm

FIG. 89

3mm

LENGTH OF TENON

WIDTH OF SAWCUT

loss in strength, caused by the glue gaps, weakens the effectiveness of the joint (Fig. 94). A wedge which is too thin leaves an exposed gap in the end grain which is unsightly and, once again, the glue gaps will weaken the joint (Fig. 92).

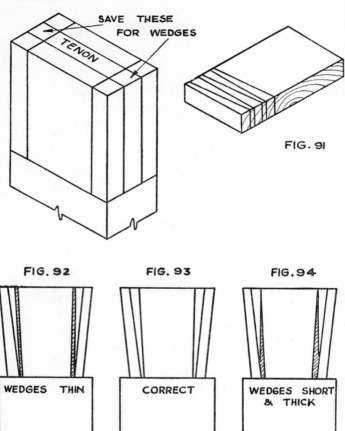

FIG. 90

SAVE THESE FOR WEDGES

TENON

FIG. 91

FIG. 92

FIG. 93

FIG. 94

WEDGES THIN

CORRECT

WEDGES SHORT & THICK

THE SHADED AREAS SHOW GLUE-FILLED GAPS WHICH CAUSE WEAKNESS (MORTICES OMITTED FOR CLARITY)

Chapter 10

MISCELLANEOUS JOINTS

The Double Tenon—Tenons with Sloping Shoulders—The Haunched M. & T. for a Grooved Frame—The Long and Short Shouldered M. & T. Joint—Cutting M. & T. Joints —The T-Bridle Joint—The Cross-halving Joint—Flat Board Joints

THE double tenon. The width of a single tenon should not exceed 65 mm, otherwise the mortice will be correspondingly long and weak. In wide rails, such as on tables, it is

FIG. 95

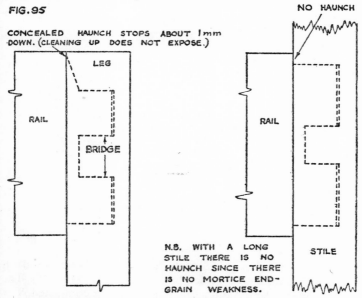

CONCEALED HAUNCH STOPS ABOUT 1mm DOWN. (CLEANING UP DOES NOT EXPOSE.)

NO HAUNCH

LEG

RAIL

BRIDGE

RAIL

STILE

N.B. WITH A LONG STILE THERE IS NO HAUNCH SINCE THERE IS NO MORTICE END-GRAIN WEAKNESS.

advisable to have two small tenons rather than one large one, thus giving greater strength and rigidity. The bridge between the two mortices (Fig. 95) must be at least 18 mm long to give adequate strength. On the example shown there is a haunch between the two tenons. This is not necessary if the bridge is not recessed.

If the construction does not call for a groove to be ploughed in the stile, the common haunch may be replaced with a secret haunch as illustrated. A secret or concealed haunch may be necessary on some recessed-top tables and stools.

FIG. 96

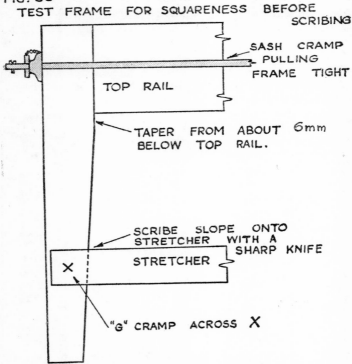

TEST FRAME FOR SQUARENESS BEFORE SCRIBING

SASH CRAMP PULLING FRAME TIGHT

TOP RAIL

TAPER FROM ABOUT 6mm BELOW TOP RAIL.

SCRIBE SLOPE ONTO STRETCHER WITH A SHARP KNIFE

STRETCHER

X

"G" CRAMP ACROSS X

Tenons with sloping shoulders. This joint is often used on small stools and tables which have tapered legs (Fig. 96). The joint between the top rail and leg must first be completed. The whole frame is then cramped up and tested for squareness, and if satisfactory the slope of the leg is scribed on to the stretcher with a sharp knife. This line is then squared across the top and bottom of the stretcher and a bevel gauge is set to give the angle on the fourth side. Normal procedure is adopted for the remaining marking out.

The haunched M. and T. for a grooved frame. If a panel has to be fitted inside a frame about 18 mm in thickness, the inside of the frame is normally grooved. This groove, on small frames, is usually as wide as the tenon is thick. In an 18 mm frame the groove would therefore be 6 mm wide and 6 mm deep.

Since both stile and rail must be grooved, the mortice must start 6 mm above the inside corner of the stile and rail. (Even if the tenon were made without a shoulder at the bottom, the plough plane would remove the bottom 6 mm of the joint.) The tenon, it will be noted from Fig. 97, carries a haunch. The haunch fills the groove made at the top of the stile by the plough plane.

This method may be used on all frames with plywood or solid panels but not with glass or mirror.

The long and short shouldered M. and T. joint. This joint is used on rabbeted frames which hold glass or mirror, so that the glass may be replaced in case of breakage. Instead of a 6 mm groove, a 6 mm rebate is run round the back inside edge of the frame (Fig. 98). Since the rebate plane is normally run right along the stile and rail, there would, with a normal mortice and tenon joint, be a gap exposed on the back of the frame. To fill this gap, the tenon is made with one shoulder longer than the other. This is seen in the plan view of the joint in Fig. 98.

The depth of the rebate must be at least 12 mm to allow sufficient room for the glass and holding fillet. (The fillet needs to be at least 6 mm wide since it must be pinned or screwed to the rebate.) The rebate depth is usually made equal to two-thirds of the rail thickness and thus coincides with the tenon proportions.

If a mirror is to be inserted, the silvered back must be adequately protected against dampness, causing grey patches, breakage and vibration. Plywood placed hard against the back of the mirror is not suitable, since vibration may cause scratches to appear on the mirror surface. The best form of protection is illustrated in the inset diagram to Fig. 98. The mirror is wedged so that it does not touch the sides of the frame; the protecting plywood panel rests against the ends of these wedges and is thus

clear of the back of the mirror. To prevent steam from lifting
the silvered surface of the mirror it should have its edges painted
with lead paint or polyurethane.

CUTTING M. AND T. JOINTS

The mortice and tenon joint is probably the most widely
used of all joints in woodwork. To ensure tight joints and clean
shoulder lines the following rules should be followed:—

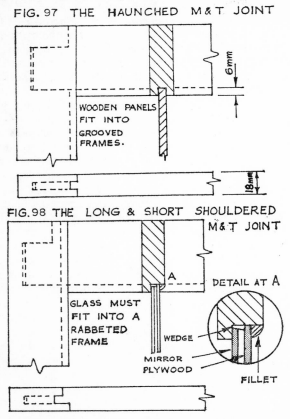

FIG. 97 THE HAUNCHED M & T JOINT

WOODEN PANELS
FIT INTO
GROOVED
FRAMES.

6mm

18mm

FIG. 98 THE LONG & SHORT SHOULDERED
M & T JOINT

A

GLASS MUST
FIT INTO A
RABBETED
FRAME

DETAIL AT A

WEDGE

MIRROR
PLYWOOD

FILLET

1. Always set the mortice gauge to the mortice chisel which
is to be used (Fig. 99). If the points of the gauge are set to a

measured distance, a slightly oversize mortice chisel will make
the mortice too wide and give a badly fitting joint.

2. The tenon shoulders should always be cut lines (Fig. 100).
It is easier to work to an exact cut line than a pencil line, which
may often be of considerable thickness.

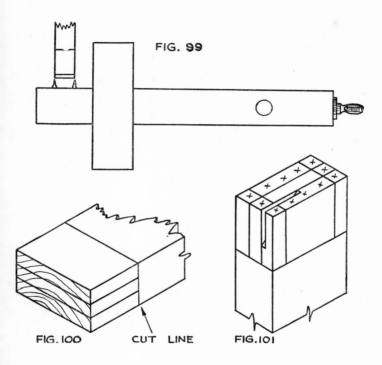

FIG. 99

FIG. 100   CUT LINE   FIG. 101

3. Remember that a saw-cut or kerf has width. This must lie
in the waste wood, with one side touching the cut line (Fig. 101).

4. Both mortice and tenon should be marked out at the same
time, with the mortice gauge running against the face side or
face edge of the work.

5. It should not be necessary to use a chisel on the tenon
cheeks and shoulders, or on the mortice sides. Constant practice will soon remove the need for this joint doctoring.

THE T-BRIDLE JOINT

This is a common form of joint on firescreens, swing mirrors and some stool constructions where a leg is bridled into a carcased seat frame.

In the marking out, the distance shown as "X" on Figs. 102

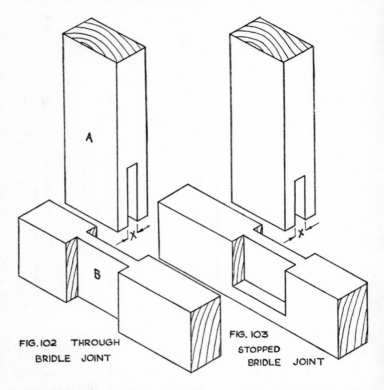

FIG. 102   THROUGH BRIDLE JOINT

FIG. 103   STOPPED BRIDLE JOINT

and 103 is best set on a mortice gauge. This should be done by using the chisel which is to do the cutting at a later stage. The principle of setting out is therefore the same as for the mortice and tenon joint described earlier. To avoid errors in measurement, it is advisable to scribe the width of piece A on to piece B. The bridle joint may be either through or stopped.

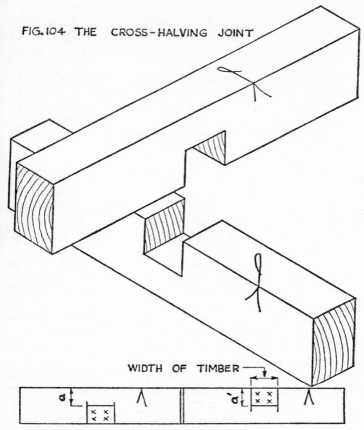

FIG.104 THE CROSS-HALVING JOINT

WIDTH OF TIMBER

FIG.105 DEPTH MUST BE GAUGED FROM FACE
SIDE <u>ONLY</u> & WASTE MARKED AS SHOWN.
THIS ENSURES THAT THE WOOD LEFT AT a
EXACTLY FILLS THE SLOT AT a'

THE CROSS-HALVING JOINT

This is a useful form of joint when two pieces of wood have
to cross over each other. It is seen on small table-lamp bases,
coffee tables with crossed feet and crossed stretchers on small
tables and stools.

The width of the slot across the grain must be equal to the width of the timber (Fig. 104). For this reason it is best to scribe the width from the one piece of wood to the other. This ensures a tight joint so that subsequent cleaning up of the sides does not make a gap in the joint.

When setting out, the depth of the cross-halving should be marked from the face side on both pieces of timber. When the waste wood is marked, it should be done on *opposite* sides as shown in Fig. 105. This ensures that the face edges will be flush when the joint is put together, even if the depth was incorrectly set in the early stages of marking out.

HOUSING JOINTS

This is normally used when a shelf has to run into the side of a carcase (Fig. 106). The housing into which the shelf fits should not be made deeper than one-third of the thickness of the side. (Usually, it is made a quarter of the side's thickness, e.g. 12 mm side—3 mm housing.)

A stopped housing presents a neater finish than a through housing since it does not break the line of the side. If the carcase is fitted with a door, the stopped housing must finish well inside the carcase to give clearance for the door.

The dovetail housing, which may be through or stopped, is a stronger joint and makes a better tie across the carcase.

For long shelves the addition of a twin tenon at the ends of the shelf helps to keep the sides from warping (Fig. 107). This makes a very strong job, particularly if the tenons are wedged. If through tenons spoil the appearance of the carcase sides they may be stopped, but this means considerable loss in strength. In a bookcase, where the shelves carry a large weight of books, it is advisable to wedge the tenons.

BUTT JOINTS

This is a quick form of jointing, used where strength is not of major importance (Fig. 108). It would be used on such objects as small boxes for use in the workshop. Skew nailing is often used to give added rigidity to the box, since the nails oppose being pulled apart. The centre vertical nail should be driven in first, to prevent the wood from "crabbing" when the sloping nails are driven in. (This method of nailing is sometimes

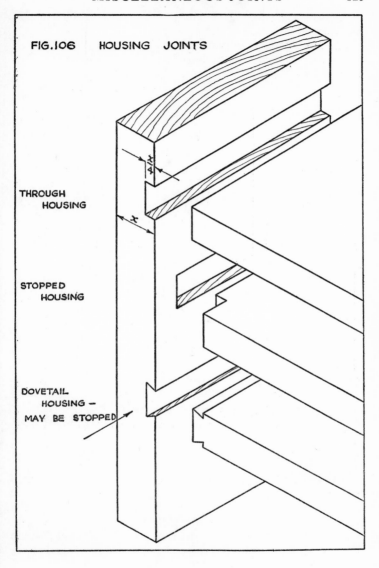

FIG.106   HOUSING   JOINTS

THROUGH
HOUSING

STOPPED
HOUSING

DOVETAIL
HOUSING —
MAY BE STOPPED

called dovetail nailing.) Since end-grain gluing has little strength, a corner block is sometimes glued inside the box.

The lapped butt joint is neater in appearance than the plain butt since it reduces the amount of end grain showing (Fig. 109). It is still a weak joint, however, which needs nailing together.

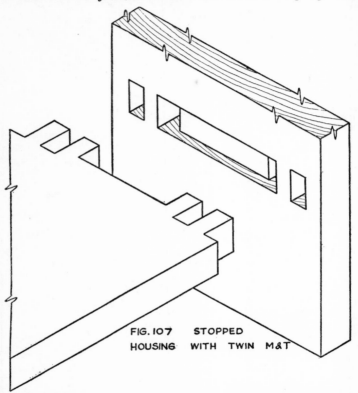

FIG. 107   STOPPED HOUSING WITH TWIN M&T

The mitred butt joint conceals the end grain entirely and is used for small picture frames which are too small to joint and small boxes which are to be veneered. The two ends are squared off, mitred and then clamped rigidly together at right angles. Cuts are made with a fine dovetail saw in dovetail fashion (Fig. 110). These saw-cuts slope to both surfaces. Small pieces of veneer are then glued and hammered into the saw-cuts.

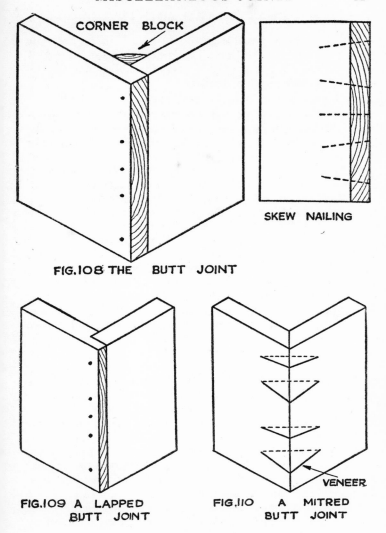

CORNER BLOCK

SKEW NAILING

FIG. 108 THE BUTT JOINT

FIG. 109 A LAPPED BUTT JOINT

FIG. 110 A MITRED BUTT JOINT

VENEER

FLAT BOARD JOINTS

It is not usually possible to obtain boards of timber wide enough for use as table tops. This means that some form of edge joint must be constructed to make invisible joints between several narrower pieces of timber:—

The rubbed joint as shown in Fig. 111.

(a) First, match up the grains of the two boards for appearance, possible distortion and ease of surface planing after the joint is made. Mark the edges which are to be joined and plane them fairly true with a trying plane.

(b) Place the two boards in the vice with the planed edges uppermost, and what will be the face edges together.

(c) With a trying plane, plane both edges perfectly true, using a very sharp blade which is finely set. (Try to take off full width shavings and plane hollow at the same time.)

(d) When no more shavings can be removed, owing to a very slight hollowness in the length of the edges, remove one board from the vice. Check for truth by balancing this board on the other. Any excessive hollowness or rocking of the upper board will be immediately apparent and should be remedied by careful planing along the edge of the board still held in the vice.

(e) If the joint is satisfactory, apply fairly thin, hot animal glue or synthetic resin glue to both edges. (The glue must not be too thin or a starved joint will result.)

(f) Slide the loose board along the fixed board, keeping it carefully in line, thus squeezing out surplus glue and effecting maximum glue penetration into the pores of the wood.

(g) After a few minutes the movement will become stiff. When this occurs the glue has jelled and the boards should now be placed against a lath as shown in the diagram.

(h) When the joint is dry, the face side may be cleaned up, unless there is another board to be edge jointed to the original boards. (It is not wise to attempt the gluing of three boards at the same time, but to make two separate operations.)

Sometimes the edges are planed hollow, with a slightly fuller cut on the trying plane. This hollowness is then removed by sash-cramping the two boards together. This gives a very strong joint, if a reliable glue is used, but it is not a true rub joint. Note that the cramps on the diagram are placed on opposite

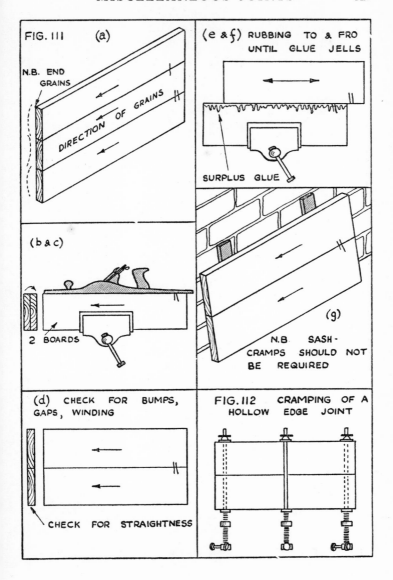

FIG. 111   (a)

N.B. END GRAINS

DIRECTION OF GRAINS

(b & c)

2 BOARDS

(d) CHECK FOR BUMPS, GAPS, WINDING

CHECK FOR STRAIGHTNESS

(e & f) RUBBING TO & FRO UNTIL GLUE JELLS

SURPLUS GLUE

(g)

N.B. SASH-CRAMPS SHOULD NOT BE REQUIRED

FIG. 112 CRAMPING OF A HOLLOW EDGE JOINT

sides to counteract the tendency of the wide board to bow and spring out of the cramps (Fig. 112).

A well-made rub joint, or a hollow-edge joint, is perfectly reliable and will not open up. Sometimes, in order to increase

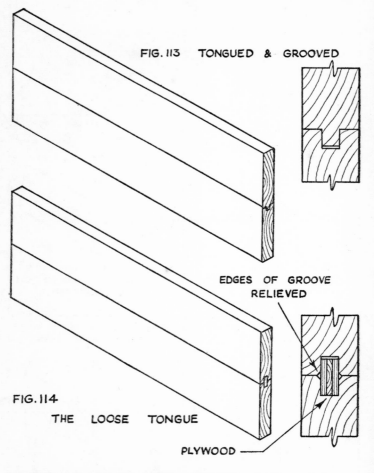

FIG. 113 TONGUED & GROOVED

EDGES OF GROOVE RELIEVED

FIG. 114

THE LOOSE TONGUE

PLYWOOD

N.B. BOTH JOINTS GIVE GREATER GLUING AREA THAN PLAIN EDGE JOINTS

the glue area between the two edges, a tongued and grooved (Fig. 113) or loose-tongued edge joint is used (Fig. 114).

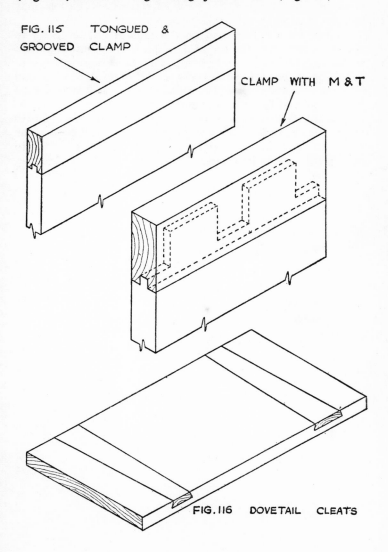

FIG. 115 TONGUED & GROOVED CLAMP

CLAMP WITH M & T

FIG. 116 DOVETAIL CLEATS

Wide boards made in solid timber are always liable to become distorted with changing humidity and temperature. In order to minimize this effect, various kinds of clamps and battens may be used. Fig. 40 shows the slot-screwed batten.

Clamps are a device used on the ends of boards to try to *prevent* movement. The tongued clamp is glued into a groove in the end grain of the wide board, thereby opposing any tendency for the board to shrink or expand (Fig. 115). This method also hides the end grain of the wide board and is therefore used on such jobs as fall-front bureaux.

Dovetailed cleats are also used in an attempt to prevent movement. The cleats, dovetailed in two directions, are glued at the wide end only, so that any shrinkage of the board tends to tighten the cleat in its groove (Fig. 116).

PART III
TOOLS

Chapter 11

CHISELS

THE FIRMER CHISEL (Fig. 117)

CHISEL handles are usually made from hardwood; box, beech or ash being the most suitable, although plastic handles, sufficiently tough even to withstand hammer blows, are obtainable.

The ferrule, which is a seamless brass ring fitting round the base of the handle, prevents the latter from being split by the tang, especially when a new handle is being driven on to the blade.

The blade is made from tool steel with a carbon content of about 1%. Tool steel contains from ·5% to 1·5% of carbon and possesses the property of becoming extremely hard when heated to redness, at 800° C. to 850° C., and then suddenly cooled by being plunged into water, brine, raw linseed oil, etc. This hardened steel is too brittle for use in most tools but can be tempered or softened by heating; the hotter the metal the greater the degree of softness until red heat is reached, when all "hardness" has been removed. If at this point the metal is allowed to cool slowly, it will remain soft, and is said to have been annealed. The degree of "softness" may be observed by first brightening the steel to be tempered and then slowly heating it until a thin film of oxide, forming on the surface of the metal, causes the steel to assume a pale straw colour at about 200° C. Further heating causes the colour to change through dark straw, to purple and then to dark blue at about 300° C. The temper of the steel between these ranges may be fixed by removing it from the source of heat and immediately quenching it in water. The greater the shock that the tool has to withstand during use, the greater must be the degree of tempering. Also, the higher the percentage of carbon present in the steel, then the more brittle the metal tends to become.

More expensive chisels may have their blades made from tungsten steel, which contains about 14% tungsten and 1%

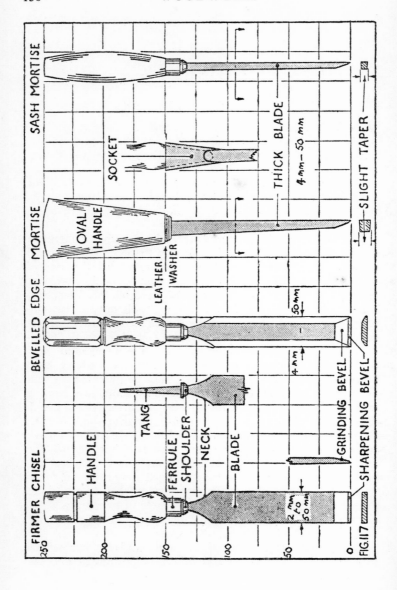

FIRMER CHISEL   BEVELLED EDGE   MORTISE   SASH MORTISE

HANDLE

TANG
FERRULE
SHOULDER
NECK
BLADE

OVAL HANDLE

LEATHER WASHER

SOCKET

THICK BLADE
4 mm – 50 mm

GRINDING BEVEL

SHARPENING BEVEL

SLIGHT TAPER

2 mm to 50 mm

4 mm

50 mm

FIG.117

carbon. This alloy has the property of retaining a keen edge for a longer period. Cobalt, as an alloying element, gives similar properties.

The shoulder prevents the tang from driving up inside the handle when the chisel is struck with a mallet.

The tang secures the blade to the handle. The tang, shoulder and blade are forged in one piece but the tang and shoulder are not hardened and tempered, thus permitting strain on these parts without fear of fracture.

The grinding bevel, which is by far the larger of the two sloping surfaces at the tip of the tool, is obtained by grinding on a wet sandstone at an angle of 25° (Fig. 118). (Cabinet makers

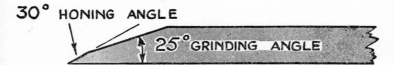

FIG. 118   ANGLES FOR AVERAGE WORK

sometimes grind at 20° and hone at 25° to give a cleaner cutting action.)

The sharpening or honing bevel is the final slope of 30° produced on the oilstone and gives a keen cutting edge to the tool (Fig. 118). It also provides a quick and easy means of restoring the cutting edge, should that edge become blunt. The honing angle is sometimes increased to 35° for heavy work such as morticing.

The cutting edge first severs the wood fibres; the grinding bevel acting as a wedge then forces away the fibres. This action by the grinding bevel provides a good example of the principle of the Inclined Plane (Fig. 236a), whereby a heavy load may be pulled up a long sloping surface with considerably less effort than raising the same load vertically to the same height.

The oblique cut is obtained by moving the chisel sideways as well as forwards, thus producing a slicing action. When a chisel is used square to the wood, the shaving travels straight up the sloping surface of the grinding bevel along the shortest path

A–A (Fig. 119). When the chisel is presented obliquely to the wood, the shaving travels across the sloping surface B–B and the angle of the bevel is, in effect, decreased. Applying the principle of the Inclined Plane (Fig. 236a), the slope has been

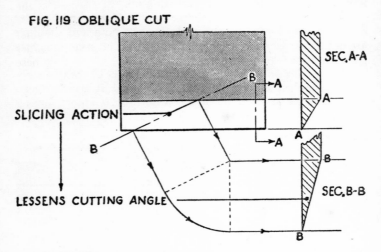

FIG. 119 OBLIQUE CUT

SLICING ACTION

LESSENS CUTTING ANGLE

SEC. A-A

SEC. B-B

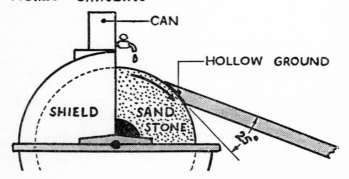

FIG. 120 GRINDING

CAN

HOLLOW GROUND

SHIELD   SAND STONE

25°

decreased, and thus the effort, although operating over a greater distance, is correspondingly decreased.

The firmer chisel is employed for all general bench work and may be used in conjunction with a mallet.

When removing the bulk of waste wood, such as chiselling a groove across the grain, it is advisable to use the chisel with its bevel reversed or facing downwards. The wedging action of the bevel tends to force the cutting edge upwards and thus helps to guard against the danger of the chisel "digging down" into the work.

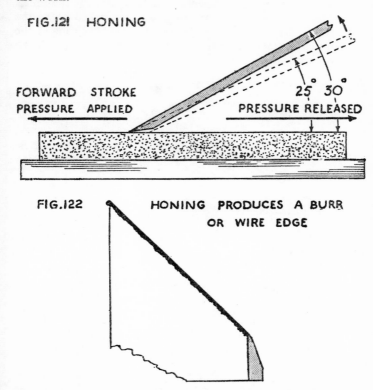

FIG.121 HONING

FORWARD STROKE
PRESSURE APPLIED   25° 30°
                        PRESSURE RELEASED

FIG.122   HONING PRODUCES A BURR
                      OR WIRE EDGE

Grinding is best carried out on a sandstone. The surface of the grindstone is constantly kept wet by a trickle of water from a drip can (Fig. 120). This water cools the blade, since any burning of the blade will destroy, or draw its temper. It also washes away the loose particles of metal and sand, preventing the stone from becoming clogged. In order to ensure that the stone is worn away evenly, the chisel should be traversed from side to side across the face of the stone.

Honing.

(a) The blade of the chisel is placed so that the grinding bevel rests firmly on the surface of the oilstone (Fig. 121).

(b) The blade is then raised about 5° and with the chisel carefully maintained at this angle, is worked along the full length of the stone. To avoid uneven wearing of the oilstone, the cutting edge of the chisel should be moved across its width.

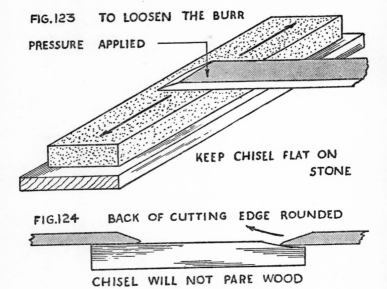

FIG. 123   TO LOOSEN THE BURR

PRESSURE APPLIED

KEEP CHISEL FLAT ON STONE

FIG. 124   BACK OF CUTTING EDGE ROUNDED

CHISEL WILL NOT PARE WOOD

The surface of the oilstone must be perfectly flat to ensure a straight cutting edge to the chisel, also the finer the stone the sharper will be the cutting edge. Some form of lubricant is necessary for the same reason that water is used on a sandstone when grinding. Thin machine oil is excellent for this purpose.

Honing produces a burr or wire edge by turning back the cutting edge (Fig. 122). The honing bevel itself also becomes longer, thus making each successive operation more tedious by virtue of the increased amount of metal to be removed. After several re-sharpenings, re-grinding will therefore become necessary.

To loosen the burr (Fig. 123) the chisel is now reversed, and, while great care is exercised to keep the back of the blade perfectly flat on the oilstone, is worked along the length of the stone in the direction shown. Any lifting of the blade will not only round the back of the cutting edge, making paring with the chisel an impossibility, but will also cause the honing angle to be increased (Fig. 124). This fault may also be caused by

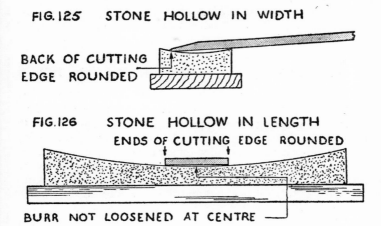

FIG. 125   STONE HOLLOW IN WIDTH

BACK OF CUTTING
EDGE ROUNDED

FIG. 126   STONE HOLLOW IN LENGTH
ENDS OF CUTTING EDGE ROUNDED

BURR NOT LOOSENED AT CENTRE

using an oilstone which has worn hollow across its width (Fig. 125). A stone which has been allowed to become hollow in its length will be equally useless, since not only will the ends of the cutting edge become rounded, but it will be impossible to remove the burr at the centre in the correct manner (Fig. 126).

To remove the burr. The wire edge produced by honing should be worn away and not broken off by stropping, or a thin jagged edge will remain. The procedure should therefore be:—

(a) The chisel is placed at the far end of a fine oilstone as for honing (i.e. at 30°), and drawn back very lightly towards the operator. This will push back the wire edge in the opposite direction.

(b) The chisel is again reversed so that its back edge is flat on the stone and, using heavy pressure, is worked along the length of the stone as previously described under loosening the burr.

(c) (a) and (b) are now repeated until the wire edge is removed, using successively lighter pressure when honing at 30° ((a) above).

Sharpening is now completed and, to test that a keen edge has been obtained, the chisel should be held so that light may play along the cutting edge. A blunt or damaged edge reflects light, and if a white line or white specks are seen, the tool is still not sharp.

THE BEVELLED EDGE CHISEL (Fig. 117)

The bevelled edge chisel is similar in construction to the firmer chisel, but has its two long edges bevelled on the same face as the grinding bevel. It is lighter in weight and easier to handle than the firmer pattern and is therefore used for paring and all fine work. Its bevelled edge makes it very suitable for cleaning out angles that are less than 90°, such as are to be found at the base of dovetails. Because of its lightness it is not as strong as the firmer chisel and therefore should *not* be used with a mallet.

THE PARING CHISEL

The paring chisel may be of the firmer or the bevelled edge pattern but the blade is thinner and much longer. Its extra length allows for deep cutting, as is required in long housings. As with the bevelled edge chisel, this chisel should not be used with a mallet.

THE MORTICE CHISEL (Fig. 117)

The blade is considerably thicker than that of the firmer chisel, to provide added strength for levering away the waste wood and to prevent its turning in the mortice when driven with a mallet. The blade tapers from the tang towards the cutting edge. It also has a slight taper in section, away from the back edge, to permit easier withdrawal from the mortice.

There are two methods by which the blade may be fixed to the handle:—

(a) *By a tang* in common with all other chisels. A leather washer is often inserted between the shoulder and the handle to assist in absorbing shock when struck with a mallet. The oval beech handle helps to keep the tool in line, thus ensuring that the mortice is square to the face of the work.

(b) *By a socket*. In this pattern of mortice chisel, the tang is replaced by a hollow conical socket into which the base of a round handle is fitted and held by friction. This arrangement avoids the possibility of the handle splitting under the heavy blows that this chisel is often required to undergo. For the same reason, the top of the handle is often encircled by a steel band, but after considerable wear this may cause damage to the mallet.

A lighter pattern of mortice chisel with a round handle is obtainable and is known as a sash mortice chisel.

THE FIRMER GOUGE (Outside Ground)

This tool is similar in most respects to the firmer chisel, but its blade is curved in section to form an arc (Fig. 127). The size of the gouge is denoted by the measurement along the chord which subtends the arc made by the curvature of the blade. The steepness of the curve may vary from almost flat to a half-circle.

Firmer gouges are used for hollowing out recesses ranging from the forming of small finger grips in door and drawer handles, to the hand finishing of the inside of wooden bowls.

Grinding. The blade is ground on the outside of the curve at 25°, the bevel being produced on the grindstone by giving a part rotary movement to the blade (Fig. 128).

Honing is carried out at 30° on an oilstone by holding the blade at right angles to the stone. The tool is moved along the length of the stone, using a similar wrist action to that employed when grinding (Fig. 129).

To loosen the burr. The burr or wire edge is loosened from the inside of the tool by means of an oilstone slip. The curve of the slip should match the curve of the blade. To avoid the

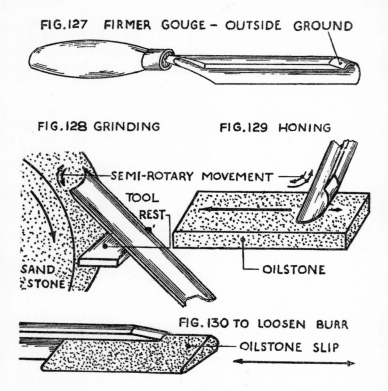

FIG.127 FIRMER GOUGE – OUTSIDE GROUND

FIG.128 GRINDING   FIG.129 HONING

SEMI-ROTARY MOVEMENT

TOOL REST

SAND STONE

OILSTONE

FIG.130 TO LOOSEN BURR

OILSTONE SLIP

possible turning over of the cutting edge, it is advisable to allow less than half of the slip to protrude beyond the cutting edge (Fig. 130).

To remove the burr. The above procedure is repeated as from "honing" until the wire edge is removed. When honing, only two or three strokes should be made, these strokes becoming successively lighter for each complete operation.

SCRIBING AND PARING GOUGE
(Inside Ground)

These gouges have their grinding and honing bevels on the inside of the curve (Fig. 131). They are used for scribing mouldings and cutting sharp concave curves such as might be required on the inside top of stool legs to take a recessed, upholstered seat with rounded corners. Paring gouges which have very long blades are very useful for running long channels.

Grinding. The grinding bevel of 25° is obtained by grinding on wheels which have been specially shaped for the purpose

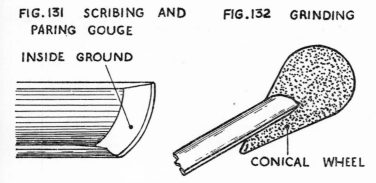

FIG.131 SCRIBING AND PARING GOUGE

INSIDE GROUND

FIG.132 GRINDING

CONICAL WHEEL

(Fig. 132). A conical wheel will allow various degrees of curvature to be obtained. If no special wheel is available, the bevel must be worn down by rubbing with a coarse oilstone slip which matches the curve of the blade; a tedious method.

Honing is carried out at 30°, using a fine oilstone slip of the correct curvature. Care must be exercised to keep the slip at the correct angle.

To loosen the burr the blade is held at right angles to the oilstone with its back quite flat. A rocking motion is imparted to the tool as it is moved along the length of the stone.

To remove the burr the above procedure is repeated as from "honing", using only two or three light strokes until the burr is removed.

Chapter 12

PLANES

THE JACK PLANE

*T*HE *stock or body* (Fig. 133) should be shaped from best quality red beech, free from all defects such as knots and shakes. The grain, which runs the length of the stock, should be straight; a condition more readily obtained if the timber has been cleft with the axe and not sawn from the log.

The sole is the working surface of the plane and therefore

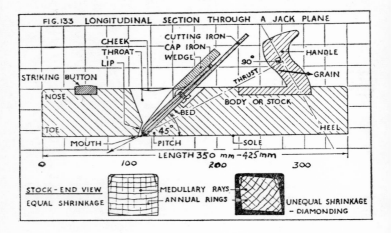

FIG. 133 LONGITUDINAL SECTION THROUGH A JACK PLANE

must be kept flat and in good condition by truing up when necessary. (See remouthing a plane.) Occasional lubrication with a wipe of raw linseed oil will aid in the smooth running of the plane.

The mouth must be fairly wide to allow the free passage of heavy shavings. If the mouth is too wide, worn or damaged, the wedging action of the blade will tend to lift and tear out the shavings in front of the cutting edge (Fig. 134), whereas a narrow mouth holds down the shavings and allows the cutting action of the blade to predominate. A narrow mouth, in

146

conjunction with a finely set blade, is necessary to obtain a satin-smooth finish (Fig. 135).

The lip slopes towards the heel of the plane so that any truing up of the sole does not greatly widen the mouth.

The bed or frog supports the blade at the desired angle or pitch (45°).

The wedge, which is made from beech, is forked to fit round the cap iron retaining nut. The prongs fit into tapered grooves cut in the cheeks of the stock. The wedge is an example of the inclined plane (Figs. 236a–f), and imparts a downward pressure on both sides of the cap iron. It is held in position by friction.

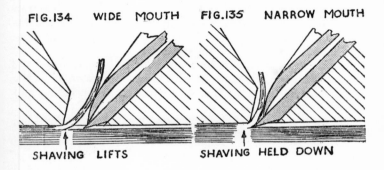

FIG.134   WIDE   MOUTH   FIG.135   NARROW MOUTH

SHAVING LIFTS   SHAVING HELD DOWN

The striking button is made from boxwood, a hard, dense wood which will withstand the blow received when releasing the wedge by the principle of inertia. This principle states that a body at rest will remain at rest unless acted upon by an external force. For example, a person standing on the back of an open cart which suddenly moves forward will, in all probability, be left behind, since that person is not a part of the cart upon which the external force is acting. In the case of releasing the wedge of the plane, the stock is held firmly in one hand with the thumb resting against the wedge, to prevent the blade from flying out. The button is then given a sharp blow with a mallet with the result that the stock suddenly moves in a downward direction and tends to leave the wedge behind.

The handle is made from beech with the grain running as shown. Maximum strength is thus obtained for the particular shape that the handle assumes. The handle is let into a long mortice cut into the stock and glued. In a good plane, a line bisecting the axis of the handle at right angles will pass through the tip of the cutting iron, thus ensuring that the maximum possible thrust is exerted at the cutting edge.

The cutting iron is made from hardened and tempered tool steel.

Sharpening of the cutting iron is carried out as for the chisel, with the grinding and honing angles at 25° and 30° respectively. The slight curve on the cutting edge may be obtained on the oilstone by imparting a slight sideways rocking motion to the blade on the backward stroke. The edge of the cap iron must fit closely against the back of the cutting iron. Any gap will trap shavings causing choking in the mouth. To recondition a damaged or worn cap iron, grind or file the edge straight and follow with a final sharpening on the oilstone.

The cutting iron is set in the plane with the bevel downwards, so that the angle at which the cutting edge is presented to the wood remains the same (i.e. 45°) whatever the grinding and honing angles may be.

The cutting edge is slightly curved along its length (Fig. 136), for two reasons:—

(a) To assist in removing coarse shavings.
(b) The slight curve in the blade is a useful aid to squaring a sloping edge, since a thicker shaving will be removed at the centre of the blade than at the ends. All that is necessary is to move the centre of the cutting edge over to the "high side" of the wood, keeping the sole of the plane flat on the surface of the work (Fig. 137).

When setting a plane blade, sight along the sole of the plane until a thin hair line of blade is visible. A light tap with a hammer on the top of the blade will suffice to increase the cut. If set too coarsely, a blow on the striking button will "pull back" the blade and also loosen the wedge. The wedge must, of course, be firmly tapped back into position.

Angle of pitch (Fig. 133). This is the angle at which the cutting iron is inclined to the sole. In a jack plane the angle is 45° and is known as Moderate Pitch.

The cap iron is secured to the back of the cutting iron by the cap iron retaining screw, which, to allow adjustment, works in a slot in the cutting iron. It strengthens the cutting edge of the cutting iron and helps to prevent chattering.

The shape of the cap iron causes the shavings to curl over.

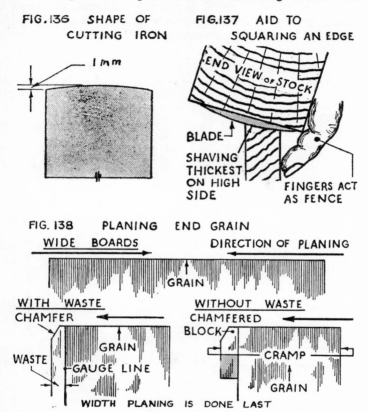

FIG. 136   SHAPE OF CUTTING IRON

1 mm

FIG. 137   AID TO SQUARING AN EDGE

END VIEW OF STOCK

BLADE

SHAVING THICKEST ON HIGH SIDE

FINGERS ACT AS FENCE

FIG. 138   PLANING   END GRAIN

WIDE BOARDS   DIRECTION OF PLANING

GRAIN

WITH WASTE   WITHOUT WASTE

CHAMFER   CHAMFERED BLOCK

WASTE   GRAIN   CRAMP

GAUGE LINE   GRAIN

WIDTH PLANING IS DONE LAST

This allows the cutting edge of the cutting iron to operate better and breaks the shavings at the mouth, thus reducing tearing out of the grain.

For a jack plane, the edge of the cap iron should be set back 1·5 mm to 3 mm from the edge of the cutting iron. If set closer than 1·5 mm, increased support at the cutting edge will be obtained, but a considerably greater effort will be required to turn back the fairly heavy shavings normally removed by this plane.

The jack plane is used for the general preparation of wood preparatory to bench work. If planing end grain, the wood fibres at the end of the stroke will be broken out very badly, unless special planing measures are adopted as shown in Fig. 138.

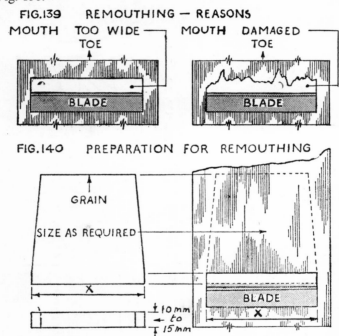

FIG.139   REMOUTHING — REASONS

MOUTH TOO WIDE — TOE

MOUTH DAMAGED — TOE

BLADE

BLADE

FIG.140   PREPARATION FOR REMOUTHING

GRAIN

SIZE AS REQUIRED

X

10 mm to 15 mm

BLADE

X

Remouthing. This becomes necessary when constant truing up of the sole has considerably widened the mouth or it has become damaged through wear (Fig. 139).

Preparation for remouthing. Cut to the required shape a piece of dense-grained hardwood (box or ebony) from 10 mm to 15 mm thick (Fig. 140).

Cramp the new mouth piece in position on the sole. The cutting iron should remain in the plane and should be set for

the removal of fine shavings. The width of the new mouth may
thus be accurately ascertained (Fig. 141).

Scribe round the new mouth with a sharp knife.

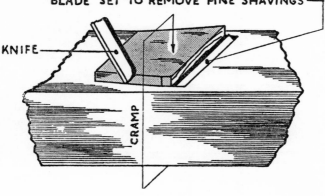

FIG. 141 NEW MOUTH CRAMPED IN POSITION
BLADE SET TO REMOVE FINE SHAVINGS
KNIFE
CRAMP

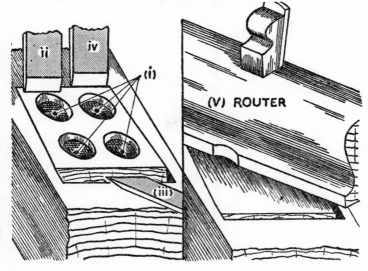

FIG.142 FORMING THE RECESS
(ii) (iv) (i)
(iii)
(V) ROUTER

Forming the recess (Fig. 142). The depth of the recess should be slightly less than the thickness of the new mouthpiece.

   i. The bulk of the waste may be removed with a twist or centre bit instead of a chisel.

   ii. Chisel almost to the scribed lines, first cutting across the grain.

   iii. Chisel just short of the required depth. (It will be found necessary to work with the bevel of the chisel reversed.)

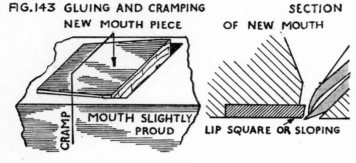

FIG. 143 GLUING AND CRAMPING NEW MOUTH PIECE

SECTION OF NEW MOUTH

MOUTH SLIGHTLY PROUD

CRAMP

LIP SQUARE OR SLOPING

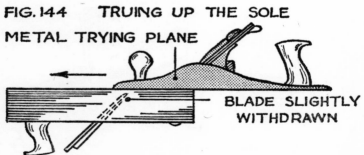

FIG. 144 TRUING UP THE SOLE

METAL TRYING PLANE

BLADE SLIGHTLY WITHDRAWN

   iv. Vertically pare to the scribed lines.

   v. Obtain an even bottom to the recess by finishing off to the required depth with a router plane.

Glue and cramp the new mouth piece into position (Fig. 143) and set the plane aside. When the glue has set, level up the new mouth piece and true up the sole. The plane to be trued up should be under actual working conditions (Fig. 144).

Chattering. This usually occurs when planing end-grain or tough wood of difficult grain, such as may arise from the presence of knots. It is felt by the operator as a vibration and causes unsightly ripple marks on the surface of the work. It is

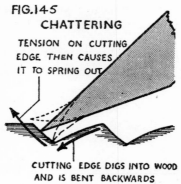

FIG.145
CHATTERING

TENSION ON CUTTING EDGE THEN CAUSES IT TO SPRING OUT

CUTTING EDGE DIGS INTO WOOD AND IS BENT BACKWARDS

FIG.146   CUTTING IRON NOT HELD FIRMLY

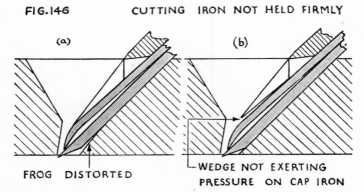

(a)   (b)

FROG DISTORTED   WEDGE NOT EXERTING PRESSURE ON CAP IRON

caused by the oscillation of the cutting edge alternately digging into the wood and then springing out again (Fig. 145).

Chattering may be caused by various faults in the plane:—

(a) The cutter may not "bed down" properly on the frog, owing to distortion in the frog itself. If this occurs (Fig. 146), the frog should be pared down to give all-over support to the cutting iron.

(b) The prongs of the wedge may not fit properly into their tapered grooves and thus may not be exerting a constant pressure on the cap iron (Fig. 146). When this happens, pare down the wedge to make a good fit in the grooves.

(c) The cutting iron may be ground at too acute an angle (θ), as shown in Fig. 147. The nearest point of support to the cutting edge is at point P, which may be too high (A) and too far

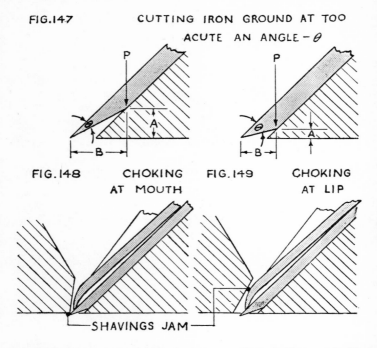

FIG.147   CUTTING IRON GROUND AT TOO ACUTE AN ANGLE – θ

FIG.148   CHOKING AT MOUTH   FIG.149   CHOKING AT LIP

SHAVINGS JAM

back (B). To remedy this fault, increase the grinding angle (θ), thus decreasing both distance A and B.

(d) The wedge may have worked loose; if so, tighten it.

(e) The cap iron may be loose and therefore fail to make the cutting edge rigid. If this is so, tighten the cap iron retaining screw.

Choking. This is a fairly common fault which occurs at the mouth of the plane. The shavings fail to curl into the escapement and jam solidly in the mouth of the plane. The plane cannot remove shavings and becomes very difficult to push along the surface of the work. This fault may be due to the causes shown below:—

(a) The mouth may be too small to allow the passage of heavy shavings (Fig. 148). To rectify this fault, increase the width of the mouth very slightly by vertical paring.

(b) Shavings may pass through the mouth but be trapped between the lip and the cap iron (Fig. 149). This must also be

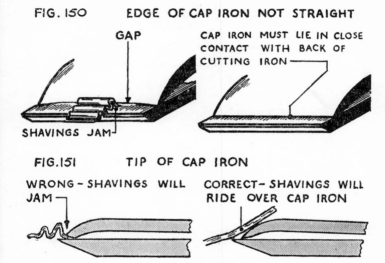

FIG. 150   EDGE OF CAP IRON NOT STRAIGHT

GAP

CAP IRON MUST LIE IN CLOSE CONTACT WITH BACK OF CUTTING IRON

SHAVINGS JAM

FIG. 151   TIP OF CAP IRON

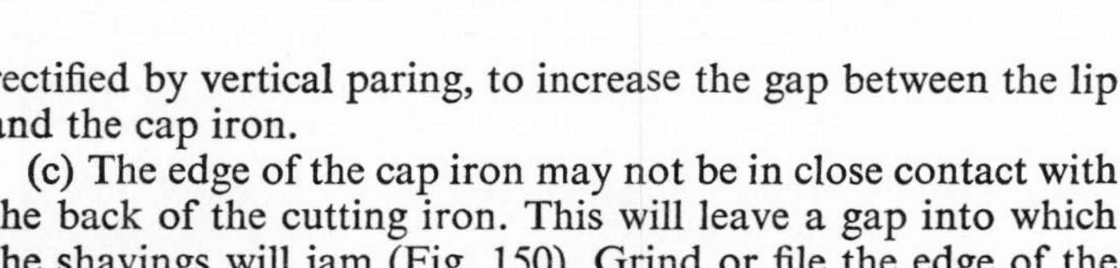

WRONG – SHAVINGS WILL JAM

CORRECT – SHAVINGS WILL RIDE OVER CAP IRON

rectified by vertical paring, to increase the gap between the lip and the cap iron.

(c) The edge of the cap iron may not be in close contact with the back of the cutting iron. This will leave a gap into which the shavings will jam (Fig. 150). Grind or file the edge of the cap iron so that it becomes a perfect fit.

(d) The tip of the cap iron may be very square and blunt. The shavings will pack against this instead of sliding over the cap iron (Fig. 151). Again, the cap iron must be ground or filed to the correct shape.

THE TRYING AND JOINTER PLANES

These two planes are similar in construction to the jack plane but are longer and heavier and are fitted with closed handles to provide greater strength when handling (Fig. 153). The mouth is narrow as it is intended to be used for the removal of fine shavings. The cutting edge of the cutting iron is straight so that a true and flat surface may be obtained, but both ends

FIG.152   USE OF TRYING PLANE ON LONG WORK

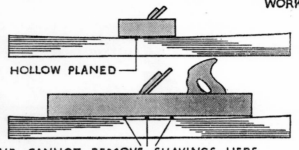

HOLLOW PLANED

PLANE CANNOT REMOVE SHAVINGS HERE

of the cutting edge are slightly rounded to prevent them digging into the work. As these planes are required to remove only fine shavings, the cap iron should be set slightly less than 1 mm back from the cutting edge of the cutting iron.

The trying and jointer planes are used for truing up large surfaces and planing long edges as would be the case when preparing a "rubbed joint". The use of a plane with a short stock would be more liable to produce a hollow in the work, since its lack of length would permit it to follow a slight curve (Fig. 152).

WOOD AND METAL JACK PLANES COMPARED

Wooden planes

(1) A wooden plane runs more easily over wood than a metal plane, especially on resinous woods.

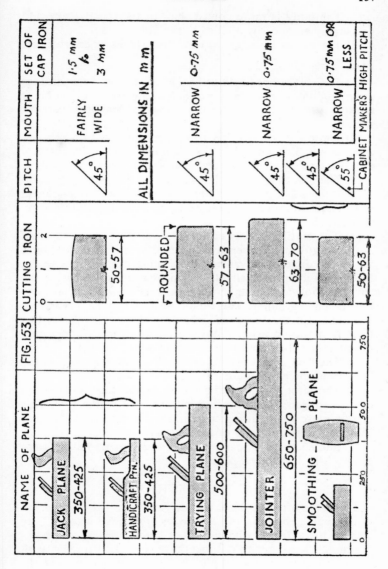

NAME OF PLANE	FIG. 153	CUTTING IRON	PITCH	MOUTH	SET OF CAP IRON
JACK PLANE	350-425	50-57	45°	FAIRLY WIDE	1·5 mm to 3 mm
HANDICRAFT PLN.	350-425		ALL DIMENSIONS IN mm		
TRYING PLANE	500-600	ROUNDED 57-63	45°	NARROW	0·75 mm
JOINTER	650-750	63-70	45°	NARROW	0·75 mm
SMOOTHING PLANE		50-63	45° / 55°	NARROW	0·75 mm OR LESS
			CABINET MAKER'S HIGH PITCH		

(2) The body is more robust than in the metal plane and pressure is more easily applied at the nose.

(3) The mouth is subject to wear and widens when trued up.

Metal planes (Fig. 154)

(1) The sole is not likely to become distorted if the castings are of good quality and it is not liable to wear. Lubrication of the sole with an oil pad helps to make it run smoothly without sticking.

(2) The body is less likely to become distorted and the increased weight is considered to be advantageous by some, a disadvantage by others. Made from cast iron, therefore brittle.

(3) The mouth is not subject to wear and is not easily damaged. If fine shavings are required, especially on double-grained timbers, the mouth may be closed up by adjustment of the frog, thus reducing "tearing".

(4) The cutting iron is easily removed and easily adjusted both laterally and for depth of cut. Setting of the plane should always be done by advancing the cutting iron, otherwise the blade may jump back slightly when used, thus decreasing the cut. The tool steel cutter is of thinner section which means less time taken in grinding. This thinner section may help to induce "chatter" but the "stay-set" iron (Fig. 154) will remedy this fault if it should arise. Alloy steel cutting irons containing tungsten or cobalt give a more lasting cutting edge.

(5) The frog is very accurately machined, which reduces the liability of the plane to "chatter".

(6) The lever cap applies pressure across the whole width of the cap iron just above the cutting edge of the tool. This gives a more rigid cutting edge and reduces the possibility of chatter. It acts as a lever of the first class (Fig. 236j).

(7) Interchangeable spare parts are obtainable to fit the well-known brands of metal plane.

THE SPOKESHAVE

The name of spokeshave was derived from the original use of the tool in rounding off the spokes of wooden wheels. They may be made from either metal or wood, the latter becoming rapidly less popular. A spokeshave is virtually a plane with a very short stock and is thus able to negotiate curved work.

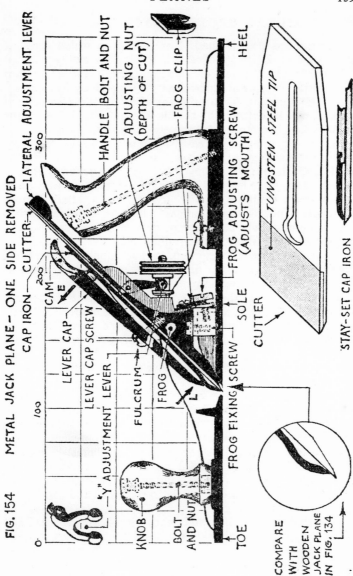

FIG. 154 METAL JACK PLANE – ONE SIDE REMOVED

CAP IRON — CUTTER — LATERAL ADJUSTMENT LEVER

HANDLE BOLT AND NUT

ADJUSTING NUT (DEPTH OF CUT)

FROG CLIP

HEEL

FROG ADJUSTING SCREW (ADJUSTS MOUTH)

SOLE

CUTTER

FROG FIXING SCREW

TOE

KNOB

BOLT AND NUT

FROG

FULCRUM

LEVER CAP SCREW

"Y" ADJUSTMENT LEVER

LEVER CAP

CAM

CUTTER

TUNGSTEN STEEL TIP

'STAY-SET CAP IRON'

COMPARE WITH WOODEN JACK PLANE IN FIG. 134

METAL SPOKESHAVES (Fig. 155)

The stock is usually made from cast iron which contains approximately 2% to 5% of carbon, either chemically combined with the iron as "cementite", making the iron extremely hard and brittle, or spread throughout the metal as free carbon (graphite). Graphite has a softening effect upon the iron and, if present, may be detected by the blackening effect it has on the hands when handling. Cast iron is comparatively cheap, but owing to its brittleness will easily fracture if subjected to a blow or to any tensile strain. It always has a hard skin formed during casting which must be removed before filing, turning, etc., to prevent damage to the tools. Stocks made from malleable cast iron, which are sufficiently tough to withstand a certain amount of rough handling, are obtainable but are more expensive. Malleable cast iron has a low percentage of carbon which is present almost entirely in its graphitic state.

The blade. There is no cap iron. On good quality spokeshaves the blade is adjustable for depth of cut and lateral movement by two knurled nuts working in the slotted blade.

The lever cap. On the fully adjustable pattern, the lever cap screw holds the lever cap in position on the blade. The screw acts as a fulcrum whereby even pressure is exerted along, and just above the cutting edge by means of the lever cap thumb screw.

The sole, or face of the spokeshave (Fig. 156), may be either flat or round.

A spokeshave is not a suitable tool for very sharp curves, since the sole of the tool is out of contact with the work and "chatter" of the whole tool will result. Even on shallow curves, heavy pressure must be exerted on the tool to prevent chatter. (With round faced spokeshaves this pressure must be exerted on the back of the tool, with flat faced spokeshaves on the front of the tool.) A skew or oblique cut is sometimes advisable, to present a greater area of the sole to the work and also give a more acute cutting angle.

Maintenance. Grinding and sharpening angles are 25° and 30° respectively. To facilitate the holding of so short a blade, a groove should be sawn in the end of a rectangular block of hardwood and the blade inserted in the saw-cut (Fig. 157).

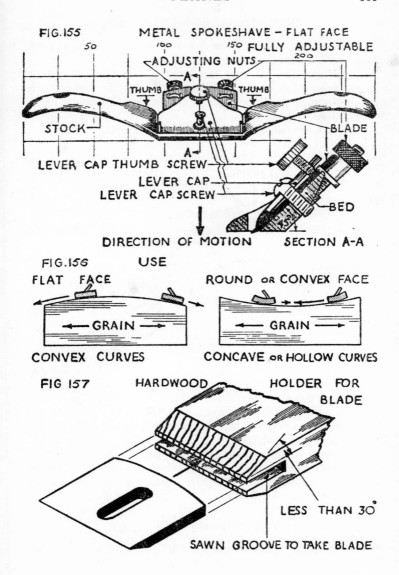

FIG.155 METAL SPOKESHAVE — FLAT FACE
FULLY ADJUSTABLE

ADJUSTING NUTS

A→

THUMB   THUMB

STOCK

BLADE

A→

LEVER CAP THUMB SCREW

LEVER CAP

LEVER CAP SCREW

BED

DIRECTION OF MOTION   SECTION A-A

FIG.156   USE

FLAT FACE   ROUND or CONVEX FACE

← GRAIN →   ← GRAIN →

CONVEX CURVES   CONCAVE or HOLLOW CURVES

FIG 157   HARDWOOD   HOLDER FOR
                                    BLADE

LESS THAN 30°

SAWN GROOVE TO TAKE BLADE

WOODEN SPOKESHAVES

The stock (Fig. 158) is usually made from boxwood, but ash or beech is sometimes used.

The blade, which is long and narrow, is hollow-ground on its top edge while the underside is quite flat. To increase the depth of cut, or set, the tangs are tapped with a piece of hardwood. To decrease the set, the flat of the blade should be tapped in a similar manner.

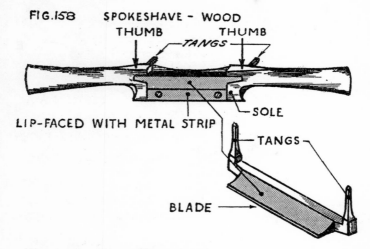

FIG.158   SPOKESHAVE - WOOD
THUMB   THUMB
TANGS
LIP-FACED WITH METAL STRIP
SOLE
TANGS
BLADE

The mouth suffers considerably from wear and damage. This wear may be reduced by facing the mouth with a strip of brass, but even if this is done, the mouth is still widened every time the blade is sharpened.

Maintenance. Sharpening is carried out in a similar manner to chisel sharpening. If the blade is too narrow for the oilstone, turn the stone on its side. A square section oilstone slip may be used in place of an oilstone.

THE CABINET SCRAPER

The blade (Fig. 159), which is made from hardened and tempered tool steel, is about 1·2 mm in thickness. If this thickness

is exceeded the blade will be difficult to bend when in use. If
less than 1·2 mm, the tool will tend to become too hot to handle
comfortably. The blade, as the name implies, has a scraping
action which is capable of cleaning up double-grained timbers
prior to polishing. It is also used on veneered surfaces.

Scraping is a difficult operation. The scraper should approach
the work at a high angle and be pushed away from the operator. The thumbs, pressing in the centre of the blade, should
force it into a curve to prevent the corners from digging in

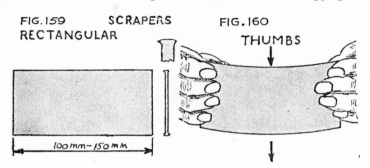

FIG. 159   SCRAPERS   FIG. 160
RECTANGULAR   THUMBS

100 mm – 150 mm

(Fig. 160). It is important that shavings, and not merely dust,
should be removed. Should the latter occur, re-sharpening is
necessary.

If a scraper blade is badly worn, the following maintenance
procedure should be carried out (Fig. 161).

1. Carefully draw-file top and bottom edges at 90°.
2. Remove the file marks on a flat oilstone.
3. Remove the burr by rubbing the blade flat on the oilstone.

For the first sharpening after having carried out the above
procedure, carry on as follows:—

1. Hold the scraper flat on the bench or vertically in a
   wooden vice (Fig. 162).
2. Make a firm stroke along the edge of the scraper with a
   burnishing tool, or the back of a gouge, holding the
   burnisher at an angle of about 85° to the face of the
   scraper.

This should give the required edge for considerable scraping but after a time it will become blunt again. For re-sharpening after use, carry out the following procedure:—

1. Remove the old burr by firmly stroking the face of the scraper with a burnisher held flat on the face (Fig. 163).

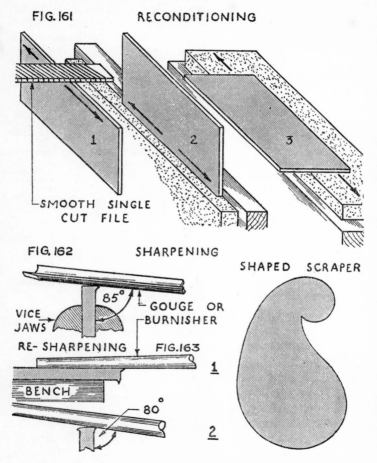

FIG. 161   RECONDITIONING

SMOOTH SINGLE CUT FILE

FIG. 162   SHARPENING

SHAPED SCRAPER

85° GOUGE OR BURNISHER

VICE JAWS

RE-SHARPENING   FIG. 163

BENCH

80°

2. Repeat the sharpening procedure in p. 163 (2), but reduce the angle between the burnisher and scraper to about 80°.

THE SCRAPER PLANE

The stock (Fig. 164) is made from cast iron.

The blade is thicker than that of hand scrapers and allows a different method of sharpening to be used. A thumbscrew, passing through the centre of the stock, bends the blade as the thumbs do in the cabinet scraper. The blade is pitched at about 70° (Fig. 165).

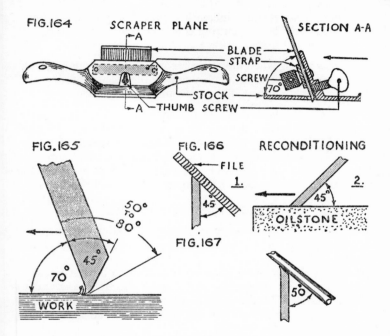

FIG.164 SCRAPER PLANE SECTION A-A

BLADE
STRAP
SCREW
STOCK
THUMB SCREW

FIG.165 FIG.166 RECONDITIONING

FILE
1.
45

OILSTONE
2.

FIG.167

50° TO 80°
45
70°
WORK

50

The scraper plane is a more satisfactory tool than the hand, or cabinet scraper, since the flat sole of the plane prevents "digging-in" of the blade edges. It is a far less fatiguing tool to use and gives a very clean finish on the most difficult grains. The tool is pushed away from the operator and is lifted on the return stroke. Chatter will result if insufficient pressure is put on the plane.

Reconditioning a much worn or damaged blade is carried out in the following manner (Fig. 166).

1. File or grind the cast steel cutting edge at 45°.
2. Hone at 45° to remove file or grindstone marks.
3. Remove the burr by honing the flat side on the oilstone.

After the correct angle and edge have been restored the edge should be turned over (Fig. 167):—

Incline the burnisher at about 50° to the face of the blade and, with steadily increasing pressure, produce a burr. This provides the cutting edge and consolidates the steel to give a tougher surface.

Re-sharpening when the blade becomes blunt through normal use, does not entail so much work as the reconditioning and first sharpening above. The procedure to adopt is:—

1. Remove the old burr on the oilstone.
2. Re-burnish the cutting edge at an increased angle of about 55°. This re-burnishing may be repeated several times before reconditioning becomes necessary, but each time it is done the angle should be increased by about 5°. When the angle reaches about 85°, reconditioning will be necessary.

SKARSTEN SCRAPERS

A very versatile scraper obtained in various patterns for specific jobs. Fig. 167a shows the type for finishing wood surfaces.

The handle consists of a suitable hardwood block (beech) to which is fixed a steel plate bent over at the operating end to take the hook or blade. Various types of handles are obtainable, long handles for heavy duty and pistol grip handles for use in inaccessible places.

Scraping hook. The following patterns are obtainable:—

1. Straight-edged, giving a smooth and even finish, superior to glasspaper.
2. Serrated, for removal of paint, varnish, enamel, lacquer and glue, scraped from wood, metal and glass without the use of heat or solvents.
3. Profile blades, for scraping mouldings etc.

The hooks are renewable and at all times should be kept sharp. They may be withdrawn to either side as shown in (a) for scraping in awkward corners.

The scraper is pulled towards the operator. Varying the angle at which the scraper is used will give various degrees of cut (b).

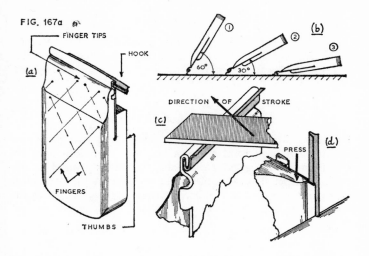

FIG. 167a

1. Heavy cut. Held with both hands; thumbs close together and pointing downwards on one side and hands over-lapping with the fingertips near the cutting edge on the other side as indicated in (a). This hold gives the firm pressure required for a coarse cut.
2. Medium cut.
3. Smooth finish. Held in one hand with the handle as low as possible, employing fast light strokes in the direction of the grain.

As with other cutting tools, a slicing cut taken parallel with the grain gives a better finish and helps to prevent clogging of the scraping edge.

Re-sharpening (c). Stroke diagonally outwards against the scraping edge, keeping the file at the original grinding angle.

Care must be taken to maintain a straight edge. A special filing guide may be obtained to assist in maintaining a constant angle.

To remove or extend hook (d). Press the end of the hook firmly down on a square edge; or drive out by the insertion of a new hook; or pull out with pliers.

THE DRAWKNIFE (Fig. 167b)

This tool is used for the rapid reduction of the width of timber. It is also used for rapid rounding of edges, such as when forming the "bucket" on the framework of an upholstered stool seat before the webbing is fitted.

THE SCRATCH STOCK

Fig. 167c shows a scratch stock made from two pieces of dense-grained hardwood such as beech. The blades may be made from old scrapers or old hacksaw blades ground to the required shape. The action is one of scraping and scratch stocks are therefore only effective when used with the grain. They may be used for:—

(a) forming small mouldings after first roughing out the shape with a plane.

(b) decoration such as "V" grooves, flutes, etc.

(c) preparation of grooves, especially if stopped to receive inlaid "lines" or "strings". It is advisable to knife or gauge the sides of the grooves first, particularly if the grain is not straight.

The blade will be more efficient if it is given a slight grinding and honing bevel. This will mean, however, that it can be used in one direction only.

Fig. 167d shows a scratch stock with an adjustable fence attached to the stem by means of a wing nut and bolt. An adjustable scratch stock may also be made from an old cutting gauge or marking gauge with a rectangular mortice cut at the point where the spur is located. The blade is held in position by a wedge in a similar manner to a cutting gauge, but in this case the width of the blade lies in the direction of the stem.

Fig. 167e shows how a bead may be scratched by using the head of a countersunk steel screw, screwed into a block of wood (the screw-slot is vertical to the work). The outside edge of the work is subsequently rounded off.

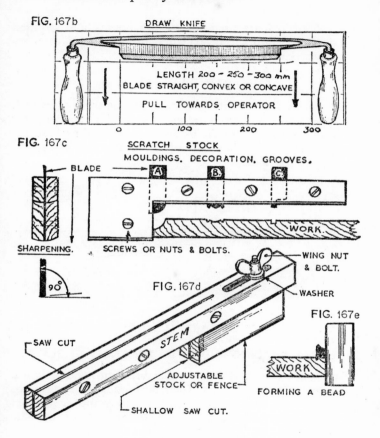

FIG. 167b

DRAW KNIFE

LENGTH 200 - 250 - 300 mm
BLADE STRAIGHT, CONVEX OR CONCAVE

PULL TOWARDS OPERATOR

0   100   200   300

FIG. 167c

SCRATCH STOCK
MOULDINGS. DECORATION. GROOVES.

BLADE   A.   B.   C.

SHARPENING.   90°   SCREWS OR NUTS & BOLTS.

FIG. 167d

WING NUT & BOLT.

WASHER

STEM

FIG. 167e

SAW CUT

ADJUSTABLE STOCK OR FENCE

SHALLOW SAW CUT.

WORK

FORMING A BEAD

Chapter 13

SAWS

HANDSAWS are used for cutting boards into required sizes preparatory to bench work. Included in this category are rip saws and cross-cut saws.

THE RIP SAW (Fig. 168)

The handle. Best quality handles are made from rosewood, but apple wood and beech are also used. In the modern saw the handle is inclined to the blade, so that the thrust exerted upon it is directed to the centre of the cutting edge and not to the front of the blade.

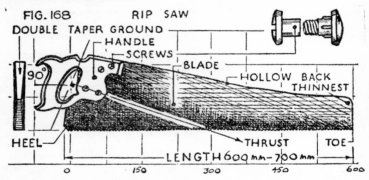

FIG. 168   RIP SAW
DOUBLE TAPER GROUND
HANDLE
SCREWS
BLADE
HOLLOW BACK THINNEST
90
HEEL
THRUST   TOE
LENGTH 600 mm – 700 mm
0   150   300   450   600

DEPTH OF SHADING INDICATES THICKNESS OF BLADE

Saw handle screws. These should be brass nuts and bolts and not rivets or imitation bolts. Their purpose is the securing of the blade to the handle and, should any play appear between the two, it is essential that it be removed by tightening the screws.

The blade should be made from the highest quality tool steel, hardened and tempered so that it is tough and elastic. If the steel is left too hard the teeth will be brittle and may fracture when being set.

During the process of manufacture, the blade is hammered,

170

partly to flatten it; but more important, to spread the metal slightly in the centre of the blade, thus placing the edges under a constant state of tension. The stretching effect thus obtained, particularly along the cutting edge, helps to keep the blade straight and rigid under working conditions.

The back of the blade may be straight or hollowed. The latter is known as a skew-back saw and is lighter in weight.

A good quality saw has its blade double taper ground. The toothed edge and the handle end remain the stoutest parts and are of equal thickness; both taper towards the front tip of the back edge, the thinnest part of the blade. Not only is a lighter saw obtained but less set need be given to the teeth to provide a sufficiently wide kerf to clear the saw.

The teeth (Fig. 169) are in the form of numerous small chisels. Their size is given by the number of points in 25 mm, and varies from 3 to 5½. Often there are 1 to 1½ more teeth at the toe than at the heel of the blade, allowing an easier start to be made when beginning a saw-cut.

The pitch or rake is the angle at which the front edge of the tooth is inclined to the line joining up all the points of the teeth. It is usually 90° but might be lowered to 80° for very tough wood.

If the angle of pitch is increased, then the teeth will be more likely to dig into the wood. If the angle of pitch is decreased there will be a greater tendency for the teeth to ride over the wood instead of cutting it.

The gullet is the space between the back edge of one tooth and the leading edge of the following tooth. The angle made by the gullet is always 60°, since a three-square or triangular (equilateral) file is used to shape and sharpen the teeth.

The kerf, although not part of the saw, is of great importance. It is the channel made in the wood by the saw teeth. It must be of sufficient width to allow the easy passage of the following blade and is determined by the degree of set given to the teeth.

The set is produced by slightly bending outwards, in opposite directions, the top half of each successive tooth.

If the set is too great (Fig. 170) the kerf will be very wide. The wood will offer a greater resistance to cutting, owing to the unnecessary extra amount of waste that must be removed. It will also be more difficult to keep the saw running straight and will not efficiently clear out the waste between each pair of alternately set points as shown at P.

If the set is too small, the saw will bind in the kerf and this may easily cause the blade to buckle.

The bevel (see under Cross-cut saw). There is usually no bevel although a very slight one is sometimes found to be

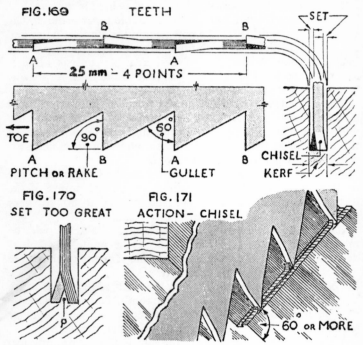

FIG. 169   TEETH

25 mm - 4 POINTS

TOE

PITCH OR RAKE   GULLET   CHISEL   KERF

SET

FIG. 170
SET TOO GREAT

FIG. 171
ACTION - CHISEL

60° OR MORE

advantageous when boards of very tough wood are being ripped.

The rip saw is used for cutting along the grain. The teeth have a chisel-like action and remove very small shavings or chips (Fig. 171). Attempts to use the saw across the grain will result in jamming of the saw and bad tearing out on the underside of the board.

Care of saws. Store in a dry place or dampness will cause the saw to rust.

Oil before putting away for any length of time. If the saw has become rusty, then remove the rust marks with fine emery paper and oil.

The teeth must always be protected and never allowed to come into contact with other tools. A wooden rack should be used for storage. If it is necessary to carry the saw about, then a grooved strip of wood to fit over the teeth will make a suitable shield.

If the saw has become slightly buckled, it may be hammered straight by placing it over a metal block and striking it very lightly with a hammer on the hollow side of the blade. (This

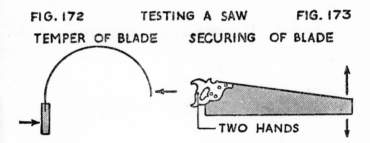

FIG. 172   TESTING A SAW   FIG. 173

TEMPER OF BLADE   SECURING OF BLADE

TWO HANDS

should not be attempted by the inexperienced.) The purpose of this operation is to stretch the metal on the hollow side.

Wood containing nails and screws should never be sawn or eventually the teeth will be badly damaged.

A saw must never be forced or the blade may buckle. Damage cannot occur if long, light, even strokes are used.

Testing a saw. A handsaw should be tested in the following manner:—

For straightness, by looking along the cutting edge.

For balance, by holding the saw in the working position and testing for "feel".

For temper of the steel: Using great care, hold the tip of the blade in one hand and the handle in the other, bend the blade in the form of a semi-circle. On release the blade should spring back to its original straight position (Fig. 172).

The blade, if of good quality steel, should give a clear ringing note when struck sharply with the tip of the finger.

For hammering and grinding, by holding the saw so that light may play on the blade. Any imperfections will readily be seen.

For security of blade to handle: The handle of the saw should be held firmly in both hands with the saw teeth pointing downwards. If the saw is moved rapidly up and down, no movement of the blade in the handle should be seen or felt, nor should any noise be heard (Fig. 173).

THE CROSS-CUT SAW

The cross-cut saw is similar to the rip saw with the following exceptions.

The teeth (Fig. 174) are shaped like numerous knives, having

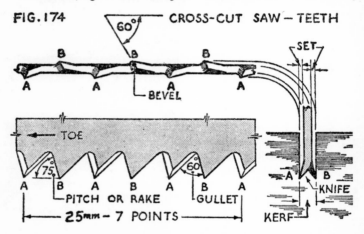

FIG. 174   CROSS-CUT SAW — TEETH

a slope or bevel on their leading edge. The number of points varies from $5\frac{1}{2}$ to 12 in 25 mm.

The pitch is 75°.

The bevel is the slope, if any, on the leading edge of the tooth. It is indicated by the angle formed between the face of the leading edge of the tooth and the face of the saw blade. If the angle is 90° there is no bevel. (See under Rip saw.) The angle of bevel may be varied from 60° for soft woods, giving a clean cut, to not less than 75° for hard woods, where the cutting edge needs to be far more rigid to prevent damage or undue wear.

The cutting edge of the tooth, with the knife-like action produced by the bevel, first severs the fibres on the outside of the kerf. This preliminary cutting prevents the grain from tearing out and might be compared to cutting down the sides of a

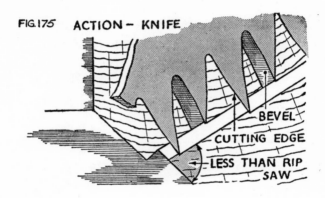

FIG. 175 ACTION – KNIFE

BEVEL
CUTTING EDGE
LESS THAN RIP SAW

groove across the grain, prior to chiselling out the waste (Fig. 175). The bevel, following up the knife edge, exerts a shearing force on the wood in the centre of the kerf and causes it to crumble away as dust.

As the name suggests, the saw is used for cutting across the grain. It can be used quite effectively with the grain but does not cut so rapidly as the rip saw.

THE TENON SAW (Fig. 176)

The blade is both thinner and finer than that of the hand saw. To allow accurate sawing to a line, the blade must be rigid and true; a condition which is obtained by tightly folding along its back edge a thick strip of brass or steel. (Hence the name of "back saw".)

The teeth are of cross-cut pattern and are usually pitched at 60°. The pitch is, however, sometimes increased to 75°.

Maintenance. No twist must be allowed to develop by the

back of the blade becoming out of line with the cutting edge.
The cutting edge itself must also be straight. These conditions

FIG. 176   TENON AND DOVETAIL SAW

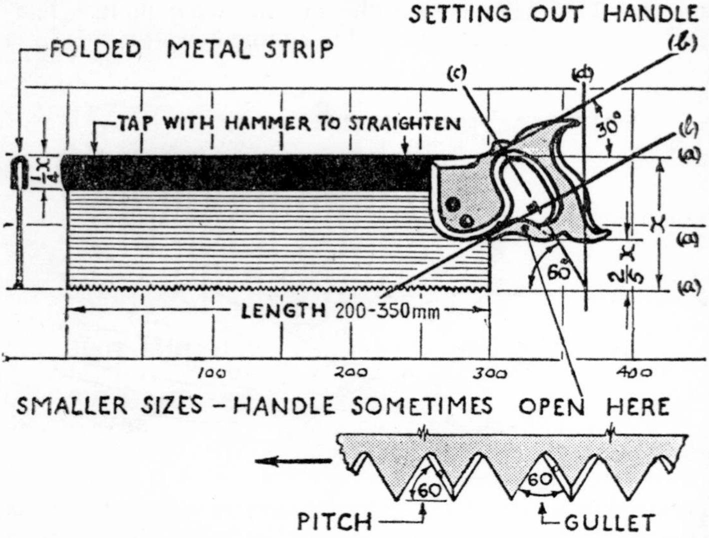

SETTING OUT HANDLE

SMALLER SIZES – HANDLE SOMETIMES OPEN HERE

PITCH —   — GULLET

may often be restored by holding the saw in one hand and
tapping the folded back edge with a hammer at the front end
of the saw. When in use, never pull a backsaw over in its
kerf to get back on the line. This will buckle the saw, which
means that it will never cut true. It is far better to turn the
wood over and start again from the other side.

Summary

Type	No. of points in 25 mm	Length in mm	Use
Tenon saw	12 to 14	200 to 400	General bench work
Dovetail saw	18 to 22	200 to 250	(a) Fine work (b) Dovetailing

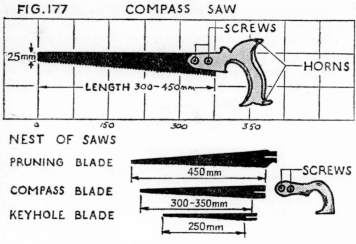

FIG.177   COMPASS   SAW

25mm

LENGTH 300-450mm

SCREWS

HORNS

NEST OF SAWS

PRUNING BLADE   450mm
COMPASS BLADE   300-350mm
KEYHOLE BLADE   250mm

SCREWS

THE COMPASS SAW (Fig. 177)

The blade is similar to the cross-cut blade but narrower so that it may follow a curved cut of large radius. The blade may be one of three in a set known as a nest of saws. A long slot, in the wide end of the blade, fits round two screws passing through the handle.

The teeth are of cross-cut pattern and are pitched at 75°.

THE PAD SAW (Fig. 178)

This saw is often called a keyhole saw, although to be strictly correct, a keyhole saw is a small version of a compass saw.

The blade is thick, narrow and slightly tapered in its length. The width and thickness at the handle end does not allow for accuracy when sawing to a line. Because of its small rectangular section it is very liable to bend if any undue force is exerted upon it. It is therefore left soft in comparison with other blades, so that it will not snap easily and it can be easily straightened should it bend when in use.

The teeth are of rip saw pattern with a pitch from 70° to 80°.

The handle is sufficiently long to allow the use of both hands if required.

Use of the pad saw. The pad saw is used for cuts which cannot

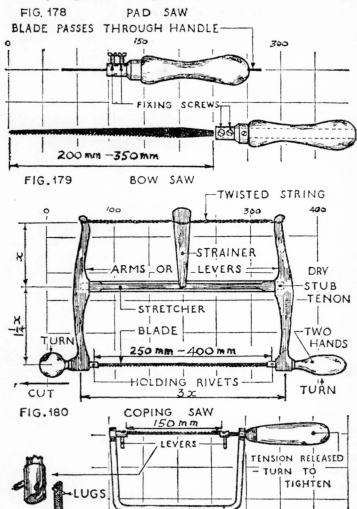

FIG. 178   PAD SAW
BLADE PASSES THROUGH HANDLE

FIXING SCREWS

200 mm – 350 mm

FIG. 179   BOW SAW

TWISTED STRING

STRAINER

ARMS OR LEVERS

DRY

STUB TENON

STRETCHER

BLADE

250 mm – 400 mm

TWO HANDS

TURN

CUT

HOLDING RIVETS

3x

TURN

FIG. 180   COPING SAW

150 mm

LEVERS

TENSION RELEASED – TURN TO TIGHTEN

LUGS

be reached with a bow saw but should not be used in preference to it. Internal cuts must be started by drilling a hole of sufficient diameter to take the blade.

THE BOW SAW (Fig. 179)

The bow saw is used for curved work, especially curves of small radius, but has the great disadvantage that it cannot work at a greater distance from the edge of the wood than the distance between the stretcher and the blade. For internal cuts, a hole must be drilled through the wood to take the blade. The holding rivet is then removed from one end of the blade, the blade is threaded through the hole and the rivet replaced.

The frame is usually made from beech. Several turns of strong string, or mason's line, are wound between the ends of the two shorter sides of the arms. A flat piece of wood known as a strainer is passed between the windings and when turned will twist the string, drawing together the arms on that side of the stretcher. The tension should always be slightly reduced when the saw is not in use.

The arms of the bow saw act as levers of the first class, but a mechanical disadvantage is obtained since the fulcrum (stretcher) is closer to the effort (tension of the string) than the load (tension exerted on the blade). This arrangement is convenient, however, since it allows the blade to work at a reasonable distance from the edge of the work.

The blade is kept constantly in tension by the twisted string. This tension allows the blade to be fairly narrow and thin, and is therefore able to negotiate fairly sharp curves. The blade may be turned to work in any direction to the frame by turning both handles. Care must be taken to see that the blade does not become twisted.

The ends of the blade fit into slotted brass collars at the base of the handles. The blades are rather too narrow to allow for easy sharpening and as new ones are cheap, worn blades are usually replaced. It is possible to sharpen the blades if they are left in the frame under tension. A pitch of 75° will be found to give a very clean cut.

The teeth are of the rip saw pattern with a pitch of 70° to 80°.

THE COPING SAW (Fig. 180)

The coping saw is mainly intended for cutting curved shapes in thin wood but has a much wider use for rapid removal of waste wood when dovetailing, or between the prongs of the bridle joint (or slot mortice). The saw must not be forced when in use; otherwise, the brittle blades will snap.

The frame, which is made from steel of a springy nature, provides tension for the blade.

The blade is fine, thereby allowing steep curves to be cut. It may be turned to work in any direction by unscrewing the handle and moving the two short levers in step with each other. If this is not done, the blade will be twisted. The handle must be tightened after the blade has been turned or there will be insufficient tension and the blade will snap. When not in use, the handle should be slightly unscrewed to reduce the blade tension. When worn out, the blades are discarded since they are so cheap to replace.

The teeth are of rip saw pattern with a pitch of 90°.

SAW RECONDITIONING

The saw blade must be held in some form of wooden or metal vice so that the teeth are rigid under the file (Fig. 180a–A). To prevent chatter during filing it is important that not more than 5 mm of the saw blade should project above the jaws of the saw vice. The wooden jaws shown at (B) are specially useful for holding tenon and dovetail saws.

Topping or jointing (Fig. 180b) is carried out with a 250 mm mill saw file, a single cut, flat file. The file must be used without a handle, since it would prevent the file from lying flat along the points of the saw teeth. To protect the hands and facilitate holding, the file may be fitted into a block of wood as shown. The file is drawn lengthwise along the top of the points of the teeth in a forward direction only, until all points are level.

Re-shaping (Fig. 180c) is carried out as shown, filing on the forward stroke only. The three-square saw file has cuts along its corners which form the slight curve at the base of the gullet. All teeth and gullets should finish the same size. It is perhaps better to file only the alternate teeth, i.e. those which have their set towards the operator and then to reverse the saw in the vice and proceed with the remaining teeth (see Fig. 180i—sharpening a cross-cut saw).

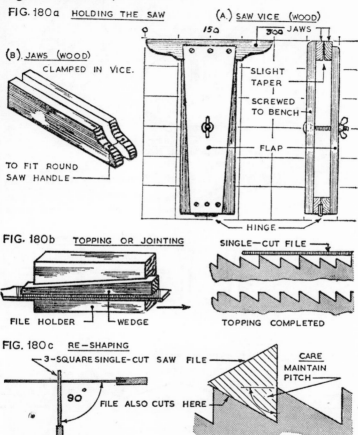

FIG. 180a HOLDING THE SAW

(A.) SAW VICE (WOOD)

300 JAWS

150

SLIGHT TAPER

SCREWED TO BENCH

(B). JAWS (WOOD) CLAMPED IN VICE.

TO FIT ROUND SAW HANDLE

FLAP

HINGE

FIG. 180b TOPPING OR JOINTING

FILE HOLDER   WEDGE

SINGLE—CUT FILE

TOPPING COMPLETED

FIG. 180c RE—SHAPING

3-SQUARE SINGLE-CUT SAW FILE

90°

FILE ALSO CUTS HERE

CARE MAINTAIN PITCH

Setting. It should be noted that the degree of set varies according to the number of teeth per 25 mm and to the use to which the saw is put. Less set is required for:—

(a) greater number of teeth per 25 mm.
(b) cross-cut saws compared with rip saws.

G

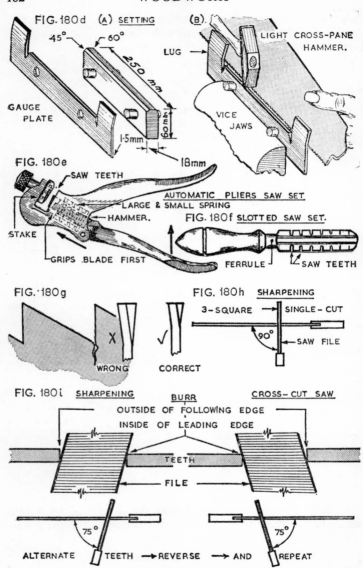

FIG. 180d (A) SETTING   (B)

45°   60°

250 mm

GAUGE PLATE

1.5mm   18mm

60 mm

LIGHT CROSS-PANE HAMMER.

LUG

VICE JAWS

FIG. 180e

SAW TEETH

AUTOMATIC PLIERS SAW SET

LARGE & SMALL SPRING

HAMMER.

STAKE

GRIPS BLADE FIRST

FIG. 180f SLOTTED SAW SET.

FERRULE   SAW TEETH

FIG. 180g

WRONG   X   CORRECT ✓

FIG. 180h SHARPENING

3-SQUARE   SINGLE-CUT

90°   SAW FILE

FIG. 180i SHARPENING

BURR   CROSS-CUT SAW

OUTSIDE OF FOLLOWING EDGE

INSIDE OF LEADING EDGE

TEETH

FILE

75°   75°

ALTERNATE   TEETH →REVERSE → AND   REPEAT

(c) hardwoods compared with softwoods.

(d) dry, well seasoned timber (woolly nature of wet sawdust and sides of kerf tend to make saw bind).

Setting may be carried out by any one of three methods:—

1. Hammer and setting stake. This is a skilled operation. Fig. 180d(A) shows a hardened steel anvil or stake together with its soft steel gauge plate. The distance between the two protruding lugs at each end of the plate should be slightly greater than the length of the stake. This allows the two lugs to be bent over at will and thus control the depth of the set. Fig. 180d (B) shows the stake and gauge plate held in the jaws of a metal vice with the positioning rods resting across the top of the vice jaws to prevent slipping. The saw blade is held flat on the top of the stake with the teeth protruding over the bevel and against the lugs of the gauge plate. With the saw in this position alternate teeth are then lightly tapped two or three times with a light cross-pane hammer as shown. The saw is then reversed on the stake and the same procedure followed for the remaining points.

2. Automatic pliers saw set (Fig. 180e). This is the best method for the less skilled. The tool follows the principle of the pliers. The stake or anvil is placed behind the teeth and against the saw blade. As the handle which operates the hammer is depressed, a cylindrical rod grips the saw blade against the anvil. Further depression of the lever causes the hammer to operate through the cylindrical rod and presses the teeth over to the required degree of set. The anvil, which is adjustable, is numbered for the number of teeth per 25 mm.

3. Slotted lever (Fig. 180f). This consists of a flat piece of metal with slots of varying widths cut into both long edges. It is not a recommended tool for a beginner, but if used, only the smallest amount of protrusion of the saw teeth above the vice jaws should be allowed or damage to the teeth may occur.

Only the top half of the tooth should be set, otherwise the saw blade may crack at the base of the gullet (Fig. 180g). When setting, the following should be noted:—

(i) the set must be uniform for all teeth on the same side of the blade to ensure even wear of the teeth (see side filing, below);

(ii) the set must be the same on both sides of the blade or the saw will tend to "run off" when cutting to a line;

(iii) the set should be just sufficient to give clearance to the following blade, otherwise too great an effort will be required when sawing.

Side filing. A file, lightly drawn along the sides of the teeth, removes any possibility of irregular setting by reducing any prominent points. If setting has been carried out skilfully, side filing should not be necessary.

SHARPENING

Rip saws (Fig. 180h). For this operation the file is held at 90° to the blade, as for shaping. Only one or two light forward strokes are necessary, filing each alternate tooth which is set towards the operator. The saw is then reversed and the remaining alternate teeth are sharpened.

Cross-cut saws (Fig. 180i). The angle shown for sharpening can be decreased slightly for cutting soft woods. The enlarged diagram shows why the tip of the file should point towards the handle of the saw. Three or four light forward strokes should suffice. When sharpening has been completed no "flats" should appear along the points of the teeth.

Back saws. Tenon saws of 250 mm and above are sharpened in the same manner as cross-cut saws. For the smaller varieties of back saw, because of the small points, sharpening without a bevel, as for rip saws, will usually prove sufficiently effective.

If, after sharpening has been completed, the saw proves to cut too fiercely, a fine oilstone may be lightly drawn along the sides of the teeth.

Chapter 14

TOOLS FOR BORING

THE BRACE (Fig. 181)

THE head, which is made from hardwood, preferably rosewood, is domed to give a comfortable grip.

The handle is also made from hardwood and revolves between two collars, but there are no bearings, since no downward pressure is brought to bear upon it. The effort exerted on the handle operates at right angles to its axis.

The chuck consists of the enlarged end of the crank rod, threaded to take a hollow casing and slotted to receive the jaw. As the casing is screwed on to the crank rod, the jaws are forced up the sloping surface of the cone by the core, and closed.

The ratchet is a special attachment on some braces which enables them to be used where a full sweep of the crank is not possible. By the movement of a stopped collar, the chuck can be engaged to turn in one direction whilst running free in the opposite direction. This enables the tool to operate with the use of only part of the sweep. To release the bit from the chuck, the ratchet is adjusted to operate in the reverse direction by turning the collar.

The mechanical principle involved in the use of the brace and bit is that of the wheel and axle, whereby a heavy load is raised on a length of rope wound round a drum of small diameter (i.e. spur of bit), by an effort applied at the end of a second rope wound round a wheel of large diameter (i.e. handle of brace). See Fig. 236k(a).

Use of the brace. When in use, the tool must be maintained square to the work so that a true hole will result. No undue force should be exerted on the brace or damage to the bit or the work may occur. Periodically the ball-race and chuck should be oiled for ease of working and to reduce wear on the moving parts.

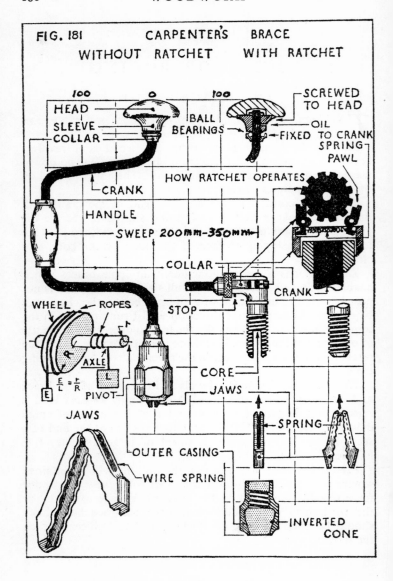

FIG. 181 CARPENTER'S BRACE
WITHOUT RATCHET WITH RATCHET

HEAD
SLEEVE
COLLAR
BALL BEARINGS
SCREWED TO HEAD
OIL
FIXED TO CRANK
SPRING
PAWL

CRANK

HOW RATCHET OPERATES

HANDLE
SWEEP 200mm-350mm

COLLAR

WHEEL
ROPES

AXLE

$\dfrac{E}{L} = \dfrac{r}{R}$

E

PIVOT

STOP

CRANK

CORE
JAWS

JAWS

OUTER CASING
WIRE SPRING

SPRING

INVERTED CONE

THE CENTRE BIT (Fig. 182)

The centre bit, made of tool steel, is used for boring shallow and through holes in thin wood. Sizes range from 3 mm to 50 mm. If used for boring deep holes, the varying density of the grain may cause the tool to drift to the side. This also applies

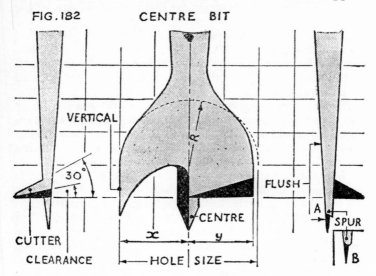

FIG. 182   CENTRE BIT

when drilling end grain, since the bit will follow the direction of the grain and produce a slanting hole (Fig. 183).

When cutting a through hole, continue the boring until the point of the centre just protrudes from the back of the work (Fig. 184). The work is then reversed and, using the small hole as a guide for the centre of the bit, remove the remainder of the core. A wooden block is sometimes placed behind the hole to prevent damage to the edge of the hole or to the bit. If the bit is sufficiently sharp the sides of the hole will appear to be polished.

The centre is in the shape of a triangular pyramid to enable it to bite into the wood. It acts as a pivot for the spur and must be longer than the spur, otherwise there will be no means of starting and holding the bit in position. The improved centre bit (Fig. 185) has a screw centre which draws the tool into the wood, reducing the pressure required to be exerted on the head of the brace and allowing quicker boring. The screw action is rather fierce, however, and as the thread crushes rather than cuts the wood on entering, splitting of thin wood is liable to occur. This may be avoided by first drilling a hole in the work equal to the maximum diameter of the core of the screw.

In the centre bit, the centre is kept sharp by an occasional stroke with a file (Fig. 186). The flat, or back side of the centre must not be touched with the file or the bit will be thrown off centre when in use. Note that smooth single-cut files are used for all bit sharpening.

The Spur has a vertical knife action and follows the centre into the wood, before the cutter operates. If this were not so, the cutter would tear the surface of the timber in a similar manner to chiselling across the grain of wood, without having first made a limiting saw-cut.

The spur is sharpened along its leading edge so that it cleanly severs the fibres round the hole to be bored. The tip or end may be at an angle, leaving the leading edge shorter than the following edge (A, Fig. 182). It may also be left round as shown at B, Fig. 182. The outer surface of the spur must be vertical since this determines the true diameter of the hole. Note that the radius from the centre to the edge of the spur (x) is slightly more than from the centre to the edge of the cutter (y, Fig. 182). This ensures that the cutter cannot lift the grain beyond the limits of the circle cut by the spur.

The spur is sharpened on the inside only (Fig. 187). The burr turned up by the file on the outside edge should be carefully removed on a fine oilstone. This outside surface must not be filed under any circumstances, since any reduction in the radius of spur to centre may cause the cutter to lift the grain beyond the limiting cut made by the spur, as previously described. It will also reduce the hole diameter.

The cutter, operating horizontally, removes the core from the hole with a chisel-like action, the mechanical principle being that of the inclined plane. The underside of the cutter slopes back slightly from the cutting edge to give clearance to the back of the blade. If this clearance is not provided, the

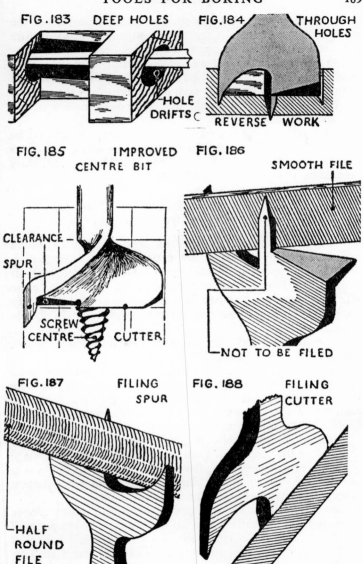

FIG. 183 DEEP HOLES

HOLE DRIFTS

FIG. 184 THROUGH HOLES

REVERSE WORK

FIG. 185 IMPROVED CENTRE BIT

CLEARANCE
SPUR
SCREW CENTRE
CUTTER

FIG. 186

SMOOTH FILE

NOT TO BE FILED

FIG. 187 FILING SPUR

HALF ROUND FILE

FIG. 188 FILING CUTTER

back of the cutter will be in contact with the surface of the
work at the same time as the cutting edge, and will therefore
rub and be unable to penetrate the work.

The cutter is sharpened on the upper side only (Fig. 188).
If an extra-keen edge is required it should be finished on a small
oilstone slip. Care must be taken not to turn over the back of
the cutting edge which would then ride over, instead of cut
into the work.

To protect the cutting edges from damage, bits should be
kept in a special canvas holder or a block of wood with holes
bored, into which the bits fit. They should also be lightly
greased as a protection against rust.

THE TWIST BIT (Fig. 189)

Twist bits are a development from, and an advance on, the
improved centre bit. They are extremely useful for boring
deep holes, especially in end grain, and by virtue of their
construction bore a truer and straighter hole than the centre
bit. They may be obtained in sizes ranging from 5 mm to
26 mm in 1 mm steps and 26 mm to 40 mm in 2 mm
steps.

The centre has a screw thread to draw the tool into the wood,
thereby giving a more rapid cutting action.

The spurs and cutter. There are two of each, giving a more
balanced cutting action, since cutting takes place at the same
time on opposite sides of the centre. The spur and cutter on
each side are in one piece with no space between them, thus
facilitating the cutting action in end grain.

Both spurs and cutters are sharpened in a similar manner
to those of the centre bit. Care must be taken not to damage
the screw centre when filing the cutters. With small bits, a thin
file will help to avoid this damage. The solid wing pattern
(Fig. 190) must be sharpened with a round file.

The body is twisted or fluted, providing a spiral groove
running from the cutting edge to the shank. The steepness of
the flute varies according to the pattern of the bit, but in all
types the purpose of the spiral is to act as a guide and keep the
bit straight in deep holes; especially those in end grain. The

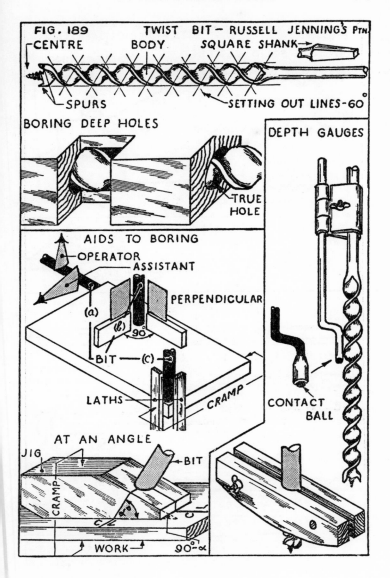

FIG. 189   TWIST BIT — RUSSELL JENNING'S PTN.

CENTRE   BODY   SQUARE SHANK

SPURS   SETTING OUT LINES-60°

BORING DEEP HOLES

TRUE HOLE

DEPTH GAUGES

AIDS TO BORING

OPERATOR
ASSISTANT
PERPENDICULAR
(a)
(b)
90°
BIT — (c)
LATHS   CRAMP

CONTACT BALL

AT AN ANGLE

JIG   BIT
CRAMP
c/L   c/L
WORK   90°-α

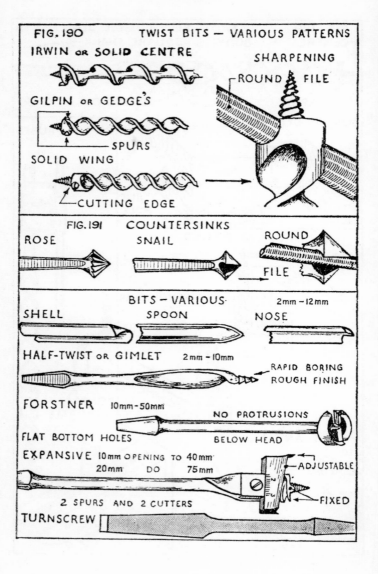

FIG. 190   TWIST BITS — VARIOUS PATTERNS

IRWIN or SOLID CENTRE

SHARPENING

ROUND FILE

GILPIN or GEDGE'S

SPURS

SOLID WING

CUTTING EDGE

FIG. 191   COUNTERSINKS

ROSE   SNAIL

ROUND

FILE

BITS — VARIOUS

SHELL   SPOON   NOSE

2mm – 12mm

HALF-TWIST or GIMLET   2mm – 10mm

RAPID BORING
ROUGH FINISH

FORSTNER   10mm – 50mm

NO PROTRUSIONS

FLAT BOTTOM HOLES   BELOW HEAD

EXPANSIVE 10mm OPENING TO 40mm
20mm   DO   75mm

ADJUSTABLE

FIXED

2 SPURS AND 2 CUTTERS

TURNSCREW

grooves raise and clear the waste wood from the cutting edge and thus prevent the bit from binding in the hole. The shank ends in a square section to fit the V-groove in the brace jaws. Twist bits, in common with the other boring tools, are made from hardened and tempered tool steel.

THE ROSE COUNTERSINK (Fig. 191)

This tool is used for countersinking in softwood, brass and aluminium, so that they may receive the heads of countersunk or raised head screws. It has a scraping, rather than a cutting action.

The end of the body is enlarged to form a cone with eight or more edges spaced round the sloping surface, terminating at the tip. The angle subtended at the tip by the sloping sides or generators may vary from 70° to 90°. (The underside of a countersunk screw head forms an angle of 90°.) The shank may end in a square section to fit into a brace or a circular section to fit into a hand drill.

THE SNAIL COUNTERSINK (Fig. 191)

The snail countersink is also used for countersinking for screw heads but is usually reserved for use in hard woods. It has a conical head and one or two cutters which give a true cutting action. The cutters are sharpened by undercutting the edge with a fine rat-tail file (Fig. 191).

THE BRADAWL (Fig. 192)

The bradawl is used for the preparation of small screw and nail holes in wood. The cutting edge should be placed at right angles to the grain of the wood so that the fibres are actually cut and not just pushed to one side. This reduces the danger of the screws splitting the wood.

The blade is round with the end flattened to form two bevels leading to the cutting edge. This causes the cutting edge to spread and thus provides clearance for the following blade. The two bevels should be sharpened to give a keen cutting edge, and the clearance should be maintained. The cutting edge first severs the wood fibres; the bevels then compress the fibres as the blade is forced into the wood and twisted.

The tang, which is square in section, should be pierced to receive a pin passing through it and the handle. This prevents the blade from being pulled out of the handle when the bradawl is withdrawn from the work and helps to resist the turning moment which would otherwise twist the tang inside the handle.

The handle, made from beech, ash or box, is of an elongated pear shape to provide the good hand grip required for the tool to be forced into the wood, turned and withdrawn.

The ferrule is of brass or mild steel.

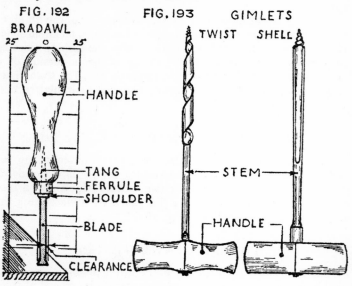

FIG. 192 BRADAWL FIG. 193 GIMLETS TWIST SHELL

HANDLE — TANG — FERRULE — SHOULDER — BLADE — CLEARANCE

STEM — HANDLE

THE TWIST GIMLET (Fig. 193)

Gimlets are used for preparing holes for screws and nails, but tend to give a rather rough finish to the edges. They may be obtained in sizes from 3 mm to 6 mm.

The stem finishes in a screw point which draws the tool into the work. The following stem tends to compress rather than cut the wood fibres and is therefore liable to split the work, especially near the edges or in thin wood.

The handle is made from boxwood, beech or ash.

THE SHELL GIMLET (Fig. 193)

The shell gimlet is similar in construction to the twist gimlet but the stem is hollowed instead of twisted. The hollow stem presents a cutting edge to the wood and is therefore less liable to split the work.

THE HAND DRILL (Fig. 193a)

The hand drill is really a metalworker's tool but is often used by the woodworker for drilling holes up to 6 mm diameter.

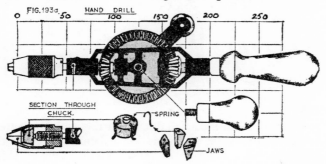

The example shown has a double pinion drive which is considerably stronger than the single pinion drive. Compare the three jaw chuck with the two jaw chuck of the carpenter's brace (Fig. 181). The three jaw chuck is designed to grip round-shanked tools while the two jaw chuck is designed to grip square-shanked tools. The three jaws, when fitted together, form a truncated cone. They fit into, and slide up, the sloping surface of an internal cone in the chuck casing. The jaws are kept in an advanced position by pressure against the threaded end of the rod which takes the chuck casing. When the chuck casing is unscrewed, the jaws are held open by the three small springs.

TWIST DRILLS

Fig. 193b shows three views of a twist drill, often known as a Morse drill, after Henry Morse who, in the U.S.A., was responsible for its development. These drills are made from carbon tool steel or high speed steel, the spiral flutes being cut on a milling machine. The drills are low in cost compared with twist bits. A useful range of sizes is from 1·5 mm to 6 mm. They provide clean, easy boring in wood but the size of the flutes does not allow the waste wood to clear easily. To prevent clogging when drilling deep holes, the drill should be withdrawn occasionally and the flutes cleared. Centres should be bradawled in wood, before starting to drill.

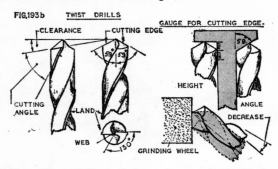

FIG.193b   TWIST DRILLS

Grinding of a drill is carried out by starting with the cutting edge horizontal. A semi-rotary motion is them imparted to the drill with the fingers and at the same time the angle at which the axis of the drill is inclined (59°) is decreased slightly to allow the clearance to be maintained (3° to 12° according to the material to be drilled). In the end view, the clearance will appear as a sloping line between the two cutting edges, at an angle of about 130°. If this angle is at 90° to the cutting edges there will be no clearance and a true cutting action will not be imparted to the tool. If the angle is greater than 130° then clearance will be excessive and insufficient support will be provided at the cutting edge. Each edge should be ground a little at a time and care taken to see that whilst grinding one edge, the other edge does not touch the stone. The length of the two cutting edges must be equal or an oversized hole will result. Carbon tool steel drills are best ground on a wet grindstone to prevent the temper of the steel from being drawn. High speed steel drills may be ground on a fast, dry stone.

Chapter 15

TESTING AND MARKING OUT

To ensure that a surface is flat in all directions the following tests are essential and should be carried out with some form of reliable straight edge (Fig. 194):—

1. Along the length of the surface.
2. Across the width of the surface.
3. Diagonally, from corner to corner, to ensure that the surface is not in "wind". Wind or twist, especially in large flat surfaces, long thin edges and framed-up work such as doors and stools, may also be detected with the aid of winding strips.

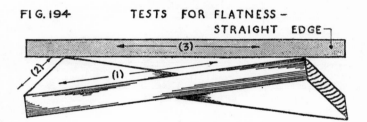

FIG. 194   TESTS FOR FLATNESS –
STRAIGHT EDGE

THE STRAIGHT EDGE

For large work the straight edge may be either a rectangular strip of steel or wood. It should be sufficiently thick to be rigid in use but, to obtain greater accuracy, the testing edge should be thinned by a bevel.

A steel straight edge, although more cumbersome to handle, is more robust and harder wearing. If, however, it should become damaged or worn, then it is far more difficult to true up. Length varies from 500 mm to 2000 mm.

Well-seasoned mahogany is a suitable material for a wooden straight edge, owing to its stability, straight grain and freedom from knots. It should be shellacked after construction to minimize re-absorption of atmospheric moisture and consequent warping (Fig. 195).

For small work. Either the edge of a steel rule or try square will suffice, but in all cases the edge must be perfectly true and reliable.

To test the edge of a straight edge, it should be held in position on a flat surface (Position I) and a fine pencil line drawn along its edge (Fig. 195). It should then be reversed on this line (Position 2) and a second line drawn. If the edge is true the two pencil lines will coincide.

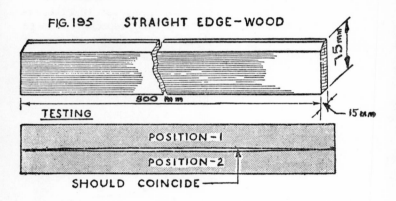

FIG. 195　　STRAIGHT EDGE—WOOD

75 mm

800 mm

15 mm

TESTING

POSITION—1

POSITION—2

SHOULD COINCIDE——

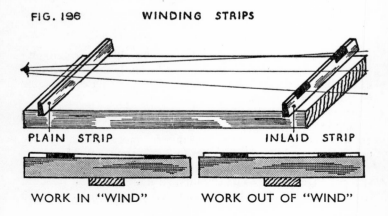

FIG. 196　　　　WINDING STRIPS

PLAIN STRIP　　　　　　　　INLAID STRIP

WORK IN "WIND"　　　WORK OUT OF "WIND"

WINDING STRIPS

These consist of two perfectly parallel strips of hardwood, preferably well-seasoned mahogany, similar in shape to a wooden straight edge and shellacked to minimize distortion (Fig. 196). A convenient size is 300 mm by 30 mm by 10 mm.

The two strips are placed parallel, and at opposite ends of the timber, with the inlaid strip at the rear. By sighting along the top of the strips any "wind" in the wood can easily be detected, since the top edges of the two strips will appear out of parallel. If the wood is out of "wind", tests for flatness must still be made as the work may be distorted in width or length.

TEMPLATES OR TEMPLETS (Fig. 197)

A template is a pattern made from thin material and used to set out and/or check work. It may be cut from thin wood, sheet metal, stiff cardboard, etc.

Mouldings. Where curved or irregular surfaces such as mouldings are to be run, a check for accuracy should be made at all points. This may be accomplished by the use of a template, its shape being the exact opposite to that of the moulding required.

Panels. When fitting a panel it is essential that its edge is a good fit along the whole length of the groove in the framework. To ensure accuracy, a strip of wood should be prepared and then grooved along the grain with the plough plane, using the same cutter employed for grooving the framework. The two grooves should match for depth as well as width. A small block, about 25 mm long, is then cut from this strip and drawn along the edges of the panel. Any inaccuracies will easily be detected.

Dovetails. See box and carcase constructions (Fig. 49).

THE TRY SQUARE (Fig. 198)

The stock is made from a close-grained hardwood such as ebony or rosewood. It is faced with a brass strip on its inside edge to prevent undue wear. This brass strip should at all times present a true edge. The heads of the securing rivets or screws must not protrude or the truth of the square will be affected.

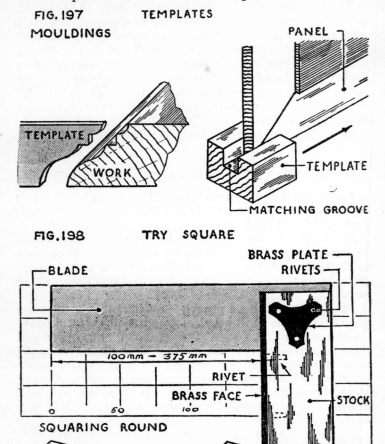

FIG.197   TEMPLATES

MOULDINGS

TEMPLATE   WORK

PANEL

TEMPLATE

MATCHING GROOVE

FIG.198   TRY SQUARE

BLADE

BRASS PLATE

RIVETS

100mm ~ 375mm

RIVET

BRASS FACE

STOCK

0   50   100

SQUARING ROUND

FROM FACE SIDE-ᵠ AND FACE EDGE-ʌ ONLY-LINES MEET

FROM ONE OTHER SIDE-LINES MAY NOT MEET

200

The outside edge of the stock cannot be regarded as reliable for testing purposes.

The blade should be of tool steel to prolong the truth of the edge, and it is "blued" to help prevent rusting. Both edges should be perfectly flat and parallel to each other, and at 90° to the brass face of the stock.

The blade must be firmly secured in the stock by means of brass or mild steel rivets. Brass plates set into both sides of the stock prevent the rivets from splitting or crushing the stock while being fixed. The plates also help to prevent damage to the square if it should be accidentally dropped or knocked.

Carpenter's steel squares are obtainable. They are more robust, subject to less wear, and the back of the stock can also be used for testing purposes. The length of the steel blade varies from 150 mm to 300 mm in 50 mm steps. The stock is made from cast iron.

Use of the try square. When squaring round a piece of wood the stock of the try square must only be used against the face side and the face edge. Failure to do so will usually result in the lines not meeting at the fourth corner, since it will be unlikely that opposite sides of the work are perfectly parallel (Fig. 198). A gap in the joint will result.

Testing the square. The stock should be held firmly in position against a perfectly straight edge of wood (Position 1) and a sharp knife or pencil drawn along the edge to be tested (Fig. 199). The square is then reversed on this line (Position 2) and a

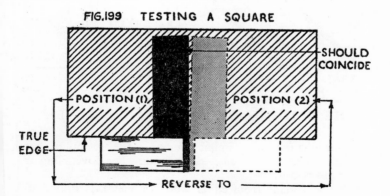

FIG.199   TESTING A SQUARE

second line knifed or drawn. If the edge is true and at 90° to the face of the stock, the two lines will coincide.

If the edge is out of square, damaged or worn by constant use of the knife, it must be trued up by careful draw-filing. The edge should then be finished with fine emery cloth to remove any marks left by the file.

If the square should be accidentally knocked, it must be tested before use. Periodic checks should also be made.

THE MITRE SQUARE

The mitre square (Fig. 200) is similar in many respects to the try square. The stock is joined to the centre of the blade and inclined to give angles of 45° and 135° on opposite sides of the stock.

The mitre square is used for setting out mitres at 45°, testing chamfers, etc., but is not an essential tool as an adjustable bevel will, with careful setting, serve these purposes equally well, if not better.

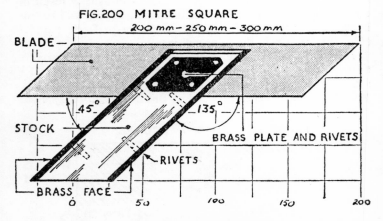

FIG. 200 MITRE SQUARE

200 mm – 250 mm – 300 mm

BLADE

45°   135°

STOCK

BRASS PLATE AND RIVETS

RIVETS

BRASS FACE

0   50   100   150   200

THE SLIDING OR ADJUSTABLE BEVEL
(Fig. 201)

This tool is used in a similar manner to the try square, but for angles other than 90° such as are found when dovetailing or setting out mitres.

The stock, made from either wood or metal, is slotted to

receive the blade. Wooden stocks have brass plates let in at both ends. Those at the round end prevent wear by the locking screw, while those at the square end take the rivets which fasten the two sides of the stock together.

The locking screw acts as a pivot about which the blade rotates and slides. At the same time it provides a method of

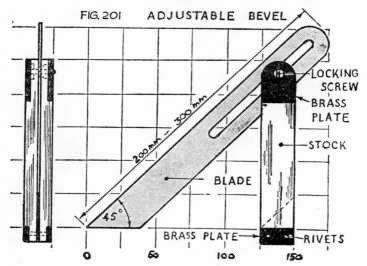

FIG. 201 ADJUSTABLE BEVEL

LOCKING SCREW
BRASS PLATE
STOCK
BLADE
200 mm - 300 mm
45°
BRASS PLATE
RIVETS
0 50 100 150

clamping the blade at any desired angle. It must be slackened before any adjustment is made.

The Blade is slotted along half of its length to permit adjustment for angle and amount of protrusion. The slot, together with the sloping end of the blade, allows it to be folded back into the stock when not in use. To set the blade to 45°, see Fig. 201a.

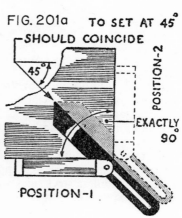

FIG. 201a TO SET AT 45°
SHOULD COINCIDE
45°
POSITION-2
EXACTLY 90°
POSITION-1

THE DIAGONAL SQUARE TEST

This is the most useful test for determining the squareness of rectangular carcases or framed work and is based on the principle that the diagonals of a rectangle are equal while those of a parallelogram are not (Fig. 202). Equal measurement is obtained between the two opposite pairs of corners by the use of a pointed lath or a rule. This is a more efficient method than using a try square, since any slight error is evenly distributed between all four corners of the job.

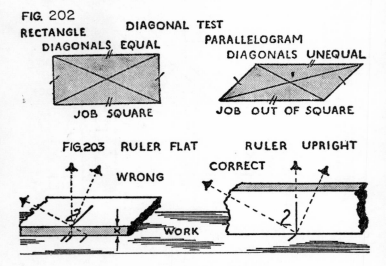

FIG. 202 DIAGONAL TEST

RECTANGLE DIAGONALS EQUAL — JOB SQUARE

PARALLELOGRAM DIAGONALS UNEQUAL — JOB OUT OF SQUARE

FIG.203 RULER FLAT — WRONG — WORK

RULER UPRIGHT — CORRECT

MARKING OUT

Rules. It is important, for the setting of gauges, etc., that all measurements should begin at the end of the rule.

Boxwood rules are obtainable in various patterns such as 1 m and $\frac{1}{2}$ m in one length and 1 m fourfold. They are tipped with brass at their ends to prevent excessive wear or damage. Steel rules are more robust, but soon become rusted and difficult to read unless kept polished with fine emery and a little oil. Stainless steel rules will overcome this difficulty but they are expensive.

To obtain the maximum accuracy in marking off measurements, the graduations on the rule or ruler should be in close contact with the face of the work (Fig. 203). If the rule is laid flat on the work, then the thickness (x) of the rule will separate the graduation marks from the surface of the work. In such a case, for accuracy to be relied upon, it must be certain that the eye of the observer is positioned immediately above the required graduation. Should the eye be slightly to one side, that is, to the left, and assuming light to travel in a straight line, then the mark on the work corresponding with the graduation on the rule will appear a little to the right of the correct position. The thicker the rule, the greater is the error, since the path of the light rays beyond the graduation is longer. For the same reason, the more the eye is inclined from the vertical, the greater will be the error.

The correct method is to hold the rule upright on the work. There will then be no light rays between the graduations on the rule and the surface of the work. Even if the eye is not vertically over the required graduation, accurate marking of the work can be carried out.

The pencil. Whenever it is necessary to work to a line with plane, saw or chisel, the line should be cut with a knife or marked with a gauge except in the following circumstances when a soft pencil should be used:—

1. For all temporary and rough marking out.
2. Where a cut line would be seen or would mark the surface of the wood.
3. For freehand curves such as run-off chamfers.
4. For marking lines which run slightly oblique to the general direction of the grain, as with the slope of a dovetail or the taper of a leg. A knife, if used, would be liable to run with the grain.
5. For marking out chamfers. If a marking gauge were used the spur would leave the edges of the chamfer damaged (Fig. 204).

The marking knife (Fig. 205). The blade is made from tool steel. It should be ground and sharpened on the outside face, thus allowing the inside face to be kept tightly against the edge of the try square. For left-handed users the knife should be ground and sharpened on the opposite side.

A penknife, similarly sharpened, makes an excellent marking knife and has the added advantage of easy use in very confined

FIG.204 CHAMFERS　　FIG. 205　MARKING KNIFE

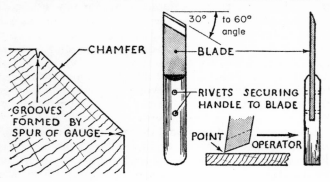

FIG.206　RODS

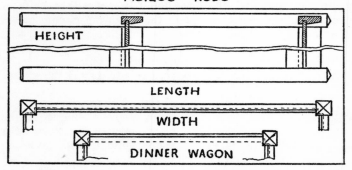

spaces such as are to be found when marking the pins from the tails of dovetails.

All lines across the grain which are to be sawn or chiselled, such as shoulders of tenons, sides of housings, ends of wood, etc., must be knifed in order that a clean edge to the joint may be obtained.

Full size drawings. When special shapes, such as might occur on the feet of a firescreen, are required, they may be traced directly on to the wood with the use of carbon paper.

Rods or skids (Fig. 206). This method is used commercially and consists of setting out on a thin board the lengths, widths and heights of a job, to be read in one direction only. These measurements can be transferred directly on to the work.

COMPASSES (Fig. 207)

Pencil compasses and wing compasses are used for marking out work of small radius. The latter are also useful as dividers for stepping off measurements.

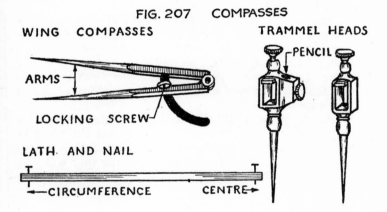

FIG. 207   COMPASSES

WING COMPASSES

TRAMMEL HEADS

PENCIL

ARMS

LOCKING SCREW

LATH AND NAIL

CIRCUMFERENCE   CENTRE

Lath and nails can be successfully used for setting out large circular work.

Trammel heads may be used to replace the nails mentioned in connection with the lath and nails above, thus making the tool adjustable.

GAUGES

These tools are used for marking lines parallel to a prepared edge.

THE MARKING GAUGE (Fig. 208)

The stock, made from beech, must have its face perfectly flat so that it will run flush against the edge of timber being gauged. It is locked to the stem by means of a thumbscrew and must be securely clamped, as any rock will lead to inaccuracy.

The thumbscrew, because of its threads, is made of boxwood. If it binds during operation the threads should be lubricated with graphite.

The stem, also made from beech, allows adjustment of the stock. Fine adjustment to the tool may be obtained by slightly tightening the thumbscrew and tapping the ends of the stem on the sides of the bench top. When the required setting is obtained the thumbscrew is firmly locked and the gauge checked before use.

The spur or tooth is made of tool steel and sharpened to a needle point. If the spur is allowed to protrude too far below the stem, the tool will become difficult to manipulate.

Use of the marking gauge. This tool is used for gauging with the grain. Its main purpose is for marking to width and thickness in the preparation of work. It must be used from face side or face edge only.

In use, the gauge is held with the spur pointing towards the operator and the stock pressed firmly against the wood to prevent the spur from wandering with the grain. Only a light forward stroke should be used, otherwise the spur will "dig in" and follow the grain.

THE CUTTING GAUGE (Fig. 209)

The cutting gauge differs from the marking gauge in that the spur is replaced by a small knife. The knife is held in a tapered mortice by means of a hardwood or brass wedge.

The knife, made from tool steel, is sharpened in a similar way to a marking knife but it will operate better if the cutting edge is slightly curved.

The ground edge may be either on the inside, facing towards the stock, or on the outside according to use. If the back edge of the knife is sharpened similarly to the front edge, the knife will be easily reversible and so fulfil either of the above conditions.

The back of the blade must be kept flat and should be

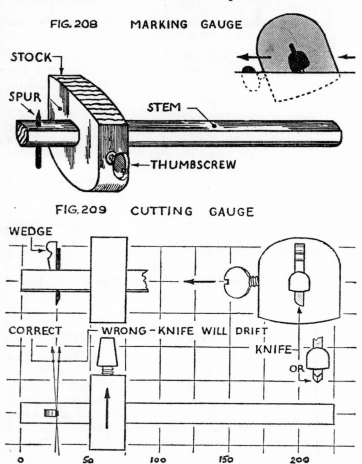

FIG. 208   MARKING GAUGE

STOCK

SPUR

STEM

THUMBSCREW

FIG. 209   CUTTING GAUGE

WEDGE

CORRECT   WRONG - KNIFE WILL DRIFT

KNIFE

OR

0   50   100   150   200

vertical when in position in the stem. The amount that the blade is allowed to project below the stem is dependent upon the depth of cut required.

The width of the blade should be inclined at a slight angle to the stock with the leading edge of the blade pointing away from it. This will pull the stock into the work during use and thus prevent the tool from drifting.

There are numerous uses to which this gauge can be put, some of which are enumerated below:—

1. Because of its knife action, this tool is primarily for cutting and gauging across the grain of timber. It is thus an essential tool for marking the depth of the dovetails in a half-lap dovetail joint.
2. For the preparation of "strings" or "lines" by splitting thin wood into strips. "Strings" are small square or rectangular sectioned strips of wood from 1 mm to 3 mm in thickness laid round the edge of a veneered surface to protect the veneer from damage.
3. For cutting small rebates such as those required for fitting the "strings" mentioned above.
4. For trimming a veneer at a given distance from the edge of work prior to the laying of cross-bandings, which are thin strips of decorative veneer with the grain running across the width of the strip. These strips thus form a border or "frame" for some central motif.
5. For cutting difficult grain which is likely to tear, before the use of a rebate plane or plough plane.

THE MORTICE GAUGE (Fig. 210)

The stock, made of ebony or rosewood, is inlaid on the face side with two brass strips to resist wear.

The locking screw, made of metal, may be sunk below the surface of the stock to prevent accidental movement or it may simply have a large round knurled head for easy adjustment. As the screw locks both the stock and the adjustable spur, care must be taken to slacken it before making any adjustment to the spur.

The stem, also of ebony or rosewood, is slotted along its length to receive the brass slide of the adjustable spur.

The spurs are both needle pointed. The outside or fixed spur is attached to a very short brass strip, let into and secured at the end of the groove in the stem. The adjustable spur is moved by means of a thumbscrew. This operates a thread which works in a circular brass nut let into the side of the stem.

Use of the mortice gauge. The mortice gauge is used wherever

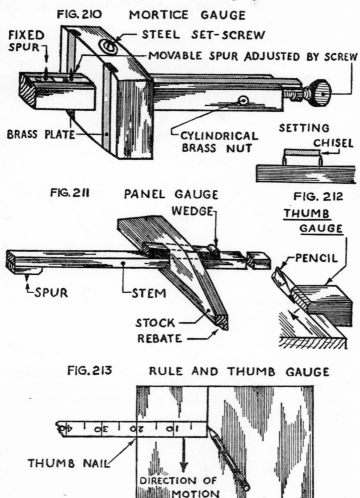

FIG. 210   MORTICE GAUGE

FIXED SPUR

STEEL SET-SCREW

MOVABLE SPUR ADJUSTED BY SCREW

BRASS PLATE

CYLINDRICAL BRASS NUT

SETTING CHISEL

FIG. 211   PANEL GAUGE   WEDGE

FIG. 212 THUMB GAUGE

PENCIL

SPUR   STEM

STOCK REBATE

FIG. 213   RULE AND THUMB GAUGE

THUMB NAIL

DIRECTION OF MOTION

two lines are required to be marked parallel to a prepared edge; for example, when marking out mortice and tenon joints, bridle joints and grooves to take panels, prior to the use of a plough plane.

The gauge should be used from face side and face edge only.

THE PANEL GAUGE (Fig. 211)

The stock is made from a thin piece of beech or similar hardwood about 200 mm in length. It is morticed to receive the stem and rebated along its lower edge. The rebate fits over the edge of the work and holds the gauge square during operation.

The stem may be up to 600 mm in length.

The wedge, made of beech, locks the stock in position on the stem but is unsatisfactory owing to the difficulty of accurate adjustment when the wedge is tapped home. If a bolt is let into the top of the stock to tighten on to a hexagonal nut, a more satisfactory adjustment is obtained. This arrangement is similar to that employed in a mortice gauge.

Use of the panel gauge. This tool is used for gauging the widths of boards which are too wide for the marking gauge.

THE THUMB GAUGE (Fig. 212)

The thumb gauge is for small work such as marking out chamfers. It is made from a small block of wood with the end rebated to the required depth.

THE RULE AND THUMB GAUGE (Fig. 213)

Used on square-edged boards. The thumb nail, held against the required measurement on the rule, is moved along the edge of the board. A pencil held at the end of the rule draws the required line.

Chapter 16

CRAMPS AND HOLDING DEVICES

THESE tools are for the temporary holding of work while gluing up, sawing, morticing, etc.

THE SASH CRAMP (Fig. 214)

The bar is made from bright mild steel and is rectangular in section. The length varies from 600 mm to 1500 mm in steps of 150 mm. A stronger bar than the above, from 750 mm to 2100 mm in length and useful for very large and heavy work, is the T section bar. (Mild steel is a soft, ductile form of steel containing up to 0·5% of carbon. Because of this low carbon content, it cannot be hardened and tempered. It can, however, be given a thin, hardened skin by the process known as case-hardening.)

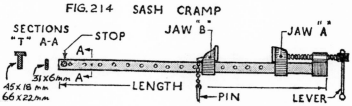

FIG. 214   SASH CRAMP

SECTIONS "T" A-A — STOP   JAW "B"   JAW "A"

A
31×6mm   A
45×18 mm ——— LENGTH
66×22mm   PIN   LEVER

The jaws, two in number, are made from malleable cast iron.

Jaw "A" is adjustable by means of a square-threaded screw operated by a lever.

Jaw "B" is adjustable by means of a tapered pin fitting into the holes along the length of the bar. A newer pattern now available consists of a spring loaded plunger which engages in the bar holes. This prevents loss of pins and chains.

The screw, of mild steel, consists of a machine-cut square thread (Fig. 215), which converts circular motion (lever) into linear motion (Jaw "A"). Action—inclined plane. (Fig. 236g.)

Use of sash cramps. Sash cramps are for cramping wide and long work, edge joints, and assembling frames and carcases.

Too much force must not be exerted in tightening up the cramp, or damage to the work or jaws may result.

The cramps should always be square to the job to prevent any twist being forced into the work, and the following points should be observed:—

Job out of square (Fig. 216). This means that the work will be leaning one way, forming a parallelogram, with one diagonal longer than the other. To pull the work square, the jaws of the cramp should be moved in the same direction as the job is already leaning.

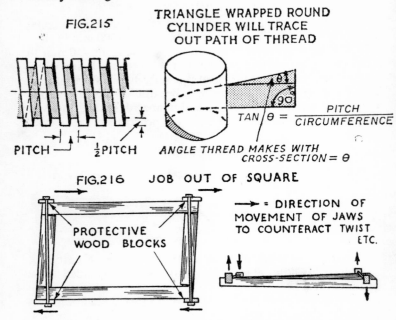

FIG. 215

TRIANGLE WRAPPED ROUND CYLINDER WILL TRACE OUT PATH OF THREAD

PITCH —   ½ PITCH

$$TAN \theta = \frac{PITCH}{CIRCUMFERENCE}$$

ANGLE THREAD MAKES WITH CROSS-SECTION = θ

FIG. 216   JOB OUT OF SQUARE

PROTECTIVE WOOD BLOCKS

⟶ = DIRECTION OF MOVEMENT OF JAWS TO COUNTERACT TWIST ETC.

Use of more than two cramps. The cramps should be placed on alternate sides of flat work to help in neutralizing any bending stresses set up by the pressure of the jaws on the job (Fig. 112).

Extra large work. To save the expense of the very largest cramps, lengthening bars are obtainable, or can be made, for the purpose of attaching to the ends of shorter cramps (Fig. 217). If neither sufficiently long cramps nor lengthening bars are available, the adjustable jaws may be removed from two shorter cramps and both bars joined end to end by means of the tapered pins, or nuts and bolts.

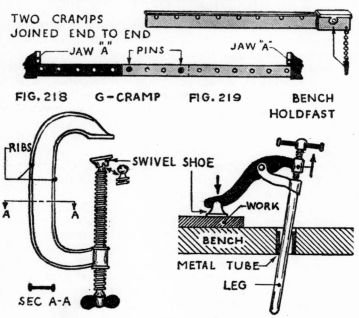

FIG.217 LENGTHENING BARS "T" SECTION

TWO CRAMPS JOINED END TO END

JAW "A" PINS JAW "A"

FIG. 218 G-CRAMP FIG. 219 BENCH HOLDFAST

RIBS SWIVEL SHOE

A A

WORK

BENCH

METAL TUBE

LEG

SEC A-A

THE "G" CRAMP (Fig. 218)

The frame, made from malleable cast iron, is ribbed on both inside and outside edges to give added strength to the G-shaped framework. Excessive pressure, if applied, will cause the frame to spring and twist, sometimes necessitating heating and forging to restore the cramp to shape.

The screw consists of a machine-cut square thread, similar to that used in the sash cramp, and terminates in a swivel shoe which enables work with opposite surfaces a little out of parallel to be held between the jaws.

The size is given by the distance between the jaws when fully opened and varies from 50 mm to 300 mm in 25 mm steps.

Deep throat G cramps are available and allow pressure to be exerted further in from the edge of the work.

THE BENCH HOLDFAST (Fig. 219)

The leg or pillar consists of a rod from 250 mm to 350 mm in length and 20 mm to 25 mm in diameter. It fits into a hole of slightly greater diameter drilled in the top of a bench. In order to resist the side pressure from the leg, the bench top should be at least 50 mm thick. Added advantage will be gained, in preventing unnecessary wear to the bench top, if the hole is lined with a metal tube. The tube must be sunk below the bench top to prevent its contacting and damaging keen-edged tools.

The arm, of malleable cast iron, projects outward from the top of the leg and allows room for work to be conveniently clamped to the bench top by means of the malleable cast iron shoe. The shoe swivels in line with the arm so that it may adjust itself to the surface of the work.

Use of the holdfast. The chief use of a bench holdfast is for holding work to be sawn by a handsaw, especially on a low sawing bench. It can also be used for holding work for such operations as boring but generally a G cramp will be found much more manageable. The holdfast may be found a useful aid for holding small carcases, drawers, etc., while they are being cleaned up. In this case it is used to cramp a block of wood to the bench top. The block should protrude beyond the bench top and be of sufficient size just to permit the job to be placed over it. The object of the block is to prevent the centre of the carcase side from sagging under the pressure of the plane passing over it.

THE HANDSCREW (Fig. 219a)

The handscrew, an awkward tool to adjust, has been replaced by the more useful G cramp. If wooden screws are used, they should be lubricated with graphite to prevent them from binding in their threads. The diagram shows the order in which the screws are tightened when cramping a job between the jaws. The centre screw acts as a lever of the 3rd class since it applies the effort (pressure) between the load (job held between the jaws) and the fulcrum (the end of the rear screw) (Fig. 236j). Because the effort is applied nearer the fulcrum than the load, a mechanical disadvantage is obtained. (This is sometimes necessary in order to gain convenience.) The rear screw then acts as a

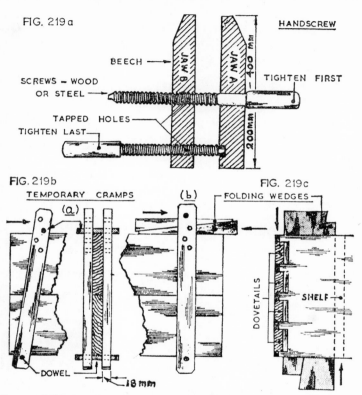

FIG. 219a

HANDSCREW

BEECH

JAW B   JAW A

SCREWS — WOOD OR STEEL

TIGHTEN FIRST

400mm

TAPPED HOLES

TIGHTEN LAST

200mm

FIG. 219b

TEMPORARY CRAMPS

(a)   (b)

FIG. 219c

FOLDING WEDGES

DOVETAILS

SHELF

DOWEL

18 mm

lever of the 1st class since it applies the effort on the opposite side of the fulcrum (centre screw) to the load.

TEMPORARY CRAMPS

Fig. 219b shows how wide boards can be glued and cramped together if no sash cramps are available. At (a), pressure is applied by merely forcing the cramp sideways, while (b) shows the more satisfactory method of knocking in folding wedges. Note the set of matching holes to make the cramp adjustable.

FOLDING WEDGES

Fig. 219c shows how folding wedges may also be used for knocking apart dovetails, where there is insufficient room to apply a hammer and a block of wood.

STRING CRAMPS (Fig. 220)

Where conventional cramps are not available, temporary cramps can sometimes be provided by using stout string and several wooden blocks.

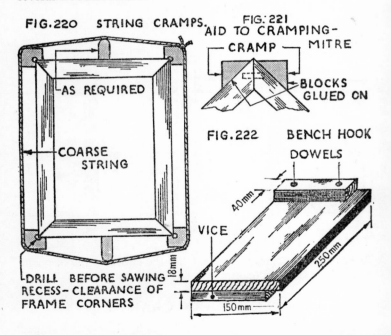

FIG. 220 STRING CRAMPS.

FIG. 221 AID TO CRAMPING - MITRE

- CRAMP -

- AS REQUIRED

- BLOCKS GLUED ON

- COARSE STRING

FIG. 222 BENCH HOOK

DOWELS

VICE

40 mm

250 mm

150 mm

18 mm

- DRILL BEFORE SAWING RECESS- CLEARANCE OF FRAME CORNERS

This form of cramping is especially useful when gluing the four corners of a small job at the same time, such as a mitred picture frame. Four wooden blocks are first prepared with a recess to fit round, and protect the corners of the work. The blocks are placed in position on the job and coarse string bound round their outside corners. Tension is then applied to the string by forcing in wooden centre blocks between the corner blocks. Care must be exercised or the carcase sides may bow. The string is then wetted and with subsequent shrinkage tightens further.

CRAMPING MITRES

Mitres can be more easily cramped for gluing if triangular blocks of wood are first glued on to the corners of the work as shown in Fig. 221. These allow a "G" cramp to be applied at each corner without the edges of the mitres slipping over each other. The blocks should be sufficiently large to permit the pressure from the cramps to be exerted about the centre of the joint and be separated from the work by a piece of paper.

THE BENCH HOOK (Fig. 222)

This is sometimes known as a sawing board and is used to steady work when sawing, especially when the cut is across the grain of the wood. At the same time it protects the bench top from damage by the saw. It may also be used to protect the bench when chiselling vertically. It is, however, better to use a separate, more easily replaceable piece of wood for this purpose.

THE MITRE BLOCK (Fig. 223)

The mitre block is used for cutting small mitres and is made from hardwood, preferably beech. There are usually three saw-cuts, one at 90° and the other two at 45° sloping in opposite directions. Suitable cuts may be made, however, at any other angle that may be required for the particular work in hand. Widening of the saw-cuts quickly makes the angles inaccurate and for this reason a faced mitre box is more suitable.

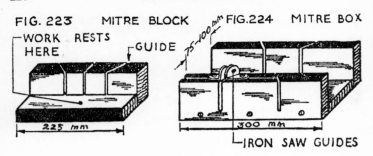

THE MITRE BOX (Fig. 224)

This is similar to the mitre block but has a double guide for cutting mitres on large, heavy work where greater guidance to the saw is needed.

The guides may contain removable facings to the saw-cuts which can be easily renewed when they have become worn. Again, to prolong the life of this device, adjustable metal guides to take any saw thickness may be fixed to the top edge of the guides.

THE SHOOTING BOARD (Fig. 225)

The platform or bed, made from beech and on which the work rests, is built up from the base on wooden blocks to form a rebate sufficiently wide to take a bench plane lying on its side.

If the block (A), at the opposite end of the shooting board to the stop is removed, a slope will be imparted to the bed. A sloping bed allows the plane to approach the work obliquely and a slicing action is obtained which offers less resistance to the cutting edge, gives a cleaner finish to the work and permits more even wear on the blade.

The fence or stop is attached at 90° to the rebate. If the stop is wedge-shaped and fitted into a tapered housing in the bed, it may be easily removed and repaired should it become damaged by tilting of the plane.

Shooting end grain. The stop prevents the fibres from breaking out at the far end of the work. If waste has been left on the

width of the work, then a chamfer may be chiselled as shown at
(B) as an extra precaution (Fig. 225).

The shooting board is best used on narrow timber, where it
would be difficult to keep the sole of the plane flat on the end
grain. For wood of sufficient width, better and more accurate
methods will be seen in Fig. 138.

Shooting edges of thin wood, planing with the grain. The edges
of long thin pieces of wood, which would bend if held in a vice,
can be easily trued on a shooting board by using a long
attachable fence screwed to the platform.

THE MITRE SHOOTING BOARD (Fig. 225)

The stop has two faces which are inclined, usually at 45°,
in opposite directions to the working edge of the bed. This
arrangement allows the mitring of mouldings, which, unlike
pieces rectangular in section, cannot be reversed.

A detachable stop can be made for use with a shooting board.
It is attached to the centre of the bed by means of stout nails
which protrude about 20 mm below its surface and from which
the heads have been sawn. The nails fit into corresponding
holes in the bed.

This device is used for shooting mitres on planted mouldings
or at the corners of picture frames, etc., if the stronger mortice
and tenon or mitred bridle joints are not used.

THE MITRE SHOOTING BLOCK (Fig. 225)

The jaws are made of beech with one face of each inclined
at an angle of 45°, so that large mitres may be shot on work
placed between them. Work is placed between the jaws and
pressure is applied to the movable jaw by means of some form
of screw. A long strip of wood is fixed to the underside of the
bed so that the tool may be rigidly held in the jaws of a bench
vice.

THE DONKEY'S EAR SHOOT (Fig. 225)

This device is for shooting wide mitres such as are to be
found on corners of boxes where the sides have been butted
together at an angle of 45°.

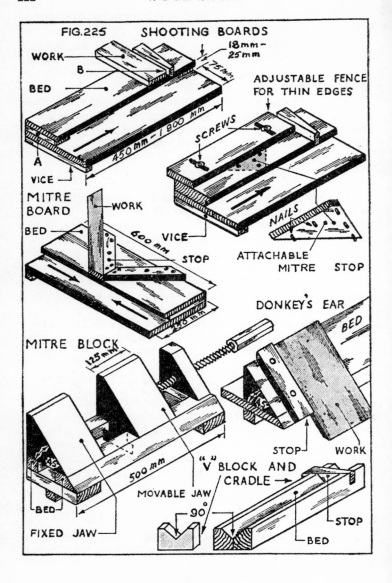

FIG. 225 SHOOTING BOARDS

WORK
B
BED
18mm – 25mm
75mm
A
VICE
450mm – 1 800 mm

ADJUSTABLE FENCE FOR THIN EDGES
SCREWS
VICE

NAILS
ATTACHABLE MITRE STOP

MITRE BOARD
BED
WORK
600 mm
STOP
VICE

DONKEY'S EAR
BED
STOP
WORK

MITRE BLOCK
125mm
500 mm
BED
45
MOVABLE JAW
FIXED JAW

"V" BLOCK AND CRADLE →
90°
STOP
BED

The bed, on which the work rests, is sloped at an angle of 45° and has the stop fixed across its sloping surface at one end.

"V" BLOCKS AND CRADLES (Fig. 225)

The bed of the cradle is made from two square sections of hardwood with one corner of each planed at 45°. The two pieces are then dowelled and glued, or glued and screwed together to give a total angle of 90°.

The Wedge should be tapered, fitting into a tapered housing cut across and near one end of the bed. It acts as a stop to hold work in the cradle.

The cradle allows cylindrical or octagonal work to be held whilst planing or chiselling. For heavy work, two "V" blocks may be used in place of the cradle.

Chapter **17**

MISCELLANEOUS TOOLS

THE MALLET (Fig. 226)

*T*HE *head.* Best quality heads are made from red beech, although white beech and ash may be used. The timber should be of dense even grain and cut as near to the heart of the tree as possible. The grain must run in a direction parallel to the sides of the head. The ends slope slightly inward from the top, so that the striking face will finish in a horizontal position at the end of the stroke.

The head is morticed through the centre to take the shaft. The mortice is tapered in its length to prevent the head from flying off by centrifugal force when the mallet is swung, and to allow the shaft to be tightened on the head should any shrinkage occur in the shaft. The end grain of the head, inside the mortice, takes the full pressure exerted by the wedging action of the shaft. To ensure that there is no pressure from the shaft across the narrowest part of the head, the mortice is parallel in width. This reduces any tendency for the head to split down the grain.

The size of a mallet is given by the length across the head and may vary from 100 mm to 175 mm. A useful weight is about 1 kilogramme.

The handle or shaft, made from red beech, ash or hickory, has its edges chamfered to provide a more comfortable hand grip.

The blow delivered by a mallet, compared with that of a hammer, is duller and, since the striking surface is considerably larger, the resultant blow is distributed over a wider area. The softer nature of the material from which the mallet head is fashioned permits chisel handles to be struck without damage. When a chisel is being driven, the greater yielding property of the mallet over the sharp blow of a hammer allows the mallet, on impact, to follow through instead of being abruptly brought to a halt. The chisel is thus driven even deeper into the wood. (For mechanical action, see page 282.)

Use of the mallet. The mallet should be swung from the

elbow, the head thus tracing out an arc. The mallet should strike the chisel with its sloping face at right angles to the axis of the chisel.

Mallets are used for driving chisels when chopping mortices, removing the waste wood from housing joints, etc. Used with the bevelled edge chisel, it can be effective in trimming the sides of housings and the base of pins and tails of dovetail joints. Care must be exercised to see that only light blows are delivered. A round-headed wood carver's mallet would serve the above purpose better.

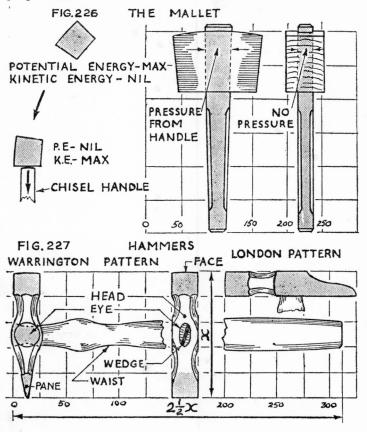

FIG. 226   THE MALLET

POTENTIAL ENERGY-MAX
KINETIC ENERGY - NIL

P.E- NIL
K.E.- MAX

CHISEL HANDLE

PRESSURE FROM HANDLE

NO PRESSURE

FIG. 227   HAMMERS
WARRINGTON PATTERN   FACE   LONDON PATTERN

HEAD
EYE

WEDGE
WAIST

PANE

WARRINGTON PATTERN HAMMER
(Fig. 227)

The head is made from tool steel, hand or drop forged and ground to shape. A useful weight is about 0·35 kilogrammes.

The face, which is hardened and tempered to resist wear, has its surface slightly curved and its edge chamfered to protect it from damage when in use.

The pane or *pein* is hardened and tempered tool steel.

The middle or centre part of the head is left in a softer, less brittle condition to prevent fracture upon impact.

The handle or shaft should be made from ash, or if obtainable, hickory, for flexibility. The waist is reduced to provide extra spring to the tool, thus helping to absorb the vibrations set up under the blow. Its oval shape allows a better grip to be obtained and assists in the correct delivery of the blow. The handle should be held at its far end so that maximum swing, and thus maximum momentum, is obtained. The hammer should be swung from the wrist (fulcrum) using the spring of the hammer to help to raise it ready for the next blow. To obtain more power, the fulcrum should be changed to the elbow, or even to the shoulder in the case of a sledge hammer.

The wedge may be made of hardwood but ragged steel is more efficient.

Use of the hammer. The Warrington Pattern is the most common general purpose hammer for carpentry and joinery.

The face is used for:—

1. Driving nails into timber, etc.
2. Adjusting the cut on wooden planes.
3. Tapping joints together and apart with the aid of a wooden block. This not only protects the surface of the work from damage by the hard metal face of the hammer, but also distributes the blow over a wider area.

The pane is used for:—

1. Starting small nails, held between the forefinger and the thumb.
2. Starting nails in corners or awkward places.
3. Straightening bent nails.

THE CANTERBURY OR AMERICAN CLAW
(Fig. 227a)

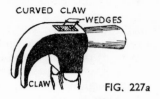

FIG. 227a

This hammer has its pein replaced by a curved pronged claw used for extracting nails. The extra strain, imposed on the shaft by the levering action, necessitates a stronger handle with greater support at the point where it is attached to the head.

LONDON PATTERN SCREWDRIVER
(Fig. 228)

This is strong but tends to be rather cumbersome.

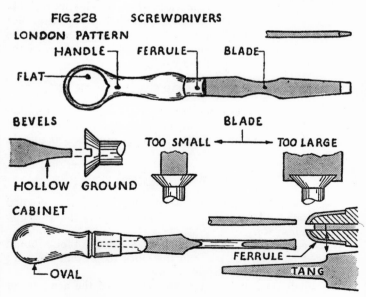

FIG. 228   SCREWDRIVERS

LONDON PATTERN

HANDLE FERRULE BLADE

FLAT

BEVELS   BLADE

HOLLOW GROUND   TOO SMALL ← → TOO LARGE

CABINET

OVAL   FERRULE   TANG

The handle, made from beech or ash, is pear-shaped and turned with opposite sides flattened in line with the width of the blade, to provide a good hand grip. Plastic handles are obtainable.

The ferrule is made from heavy gauge brass or steel. It is slotted to receive the flat and widened end of the blade, thus ensuring no movement of the tang in the handle.

The blade, from 75 mm to 350 mm long, is flat and is waisted about the centre to give lightness and spring to the tool. It is also tapered in width from the waist to the tip.

The blade is made of tool steel with the stem of spring temper (i.e. steel, tempered to a light blue colour), while the tang is left soft. The tang is much wider than the tang of a chisel to resist any turning tendency in the handle. There is no shoulder as the screwdriver is not for use with mallet or hammer and therefore there is no danger of the blade being driven up into the handle.

The blade is bevelled at its tip on both sides; the bevels being hollow ground so that the tip of the blade will not ride out and burr the slot in the screw. If the width of the bevel is appreciably less than the length of the slot in the screw, burring of the slot may again occur. If, however, the bevel is wider than the length of the slot in a countersunk screw, the corners of the blade will mark the face of the work.

CABINET PATTERN SCREWDRIVER (Fig. 228)

This is a light type of screwdriver compared with the London Pattern. The handle is pear-shaped and turned oval or round. The blade is round and varies from 75 mm to 300 mm in length.

PINCERS (Fig. 229)

Made from tool steel, comprising two bent levers pivoted towards one end by a holding rivet acting as the fulcrum. See also Fig. 236j.

When extracting nails with the jaws, a wooden block should be placed between the jaw and the work to prevent the hard jaw from bruising the surface of the work.

The small claw at the extremity of one of the arms is for

withdrawing small nails or starting the withdrawal of larger ones.

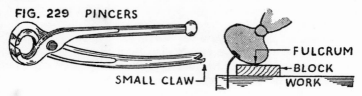

FIG. 229   PINCERS

SMALL CLAW

FULCRUM
BLOCK
WORK

GLASS PAPER

Glass paper is manufactured by first crushing glass to a fine powder under a revolving stone. Black, green or amber bottle glass is used as this breaks up into chunky fragments presenting cutting points all round. Window glass fractures into needle shaped splinters, pointed at each end. The powdered glass is then graded by sieving and sprinkled from a hopper over a continuous roll of stiff paper, previously coated by rollers with glue. The sheets of glued paper are then hung in a drying room in which air at a temperature of 38° C is circulated. Sometimes a further sizing coat of thinner glue is applied and the above drying procedure repeated. The rolls are then guillotined into required sizes, i.e. 275 mm by 250 mm. Sold in cartons of 25 sheets. Fine sand was originally used instead of glass, thus the name of sand paper which is often wrongly used.

The following chart shows the various grades of glass paper and cloth.

Sieve sizes	Grade	Continental grit number
200	00	2/0
180	0	—
140	F1	0
120	1	1
100	$1\frac{1}{2}$	2
70	F2	3
54	M2	4
46	S2	—
40	$2\frac{1}{2}$	5
36	3	6

The action of glasspaper is not that of a cutting tool but of an abrasive. It is important, therefore, that it be used with great discretion. A surface left straight from a cutting tool gives a better finish.

Glasspaper should always be used on some form of "rubber" so that pressure is more evenly distributed and a flat surface more easily obtained. The use of a "rubber" also aids the preservation of sharp edges, an important factor if a finished article is to preserve its appearance of clean lines (Fig. 230).

With the exception of glasspapering very curly grain, when a circular motion should be adopted, the glasspaper must always be used in the direction of the grain. If used across the grain, unsightly scratches, far more difficult to remove than to make, will appear on the surface of the work.

For sized or polished work the "rubber" should be dispensed with, as too much pressure may cause the glasspaper to pick up small particles and scratch the surface of the job. Instead, the glasspaper should be used with light pressure of the finger-tips only.

Glasspaper should always be stored in a dry place. If allowed to become damp it will not perform its task to the best advantage.

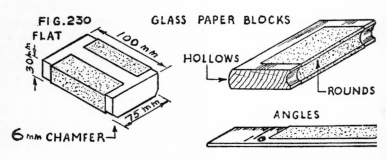

FIG. 230

GLASS PAPER BLOCKS

FLAT

30 mm

100 mm

75 mm

6 mm CHAMFER

HOLLOWS

ROUNDS

ANGLES

OILSTONES (NATURAL)

A convenient size of stone is 200 mm by 50 mm by 25 mm. There are various types of natural stone which are hewn directly from natural rock formations. Some of these are listed below, together with their chief characteristics:—

Washita

    Colour: white, streaked with red or yellow.

    Cutting quality: slow but gives a good edge to the tools.

Arkansas

    Colour: white.

    Cutting quality: finer and slower than Washita.

Turkey (a very soft stone)

    Colour: deep olive green.

    Cutting quality: fairly rapid but poorer grades wear unevenly.

Stones should be kept clean and free from dirty oil, which will tend to glaze their surface and considerably reduce their cutting properties.

For ease in handling, and protection against damage and dirt, an oilstone should be housed in a shallow wooden box with a deep fitting lid (Fig. 231). A block of wood with its end grain uppermost and its surface flush with that of the oilstone may be inserted at each end. This allows the full length of the stone surface to be worked, without damage to the cutting edge of the tool.

The use of the long edge of the oilstone for sharpening narrow tools minimizes unequal wear to the main surface and results in less frequent truing up of the stone.

The surface of the stone must at all times be maintained in a perfectly flat condition (see Figs. 125 and 126).

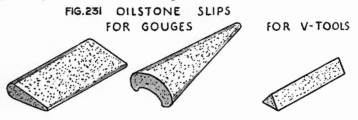

FIG. 231 OILSTONE SLIPS
FOR GOUGES   FOR V-TOOLS

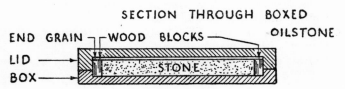

SECTION THROUGH BOXED OILSTONE

END GRAIN — WOOD BLOCKS —
LID —
BOX —
STONE

Reconditioning a glazed or clogged stone. The stone should be either scrubbed with a stiff brush dipped in paraffin or allowed to soak in a bath of the same liquid.

Reconditioning a worn stone. Either rub the face of the stone on a sheet of coarse emery cloth held firmly on a flat surface (i.e. wood, plate-glass, surface plate, etc.), or on a slab of marble or smooth paving stone, using silver sand or carborundum powder as an abrasive and water as a lubricant.

The action of a lubricant. When sharpening tools on an oilstone the surface should be lubricated:—

1. To wash away the small particles of stone and steel and prevent them clogging the pores of the oilstone.
2. To help burnish the sharpening bevel of the tool, giving a cleaner cutting edge.
3. To help dissipate the heat set up by friction, which would otherwise draw the temper of the steel.

Types of lubricant. Neat's foot oil obtained from the hooves of the ox and cow is excellent. Sweet oil or olive oil, sometimes mixed with about 10% paraffin oil, is good. A good quality thin machine oil is excellent, but ordinary lubricating oil with the addition of paraffin oil is cheaper. The paraffin not only thins the oil but cleans the stone, thus preventing it from becoming "gummed". (Paraffin may cause rust if left on tools for long periods.)

MANUFACTURED OILSTONES

A convenient size for sharpening bench tools is 200 mm by 50 mm by 25 mm. These stones consist of graded particles of some form of abrasive, cemented together to give any desired shape or size. (Note the oilstone slips for sharpening gouges, etc. (Fig. 231). The two main types of stone are:—

India, made from alundum, an oxide of aluminium
    Colour: mustard yellow to orange brown.
    Cutting quality: rapid and wears well.
Carborundum, the most difficult stone of all to reface
    Colour: dirty grey.
    Cutting quality: the most rapid of all stones but tends to
    give a rougher finish than the India stone.

The care and maintenance of artificial stones is similar in most respects to that of natural stones.

Clean oil, if allowed to soak into a stone, is inclined to have a hardening effect. Under certain conditions this may be advantageous in reducing the cutting rate of a quick cutting stone.

Reconditioning a worn stone. Usually artificial stones are too hard to respond to the treatment described under natural stones. They may, however, be re-surfaced by rubbing on a slab of marble or smooth paving stone using carborundum powder and water or carborundum paste and paraffin oil. The finer the stone, the finer should be the grade of carborundum powder used for the final truing-up.

GRINDSTONES (Fig. 231a)

Natural grindstones are shaped from naturally formed stone such as York, Newcastle or Blue Grit, and operate by means of a scraping action.

Some typical sizes are:—

450 mm diameter by 75 mm in thickness (Speed 95 r.p.m.)
900 mm diameter by 150 mm in thickness (Speed 40 r.p.m.)

A square hole is cut in the centre of the stone to take a smaller, square sectioned steel shaft. The stone is held in place

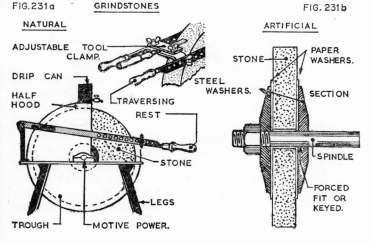

FIG.231a   GRINDSTONES   FIG. 231b

NATURAL   ARTIFICIAL

ADJUSTABLE TOOL CLAMP.
STONE   PAPER WASHERS.
DRIP CAN
STEEL WASHERS.
HALF HOOD
SECTION
TRAVERSING REST
STONE
SPINDLE
LEGS
FORCED FIT OR KEYED.
TROUGH   MOTIVE POWER.

on the shaft by wooden wedges driven between it and the shaft. Adjustment of the wedges allows concentricity of the stone to be maintained. The drive is connected at one or both ends of the shaft and may be supplied by a cranked handle, a treadle or an electric motor. The shaft rotates in bearings at the centre of the trough, the trough being designed to catch the water used as a coolant when the stone is in use.

To minimize splashing, a half-hood is fixed to the back of the trough. A drip-can fixed on top of the half-hood provides a constant supply of water which can be easily regulated by means of a tap.

An attachable tool rest is often provided which allows the blade being ground to be clamped and held at the correct angle to the stone. It consists of an open rectangular steel frame which fits over the stone. It is fixed at the back of the trough by a pivot, permitting both vertical and horizontal movement.

When not in use the stone must not be left standing in water or it will become soft, nor must it be continually exposed to the heat of the sun or it may crack.

Dressing, or truing up the stone, is carried out by forcing a hard steel tube against the revolving surface of the stone. The stone should be rotated towards the operator at its maximum speed.

ARTIFICIAL OR MANUFACTURED GRINDSTONES

High-speed wheels were first generally made from natural emery or corundum (impure forms of aluminium oxide—emery is about 60% pure corundum).

Modern wheels are made from silicon carbide and aluminous oxide and are products of the electric resistance and arc furnaces respectively. Silicon carbide (dark greenish crystals) is produced from sand and coke which provide the silicon and carbon respectively. Sawdust is added to provide porosity, thus allowing the escape of gases; and salt to form volatile salts of any impurities such as iron. The operation takes about 36 hours at 2000°C. Aluminous oxide (a reddish brown colour) is produced by melting down a clay-like material known as bauxite at a temperature of about 1800°C. After about 36 hours it is poured into ingots and allowed to solidify.

Silicon carbide (classified C) is the harder and more brittle of the two materials. Alumina (classified A) is tougher and suitable for most steels. The materials are first powdered, then graded by sifting and finally bonded together to form the desired shape of stone. The powdered grit presents many cutting edges to the work and removes minute particles of metal which are thrown clear, by centrifugal force, in the form of red-hot sparks.

The coarseness of the sifted particles is denoted by numbers, usually ranging from about 5 to over 200. A No. 40 means that the particles would just pass through a sieve of 40 meshes to 25 mm. The larger meshes are made from wire and the finer ones from silk. Grits finer than 200 are separated by water floatation.

Hardness is entirely independent of the coarseness or hardness of the particles and depends on the bond, the substance cementing the particles together. In a soft stone, the grit is easily dislodged and for this reason is used for grinding the harder steels so that a new cutting surface is maintained on the stone. Hard wheels are used to grind "soft" metals where the cutting edges of the grit are not easily blunted. Wheels are usually graded for hardness by letters running from very soft at "A", through medium at "M" to "Z", which is the hardest.

TYPES OF BOND

Synthetic Resin—Powdered bakelite mixed with grit and heated in moulds under pressure.

Rubber—The abrasive is spread over a sheet of rubber to which sulphur has been added as a vulcanizing agent. The sheet is folded and rolled to press the grit into the rubber; more abrasive is added and the sheet again folded and rolled. The process is repeated until the desired quantity of grit is obtained. The wheels are then cut from the sheet and vulcanized under heat and pressure.

Shellac—A mixture of flake shellac and grit, heated and rolled into thin sheets 3 mm or less. The wheels are then cut out with a die. Thick wheels are pressed in steel moulds.

Silicate—Sodium silicate (water glass) mixed with grit and zinc oxide (water proofing agent) and baked for several days.

Vitrified—Generally used for tool grinding. The abrasive grains are mixed with clay and baked in a mould until the clay becomes vitrified, producing a porous bond.

The density of the wheel, or closeness of the abrasive particles, depends upon the amount of bond used and may vary from 10% to 30%. Numbers range from 1 (greatest density) to 15 (open).

Wheels made by the vitrified or silicate process of bonding will give a ringing note when lightly tapped with a piece of wood and should therefore be tested for soundness when purchasing and again before fitting on the grinder.

A typical wheel for the workshop would be:—

ABRASIVE	GRAIN SIZE	BOND	BOND TYPE	DENSITY
Bauxilite	Medium	Medium	Vitrified	Medium
A	50	M	V	8

A hole in the centre of the stone passes over the shaft or spindle of the grinder (Fig. 231b) and should be an easy sliding fit. The stone is held in place by friction between the two large washers, pressure being supplied by a nut at the end of the spindle. The nut must not be tightened too tightly or damage to the wheel may result. Thin paper washers inserted between the steel washers and the stone will increase the frictional grip.

Grindstones are now usually motorized to give 2000 r.p.m. and upwards. Typical speeds are:— 150 mm wheel—about 2500 r.p.m. and 200 mm wheel—about 2000 r.p.m. Special low speed stones are available.

The tool rest, of mild steel, should be kept as close to the stone as possible to prevent tools becoming jammed between the stone and the rest.

Truing up of the stone is carried out by a "dressing" tool which consists of either a small hardened toothed wheel or an industrial diamond inserted into one end of a steel rod. The dressing tool should rest on the tool rest and be pressed very firmly against the surface of the wheel while the wheel is revolving at the maximum possible speed.

If the wheel becomes glazed during grinding it is an indication that it is too hard. If it wears away too rapidly, then it is too soft. As a wheel wears down, its peripheral speed (speed of a point on the circumference) is decreased and the wheel may appear softer towards the centre. The revolutions per minute should therefore be increased.

After mounting a new wheel it should be allowed to run freely at its operating speed for a short time, thus ensuring that it has not been damaged during mounting.

Work should never be forced against a cold wheel as the rapid heating may cause it to burst.

Grinding on the side of a wheel should be avoided, especially if it has been badly worn. This may also cause a wheel burst. Ring wheels should be used for side grinding since they are specially designed for the different stresses encountered.

COMPARISON BETWEEN NATURAL AND ARTIFICIAL STONES

Natural stones, although slow in operation, give a better finish to tools and with reasonable care the edges of even fine tools will not burn. They are comparatively easy to true up and require little maintenance, but are dirty in operation due to continual splashing.

Artificial stones with their rapid cut are very liable to draw the temper of tool edges, especially in the case of high speed grinders where the use of water as a coolant is impracticable. This necessitates the added disadvantage of constantly having to dip the tool into water. They provide the only means of grinding certain high speed steels.

The stones may be of small diameter and are therefore economical in space, but the small wheel surface makes it difficult to obtain a uniform bevel on wide tools such as plane irons.

For woodworking tools, there is a horizontal grinder which has a circulating drip feed, employing a special lubricating oil which also cleans the stone. However, uneven wear is likely to occur due to a natural tendency to work on the outside of the stone to gain maximum speed of cut. Most stones appear rather on the coarse side and the impossibility of hollow grinding might be considered a great disadvantage by some. Perhaps a better arrangement is the traverse grinder whereby a narrow grinding wheel moves slowly from side to side while the tool remains stationary.

Although artificial stones are much cleaner in use than natural stones, there is always danger to the eyes from flying particles. Protective goggles must always be worn.

Chapter 18

NAILS, SCREWS AND GLUE

NAILS and pins (Fig. 232) are usually sold by weight. There are many different kinds with names which may vary with trade and locale.

Method of nailing. Wherever possible, nails should be driven home in dovetail fashion (see Fig. 108).

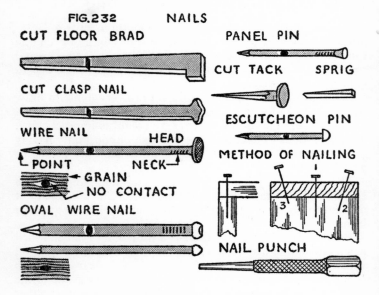

FIG. 232   NAILS

CUT FLOOR BRAD   PANEL PIN

CUT CLASP NAIL   CUT TACK   SPRIG

WIRE NAIL   HEAD   ESCUTCHEON PIN

POINT   NECK   METHOD OF NAILING

GRAIN   NO CONTACT

OVAL WIRE NAIL

NAIL PUNCH

Punching. Nail heads are best sunk below the surface of the work as they are inclined to work out a little after a time. The head may then be completely hidden by some form of stopping, finished flush with the surface of the work. If punching is intended, small headed nails should be used since those with large round heads will leave unsightly cavities.

Nail punches, or sets, can be obtained with different shaped points for various types of nail head:—

Square point: for cut brads
Round point: for French or wire nails
Cup point: for panel pins

Clenching. An extra strong joint can be obtained by selecting nails sufficiently long to pass right through the job. The head of the nail is supported on some form of anvil to prevent it rising while the point is clenched, or turned over with a hammer.

Advantages and disadvantages of nails:
While nails provide the quickest and easiest means of jointing they are difficult to withdraw without damage to the work. They give an unsightly finish and there is always the danger of splitting the work when driving them home.

Nails are preferable to screws for use in end grain, giving a stronger grip. The threads of a screw cut across the wood fibres dividing them into small pieces. These pieces, under tension, will soon shear away leaving the screw loose in its socket.

There are many stronger methods of jointing.

CUT FLOOR BRADS (40 mm–75 mm) AND CUT CLASP NAILS (20 mm–200 mm)

Both of the above patterns of nail are stamped from black mild steel strip. They are used for strong rough work, such as nailing floorboards to joists. They must be used with their width running parallel to the grain of the wood to minimize any splitting tendency. Their frictional grip is some 200% greater than other types of nails.

FRENCH OR ROUND WIRE NAILS (15 mm–200 mm)

These nails are made from bright mild steel. Their circular shape offers less surface contact between nail and timber, resulting in a certain amount of frictional loss in power to grip. The point provides easy entry into the wood.

The head, which is large and circular, has a corrugated top to reduce the danger of the hammer slipping and bruising the work.

The neck is roughened to increase the frictional grip of the nail in the wood.

Wire nails are used for all kinds of rough carpentry, including the nailing of packing cases and general household purposes.

Length (mm)	Gauge (mm)	Head size (mm)	Length (mm)	Gauge (mm)	Head size (mm)
200	8·0	16·0	60	3·35	7·5
180	6·7	13·0	60	3·0	6·5
150	6·0	12·0	60	2·65	6·0
150	5·6	11·0	50	3·35	7·5
125	5·6	11·0	50	3·0	6·5
125	5·0	10·0	50	2·65	6·0
115	5·0	10·0	50	2·36	5·5
100	5·0	10·0	45	2·65	6·0
100	4·5	9·0	45	2·36	5·5
100	4·0	8·0	45	2·0	4·5
100	3·75	8·0	40	2·65	6·0
90	4·5	9·0	40	2·36	5·5
90	4·0	8·0	40	2·00	5·0
90	3·75	8·0	30	2·36	5·5
90	3·35	7·5	30	2·00	5·0
75	4·0	8·0	30	1·8	4·5
75	3·75	8·0	25	2·00	5·0
75	3·35	7·5	25	1·8	4·5
75	3·0	6·5	25	1·6	4·0
65	3·75	8·0	20	1·6	4·0
65	3·35	7·5	20	1·4	3·8
65	3·0	6·5	15	1·4	3·8
65	2·65	6·0			

OVAL LOST OR BRAD HEAD WIRE NAILS
(20 mm–150 mm)

Made from bright mild steel, this nail has a small head and is therefore easily punched. Its oval section presents a greater gripping surface to the timber and makes it specially useful for nailing near ends and edges of wood. The nail should enter the wood with the long axis of its section in line with the grain, so that it will be less liable to split the wood.

PANEL PINS (15 mm–75 mm)

Made from bright mild steel, or brass for use with acidic woods. The head is small, round and smooth and is therefore easily punched. It is used in cabinet work, particularly of a light nature.

OVAL WIRE NAILS			PANEL PINS	
Length (mm)	*Gauge* (mm)	*Gauge* (mm)	*Length* (mm)	*Gauge* (mm)
150	7·1	5·0	75	3·75
130	6·7	4·5	65	3·35
100	6·0	4·0	65	3·0
90	5·6	3·75	60	3·35
75	5·0	3·35	60	3·0
65	4·0	2·65	50	3·0
60	3·75	2·36	50	2·65
50	3·35	2·00	40	2·36
45	3·35	2·00	30	2·00
40	2·65	1·6	25	1·0
30	2·65	1·6	20	1·0
25	2·00	1·25	15	1·0
20	2·00	1·25		

It is understood that the head diameter would be 1·4 times the wire diameter.

CUT TACK (20 mm–30 mm)

Made from black mild steel. It is blued, tinned or galvanized to prevent rusting. Copper tacks are also obtainable. The head is large and roughly circular. Its main use in cabinet making is for fixing upholstery fabric to wood.

ESCUTCHEON PIN (15 mm–30 mm)

Made from brass or iron. It may have either a round, domed or ornamental head and is used for attaching metal fittings such as escutcheon plates to a wooden background.

SPRIGS (15 mm–20 mm)

These are headless tapered nails made from mild steel and used for holding glass in a framework.

WOOD SCREWS (Fig. 233)

Screws may be made from:—

Bright mild steel. These are among the cheapest of screws. Although quite strong they are liable to rust, especially when used in acidic woods such as oak.

Brass. This is an alloy of copper and zinc and should be used in place of steel screws for all acidic woods. Brass screws are comparatively soft. To prevent the possibility of the heads breaking off when being driven into hardwood, a steel screw of

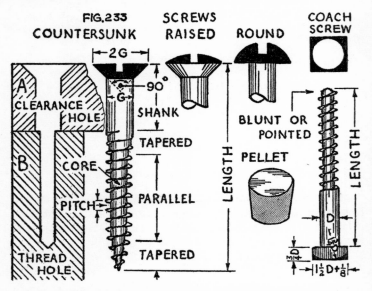

FIG. 233 SCREWS

COUNTERSUNK RAISED ROUND COACH SCREW

the same gauge should first be used, then withdrawn and replaced by the brass screw. This method also helps to ensure that the slot in the head of the brass screw does not become damaged.

Copper. As for brass.
Stainless steel. Excellent but expensive.
Aluminium. Fairly cheap and non-corrosive.
Gunmetal. An alloy of 90% copper to 10% tin.

Some screws are given a form of protective covering or finish such as:—

Galvanized. A coating of zinc as a protection for outside use.

Japanned (baked enamel). For outdoor use where timber is likely to be wet.

Chromium plated (on brass).

Nickel plated.

The head must be sufficiently large to take the slot for the screwdriver blade and strong enough to resist the turning force set up when driving the screw. There are three types of head:—

1. *Countersunk head.* The slopes of the underside of the head should meet to form an angle of 90°.
2. *Raised head.* This screw is often used with "screw cups", a form of hollow washer which not only increases the gripping area of the head but also presents a neat appearance. Often chromed for use in bathrooms and other damp atmospheres.
3. *Round head.* The head is equal to three-quarters of a hemisphere. These screws are mainly used for fixing metal to wood.

The length, which varies from 5 mm to 150 mm is measured from the tip of the screw to that part of the head which normally lies flush with the surface of the wood when the screw is in position.

The shank is the unthreaded portion of the screw and extends for one-third of the length of the screw.

The gauge (G) of a screw, which may vary from 0000 to 50, denotes the diameter of the shank. The diameter of the shank is equal to half the diameter of the head taken at its greatest width (2 G).

The thread is triangular in section to provide an edge that will cut its way into the timber. The following V-shaped portion of the thread compresses the wood fibres.

The core of the screw, the diameter between the base of the threads, is equal to 0·6 of the shank diameter. The thread is parallel for the major part of its length and only tapers at the start of the screw, to provide a sharp point of gimlet form for initial entry into the work, and at the end as a lead from the parallel screw to the shank.

Screwing into hard woods (Fig. 233). Wherever possible the thinner piece of work (A) should be screwed to the thicker piece (B). The screw used should have the length of its shank equal to the thickness of the top piece (A).

The drill clearance hole should be the same diameter as the shank, thus presenting a sliding fit to the shank so that the screw thread, working in the lower piece (B), pulls the top piece (A) into close contact.

If the clearance hole is too large, the gripping surface of the head will be greatly reduced. If too small, the outward pressure of the shank may cause the wood to split or prevent the two pieces of wood from being pulled into close contact.

The thread hole should not be greater than the core diameter of the screw and its depth should be exclusive of the tapered point of the screw.

Countersinking is necessary to house the head of a counter-sunk or raised head screw and should be carried out with a snail countersink bit.

SI METRIC DRILL SIZES FOR WOOD SCREWING

Screw Gauge No.	2	4	6	8	10	12	14
Clearance Drill (mm)	2·2	2·8	3·6	4·4	5·0	5·8	6·4
Counter Drill (mm)	1·2	1·4	1·8	2·2	2·6	3·0	3·2

The approximate size of drill for the clearance hole may be obtained from the gauge (G) as follows:—

Clearance hole = (G + 2) × 0·4 mm
i.e. (10 + 2) × 0·4 mm = 4·8 mm.

For screws, gauge No. 12 or below, the above clearance hole will be found to be a little too small, therefore add 0·2 to 0·4 mm.

Screwing into soft woods is the same as for hard woods with the following exceptions:—

1. The thread hole may be slightly smaller, it sometimes

being sufficient to merely sever the wood fibres with a
bradawl.

2. Countersinking is not normally necessary, as the softer
   nature of the wood allows the screw head to crush the
   fibres beneath it and countersink itself.

Advantages of screwing:—

1. It is a quick method of joining two pieces of wood
   together, and is both strong and rigid, except when screws
   are used in end grain.
2. Metal parts and fittings can be attached to wood
3. Slot-screwing allows for shrinkage.
4. For fixing "buttons" to table tops, etc., to allow shrinkage.

Ordering screws. The following facts must be given to the
dealer:—

Quantity	Length	Gauge	Head	Material
100	40 mm	No. 10	Countersunk	Steel

Lubrication. Screws should be lubricated with petroleum
jelly (Vaseline) before being driven. This facilitates entry and
helps to prevent the formation of rust in steel screws.

A pellet is a slightly tapered, cylindrical plug to cover the
head of a sunken screw. It should be finished flush with the
surface and match the grain of the work.

Rusted screws which have become difficult to remove can
often be loosened sufficiently to allow them to be turned with a
screwdriver, by first tapping the head of the screw with a
hammer.

The coach screw is for use on large work, where the heavy
nature of the screw does not permit the use of a screwdriver.
It is therefore provided with a square head, similar to that of a
bolt, for use with a spanner (Fig. 233).

ANIMAL GLUES

Glues have been used by man for over 3,000 years. There is,
however, little evidence of their use during the Middle Ages
when joints were usually dry tenoned and draw-pegged or
butt-jointed edge to edge with iron straps. Glue was first

commercially produced in Holland about A.D. 1700. Prior to this, craftsmen made their own glue and many continued to do so after 1700 by boiling pieces of skin and hide in open vessels over a fire, the grease and hair being roughly skimmed off.

BONE AND HIDE GLUE

Cleansing of the waste pieces of hides from abattoirs and tanneries is carried out by first swelling them in lime in large vats at normal temperatures. This process allows for easier extraction of the glue or gelatine. The hides are then washed in water and acid to get rid of the lime and finally in water to free them from any traces of acid.

The bones are sorted for size, grease and moisture content, the hoofs and horns and large pieces of meat being discarded. Any ferrous metal present is removed by a magnet. The bones are then broken to a suitable size and treated with benzine to extract the grease which, after refining, is used in the manufacture of soap. Any remaining meat or hair is removed by rotating the bones in a circular drum lined with spikes and known as a "polisher".

Extraction. Both polished bones and hides are subjected to similar treatment—that of the action of steam and hot water at varying temperatures in large cookers called digesters. A high temperature will extract more glue, but of an inferior quality. The liquor which is weak, about the consistency of size, is then run off and the above process repeated several times giving increasingly thinner "runs" of poorer quality glue.

Evaporation. The weak solution of glue must be concentrated to bring it up to its required consistency. If this was carried out by evaporating the water at boiling point, the glue would deteriorate. This operation is therefore carried out under a vacuum at a reduced temperature.

Preparation. After concentration, the glue is filtered and pumped into vats to undergo any required chemical treatments such as the addition of a preservative or bleaching. It can then be either introduced into tubes as liquid or jelly glue, the tubes or tins being sealed to prevent drying out. If the glue is to be dried it may first be run into glass trays. As soon as it has set, it is removed from the trays, cut to size and stacked on wire racks in a current of warm air until the correct moisture content is reached. It is then marketed as cake glue and may be sold under such names as Salisbury, Scotch or French glue.

Bead, grain or pearl glue is made by rapidly chilling small drops of the above glue instead of running it into trays. Glue in powder form is obtained by grinding up roughly made cake glue.

Action and use of glue. Glue penetrates the pores of the wood and thus forms countless very small dowels (Fig. 234). A surface left from the saw provides a greater gluing area and thus a stronger joint. The joint itself must be a good fit as glue is not a means of filling gaps in bad joints. This is because a thick layer of glue allowed to form between two surfaces to be joined

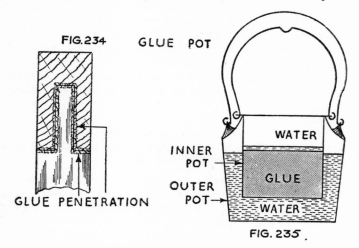

FIG.234   GLUE POT

GLUE PENETRATION

INNER POT →
OUTER POT →

WATER

GLUE

WATER

FIG. 235

has a weakening effect. Glue is fairly brittle and such a joint may break apart under pressure. The use of cramps as an effective means of squeezing out surplus glue is, in most cases essential to a strong joint. A glued joint, if properly made should be stronger than the surrounding timber.

Glue has a dulling effect upon cutting tools. Surplus glue should therefore be removed before any final cleaning up operation takes place.

Surfaces which the plane cannot reach for cleaning up after

gluing, should be completed and wax polished before assembly. The surplus glue should be allowed to harden, when, by the careful use of a chisel, it will be found to break away without causing any superficial damage to the work.

Alternatively, if surplus glue is allowed to set until it reaches a rubbery state, it may be peeled away from the surface of the job. This procedure is useful when surfaces are not prepolished.

A further method is to use a rag soaked in clean hot water to wipe away any excess glue immediately after gluing up. This does not remove all the glue, however. A thin diluted layer, spread over the surface of the work, remains and amounts to a very thin coating of size.

Preparation. If cake glue is used it should first be broken into small pieces by wrapping it in a clean cloth and striking with a hammer. The cloth prevents any splinters from flying.

Place the required quantity of glue in the inner pot of a glue kettle and steep in water until it jellifies. Cake glue is best left soaking overnight while powdered glue only requires about one hour. Glue subjected directly to heat tends to deteriorate in quality due to the promotion of harmful bacteria. Preliminary soaking also allows speedier preparation when the glue is required for use.

When required for use, a little clean cold water should be added to the glue and the mixture slowly heated in a glue kettle (Fig. 235). The glue kettle consists of:—

1. An inner pot, usually made of cast iron, but copper is preferable being a better conductor, and distributing heat more evenly. The inside of an iron pot, which is in contact with the glue, should be tinned to prevent any oxidation of the metal from discolouring the glue.
2. An outer pot, made from cast iron. It contains water, which maintains the glue at an even temperature and prevents it from over-heating.

The correct heat at which glue should be used is about 60° C (Celsius). At this temperature the finger can be dipped into the hot glue without any undue discomfort being felt.

The outer glue pot must never be allowed to boil dry or the glue will burn, causing rapid deterioration and loss of adhesive properties.

Re-heating for re-use. Add a small quantity of clean cold water for the purpose of thinning. This replaces the moisture lost by evaporation.

Tests for good quality glue. Good quality glue will absorb more water than glue of an inferior quality and should:—

1. Be clear and light in colour, the best quality usually being of an amber hue.
2. Be free from specks of impurities.
3. Feel sticky to the touch of a wet finger.
4. Not feel greasy to the touch.
5. Be fairly brittle and when broken should show a sharp and glistening fracture.

Gluing precautions. Glue must be stored in a dry place otherwise it will deteriorate. Both the inner glue pot and used brushes should be regularly cleaned by boiling them in a bucket of water. If this precaution is not taken, any harmful bacteria will multiply rapidly.

Heating for long periods will cause deterioration. Too many re-heatings will also have the same harmful effects, therefore only sufficient glue for the work in hand should be prepared. During heating, any scum of unfiltered waste appearing on the surface of the glue should be removed.

Correct consistency or viscosity is obtained when the glue will just run off the brush without forming drops. It is possible to use glue a little thicker for softwoods where the nature of the cells tend to absorb more moisture. If the glue is absorbed too quickly a "starved" joint will result.

To ensure maximum jelling time the glue should not be allowed to chill during gluing-up operations. The room should be warm and the joints brought to body heat 36° C (Celsius) by careful heating over a gas ring. This allows up to 10 minutes before jelling commences. Speed is essential; any movement of the joint between jelling and hardening, or curing, will break the small glue threads. This causes joint failure.

Glue should be applied sparingly—just sufficient to fulfil the purpose without running all over the job and note should be taken of the following properties:—

Water resistance: Poor and should not be used for outdoor

work or in places where the atmosphere is humid or the glue will revert to a gelatinous state.

Setting time: 12 hours. It is advisable not to remove cramps until this period of time has expired.

How used: Hot. (Cold varieties are obtained in tubes, e.g. Croid glue.)

Resistance to bacteria: Poor.

Staining property: Does not stain if good quality glue is used. Should a glue stain appear on work through the use of dirty glue, the stain can be removed by the application of oxalic acid. The acid is poisonous, necessitating great care in handling.

SYNTHETIC RESIN GLUES—UREA FORMALDEHYDE RESINS

Glue proper is a chemical compound of synthetic urea and formaldehyde. Urea is produced by the reaction of ammonia prepared from the nitrogen in air, with carbon dioxide. Formaldehyde is prepared from wood alcohol. It may be marketed as a powder to be mixed with water, or as a thick whitish syrup. The latter becomes rubbery after three or four months and is then rendered useless. This is because the reaction between the urea and the formaldehyde, set up during manufacture and arrested before it has caused the chemicals to solidify into a hard resin, is never completely stopped.

The hardener or catalyst may be either a transparent or coloured liquid. When brought into contact with the glue proper, the chemical action set up continues the reaction which was arrested during the process of manufacture and causes the formaldehyde to solidify.

The glue has a high adhesive strength due to the greater contractive force which is set up within itself. A thin film of glue between two surfaces will literally pull the surfaces together.

Glue in large quantities, such as may be found in poorly fitting joints, will contract within itself; the internal stresses thus set up cause crazing or the breaking up of the glue into many small pieces. Such a joint will not hold but gap-filling glue is available.

This glue may be used on both small and large work. The

method of application of urea formaldehyde glues varies according to type and make, but the methods shown below will be found successful:—

1. Hardener to one surface; glue to the other surface.
2. Hardener applied first, followed by the glue to the same surface. (Care must be taken not to use the hardener brush in the resin jar.)
3. Hardener and glue mixed together before application. This is only applicable to the slow setting varieties.
4. Single application resin glue and hardener combined in powder form, needing only the addition of water to activate them. Approximate pot life is only 30 minutes, so do not mix more than is needed.

Precautions:—
1. Pressure must be applied to joints during the setting period.
2. The glue must not be kept in containers of an alkaline nature (e.g. brass), or the setting qualities may become affected.
3. The hardener must not be kept in any type of metal container.

Summary of properties

Water resistance: Very great. (Unaffected after 30 days complete immersion in water.)

Setting time: Varies. There are usually three hardeners available for the glue:—

(a) Quick setting, for gluing joints on which it is required to begin work at the earliest possible moment. (Cramps may be removed after about 15 minutes.)
(b) Medium setting, hardens in about 2 hours.
(c) Slow setting, for gluing work containing many joints which require assembling at the same time. Cramps should not be removed for many hours, the glue taking about 96 hours to mature.

How used: Cold.
Resistance to bacteria: 100%.

Staining property: Does not stain softwoods but some hardeners tend to stain acidic woods.

PHENOL FORMALDEHYDE RESINS

Phenol is manufactured from coal. These glues are similar in most respects to the urea formaldehyde resins, but are much more sensitive to variations in temperature. They are used extensively in industry where rapid setting under controlled temperature is possible.

RESORCINOL FORMALDEHYDE RESINS

Resorcinol formaldehyde resins are similar to phenol formaldehyde resins but do not have the disadvantage of temperature sensitivity. They are, however, more expensive.

EPOXY RESINS

Epoxy resins have the added advantage of enabling non-porous materials such as metal and glass to be bonded together. They are water-proof, acid and alkali-proof, but are expensive to produce. The hardener, or catalyst, is usually a viscous liquid which is mixed with the glue proper before use. Drying time may be up to three days at room temperature.

POLYVINYL ACETATE EMULSION GLUE
(P.V.A.)

The basic raw material is acetylene, produced either by the carbide process or as a petrochemical. In the carbide process, carbon and limestone are fused together in an electric arc furnace to produce calcium carbide which is then reacted with water to evolve acetylene gas. The acetylene is reacted with acetic acid, under the influence of catalysts, to produce the monomer, vinyl acetate, a colourless, pleasant-smelling liquid. A monomer is a chemical in which the molecules can be made to join together to produce long molecular chains or networks. The substance almost always changes state during this reaction. The vinyl acetate is then emulsion polymerized (see "Impact" adhesives) to produce a synthetic latex, or emulsion, consisting of microscopic specks of the resinous polymer, polyvinyl acetate, dispersed in water. By further compounding in different ways, this basic polyvinyl acetate emulsion can be converted to other products such as emulsion paint, synthetic starch or wood glue. The wood glue is a white, free-flowing liquid with a reasonably pleasant smell. It may be applied by brush, hand roller, extruder or roller-coating machine. Application equipment may be easily cleaned before the adhesive sets, by using water to which a little detergent has been added.

Assembly should be made while the glue is wet. Open assembly time is 10 to 25 minutes, depending upon the porosity of the timber and the temperature. Only light cramp pressure is required, hard woods requiring more pressure than soft woods. Surplus adhesive can be removed, while wet, with a damp cloth.

Water resistance. Not suitable for damp or exterior conditions although special grades can be formulated giving improved performance.

Setting time. After about 15 minutes it reaches the stage when wood failure will occur if a joint is forced apart. Cramps may be removed after 30 minutes. At 20°C, maximum strength is reached in about 20 hours. By applying radio frequency electric currents to the joint, setting time may be reduced to between 30 and 60 seconds.

How used. Cold. There is no mixing, the glue is always ready for immediate use. It may be applied to one surface only, for example to a mortice, so that the adhesive spreads onto the tenon as it is inserted. When using the "single application" method of gluing care must be exercised to prevent glue starvation in the joint.

Staining property. None, a transparent bond is provided.

Note: The temperatures and times mentioned above apply to "EVO-STIK Resin W" one-way, wet adhesive and may not apply to other P.V.A. glues (check maker's instructions.)

CONTACT OR IMPACT ADHESIVES
(EVO-STIK "IMPACT" ADHESIVE)

These adhesives are produced by dissolving polychloroprene, a synthetic rubber (often referred to by its original trade name of "Neoprene"), in organic solvents such as toluene or methyl ethyl ketone together with tackifying resins and other chemicals. Polychloroprene is manufactured from acetylene which is dimerized (two molecules are joined together) under the influence of catalysts to form monovinylacetylene which is next reacted with hydrochloric acid to produce the monomer, chloroprene. The monomer is first dispersed in water and then polymerized to form a synthetic latex of polychloroprene. The synthetic latex is then coagulated, usually by the addition of acid, to precipitate the solid polychloroprene rubber. The polymerization process entails the joining together of hundreds of chloroprene molecules to form long molecular chains of polychloroprene. The polymerization reaction generates a large amount of heat, which is one of the main reasons for dispersing the monomer in water, in the form of microscopic droplets. The water acts as an efficient heat transfer medium.

With contact types of adhesive a "dry" bond can be made. The adhesive is spread with the aid of a serrated spreader onto both of the surfaces which are to be joined. Spreaders are supplied by the makers but are easily made from a piece of hardboard or tinplate. The coated surfaces are left for about 20 minutes, after which most of the solvent will have evaporated. The surface is then covered with a dry film of adhesive which does not feel particularly tacky when touched. When the two surfaces are brought together, instant bond is achieved. It is therefore essential that the surfaces are placed together in the correct position at the start of the operation. Pressure may be applied by a vice, cramps, hammer and wood block, weights or even the hands. The source of pressure may be removed immediately the bond has been made.

The separate surfaces should not be left to dry for more than 45 minutes or the "contact" will begin to fade. Should this occur, either wipe over the surface with a rag moistened with the recommended solvent or warm the coated surface for a few minutes in front of an electric fire. *Warning*. Great care must be exercised because of the fire risk. This is due to the highly inflammable nature of the solvents in the adhesive and of the solvents used for thinning, cleaning and reactivating. Because of this, it is essential that any heat reactivation, such as warming, is only carried out on thoroughly dry adhesive coatings.

Any liquid contact adhesive or solvent should be removed from the vicinity. Contact adhesives will join almost any material, with the exception of some plastics. It is used extensively in the building industry for fixing wall panels into position or melamines (such as Formica, etc.) to wood and metal surfaces. It is also widely used in the footwear industry and is one of the most popular "do-it-yourself" adhesives.

Water resistance. Fairly resistant to humid conditions, oil-proof and will withstand temperatures of up to 70°C normally, higher if specially formulated.

Setting time. Instant bond after initial surface drying time. The bond continues to improve after it has been made.

How used. Cold, applied to both surfaces.

Chapter 19

SPECIAL PURPOSE PLANES

IN addition to the bench planes described previously, there are several planes in common use which have been designed for a specific purpose. Some are of new design, some have evolved over a period of many years, but all have been used to extend man's ability to work in wood, and adapt it to his needs.

REBATE OR RABBET PLANES

The wooden rebate plane (Fig. 235a) has a cutting iron which extends across the full width of the stock at the mouth, thus allowing the plane to operate against a shoulder. The skew pattern cutting iron lowers the cutting angle by making a slicing cut. This reduces any tendency to tear the wood fibres, especially when planing across the grain. It also helps to pull the plane into the work when used with the leading tip of the cutting edge on the inside of the rebate being formed. The plane has been designed to form rebates, step-shaped reductions, along the edges, ends or faces of timber. A temporary fence or straight-edge cramped to the face of the work will act as an efficient guide for the plane, otherwise the fingers held under the sole of the plane must act as a fence. When working across the grain, the wood fibres should first be severed by a knife or cutting gauge to prevent tearing.

The metal rebate plane has both sides ground flat and at right angles to the sole (Fig. 235b). This allows the plane to be used on its side.

THE SHOULDER PLANE (Fig. 235c)

The cutting iron is adjustable (for depth of cut only) by a knurled nut attached to a collar, the latter operating in a horizontal slot cut in the end of the cutting iron. Due to the rigid support given to the cutting edge by the low angle at which the blade is inclined, this plane requires no cap iron and will cut very sweetly on end grain. It is therefore invaluable for

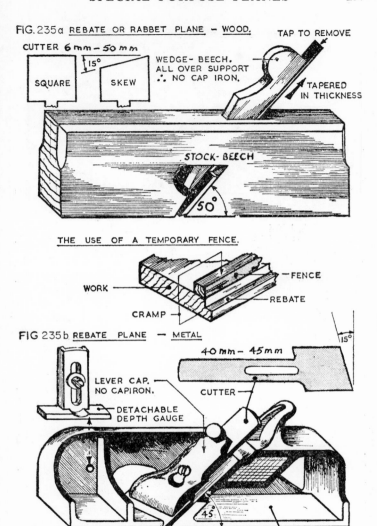

FIG. 235a REBATE OR RABBET PLANE — WOOD.

CUTTER 6mm – 50mm

SQUARE

15°

SKEW

WEDGE – BEECH. ALL OVER SUPPORT ∴ NO CAP IRON.

TAP TO REMOVE

TAPERED IN THICKNESS

STOCK – BEECH

50°

THE USE OF A TEMPORARY FENCE.

WORK

FENCE

REBATE

CRAMP

FIG 235b REBATE PLANE — METAL

15°

40mm – 45mm

LEVER CAP. NO CAPIRON.

CUTTER

DETACHABLE DEPTH GAUGE

45

MOUTH — STRAIGHT OR SKEW

STOCK – C.I.

truing wide shoulders on tenons. Other uses include cutting rebates, fielding panels if a badger plane is not available and for preliminary roughing out when forming mouldings.

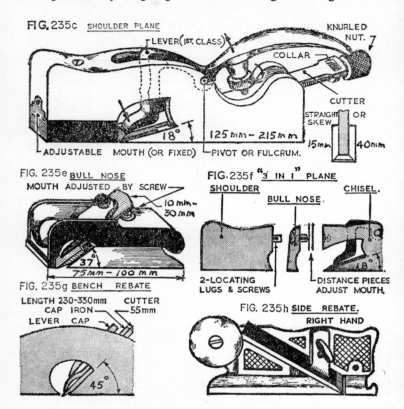

FIG. 235c SHOULDER PLANE

LEVER (1ST. CLASS)

KNURLED NUT.

COLLAR

CUTTER

STRAIGHT OR SKEW

15 mm — 40 mm

18°   125 mm — 215 mm

ADJUSTABLE MOUTH (OR FIXED)   PIVOT OR FULCRUM.

FIG. 235e BULL NOSE

MOUTH ADJUSTED BY SCREW

10 mm — 30 mm

37

75 mm — 100 mm

FIG. 235f "3 IN 1" PLANE

SHOULDER   BULL NOSE   CHISEL.

2-LOCATING LUGS & SCREWS   DISTANCE PIECES ADJUST MOUTH.

FIG. 235g BENCH REBATE

LENGTH 230-330mm   CUTTER 55mm

CAP IRON

LEVER CAP

45°

FIG. 235h SIDE REBATE.

RIGHT HAND

THE BULLNOSE PLANE (Fig. 235e)

This is, in effect, a small shoulder plane with a very short nose. This enables it to be used near the ends of stopped chamfers, for forming small rebates, shaping tapered legs with spade feet or working diminished stiles. Some patterns have the bevel of the cutting iron reversed or facing downwards when the blade is pitched at about 37° as shown.

THE CHISEL PLANE (Fig. 235f)

This is really no more than a bullnose plane with a detachable nose, thus allowing the cut to be taken right up to the shoulder of the work.

THE "THREE IN ONE" PLANE (Fig. 235f)

In this plane a shoulder, bullnose and chisel plane are combined in one tool by means of detachable nose pieces.

THE BENCH REBATE OR BADGER PLANE
(Fig. 235g)

The badger plane resembles a metal jack plane except for the mouth which extends the full width of the sole. Owing to the weakness of the stock at the mouth, the body is made from malleable cast iron which, although more expensive, is much less brittle. The badger plane is used for forming very wide rebates and for fielding panels.

THE SIDE REBATE PLANE (Fig. 235h)

In this plane the cutting iron protrudes from the side of the stock instead of from the sole, thus enabling the sides of rebates and grooves to be adjusted. Right hand, left hand and combined right and left hand patterns are available.

FILLISTER PLANES

A wooden fillister plane is shown in Fig. 235i. In effect it is a rebate plane to which has been added:—
1. An adjustable fence to control the width of the rebate.
2. An adjustable depth stop to control the depth of the rebate.
3. A spur to cut the fibres on cross-grain work.

The metal fillister plane (Fig. 235j) often includes two beds or frogs, one in the normal working position and one situated in the nose of the plane.

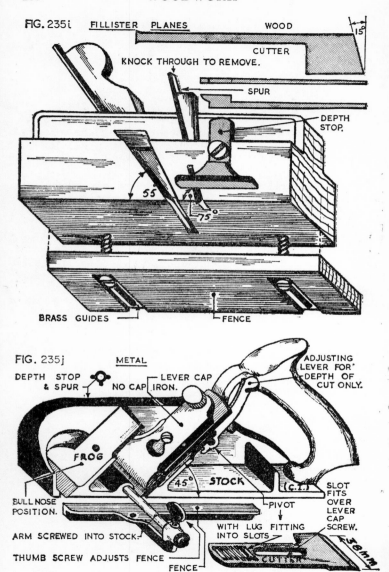

FIG. 235i   FILLISTER PLANES   WOOD

15

CUTTER

KNOCK THROUGH TO REMOVE.

SPUR

DEPTH STOP.

55

75°

BRASS GUIDES   FENCE

FIG. 235j   METAL

DEPTH STOP & SPUR   LEVER CAP   NO CAP IRON.   ADJUSTING LEVER FOR DEPTH OF CUT ONLY.

FROG

BULL NOSE POSITION.

45°   STOCK   (C.I.)   SLOT FITS OVER LEVER CAP SCREW.

ARM SCREWED INTO STOCK.

THUMB SCREW ADJUSTS FENCE   FENCE   PIVOT

WITH LUG FITTING INTO SLOTS

CUTTER   38mm

PLOUGH PLANES

The plough plane is used for working grooves to take panels or sliding glass doors. It can also be used as a rebate plane for general rebating and for roughing out, prior to forming mouldings. In both wooden and metal plough planes the sole is slightly thinner than the narrowest blade.

Wooden plough planes (Fig. 235k) look very cumbersome but in fact run very sweetly. The two arms which adjust the fence may be locked in position by wooden wedges (see end view) or may be threaded. In the latter case, wooden nuts on both sides of the stock replace the wedges. The nuts on the fence side of the plane are similar to those shown and are recessed into the stock. A long rectangular brass bar running parallel to, and below the main stock, acts as a depth stop. The bar is freely attached at its centre to a long screw. The screw passes right through the stock and terminates in a thumb screw situated on top of the stock.

In metal plough planes (Fig. 235 l) the cutting iron is adjusted for depth of cut by a screw and collar, the collar working in horizontal grooves cut across the underside of the blade as shown. A set of cutters is provided ranging from 4 mm to 15 mm. The width of the cutters is too narrow to permit the use of a cap iron. The cutters are held in place by a lever in the form of a small cranked arm, the fulcrum being provided by the point at which the arm butts up against a protrusion in the stock.

MOULDING PLANES

Moulding planes, together with various types of moulding, are shown in Fig. 235m. Mouldings of this type are rarely seen in modern cabinet work although the rule-joint edge for drop-leaf tables is sometimes used. English pattern moulding planes, about 240 mm long, are held at an angle to the work instead of in the vertical position. The sole, which is shaped to match the particular moulding to be cut, is sometimes faced with a shaped boxwood strip to reduce wear. This is particularly so with the more complicated shapes. Metal moulding planes are very similar in appearance to metal plough planes but provision is

FIG. 235k   WOOD.

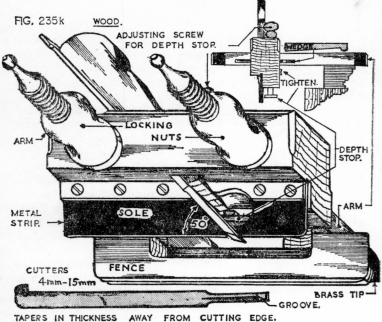

ADJUSTING SCREW FOR DEPTH STOP.

WILSON

TIGHTEN.

LOCKING NUTS

ARM

DEPTH STOP.

ARM

METAL STRIP.   SOLE   50°

FENCE

BRASS TIP

CUTTERS 4mm–15mm

GROOVE.

TAPERS IN THICKNESS AWAY FROM CUTTING EDGE.

FIG. 235l   PLOUGH PLANES   METAL

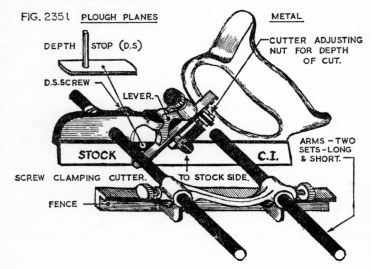

CUTTER ADJUSTING NUT FOR DEPTH OF CUT.

DEPTH STOP (D.S)

D.S.SCREW

LEVER.

STOCK   C.I.

ARMS – TWO SETS – LONG & SHORT.

SCREW CLAMPING CUTTER.   TO STOCK SIDE.

FENCE

FIG. 235m

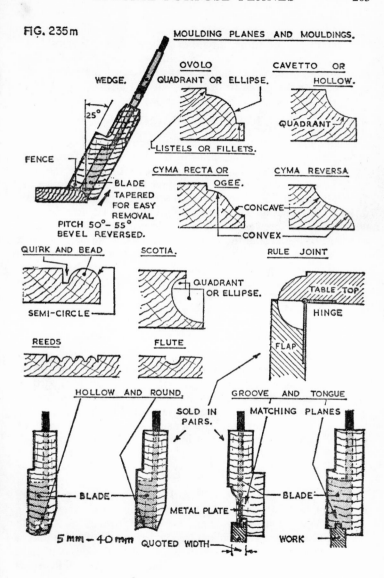

MOULDING PLANES AND MOULDINGS.

WEDGE.

25°

FENCE

BLADE
TAPERED
FOR EASY
REMOVAL
PITCH 50°- 55°
BEVEL REVERSED.

OVOLO
QUADRANT OR ELLIPSE.

LISTELS OR FILLETS.

CAVETTO OR
HOLLOW.

QUADRANT

CYMA RECTA OR
OGEE.

CONCAVE

CONVEX

CYMA REVERSA

QUIRK AND BEAD

SEMI-CIRCLE

SCOTIA.

QUADRANT
OR ELLIPSE.

RULE JOINT

TABLE TOP

HINGE

FLAP

REEDS

FLUTE

HOLLOW AND ROUND.

BLADE

5 mm - 40 mm QUOTED WIDTH

SOLD IN
PAIRS.

GROOVE AND TONGUE

MATCHING PLANES

METAL PLATE

BLADE

WORK

made for more attachments which allow it to be used as a rebate, fillister, plough, beading, matching and moulding plane.

When using moulding, rebate or plough planes, work should always begin at the far end of the job and the plane brought a little further back with each successive stroke. This reduces the tendency for the plane to drift and gives a cleaner, truer cut.

ROUTER PLANES

Router planes are used for levelling the bottoms of recesses on through and stopped housings. The wooden form (Fig. 235n) is often called the "old woman's tooth". Note the high angle of pitch of the blade. The higher the pitch, the more the action becomes one of scraping rather than cutting. Some patterns of metal router plane (Fig. 235o) have an adjustable fence which may be screwed to the underside of the sole. The fence can then be used for gauging the distance from the edge of work or as a guide in following a curved edge. The cranked cutters consist of two with normal chisel edge and one pointed for working in awkward corners. By virtue of their shape, the pitch is very low.

COMPASS PLANES (Fig. 235p)

Compass planes are used for circular work of large radius such as long table rail curves, and bowed drawer fronts. Pressure is brought to bear about the centre of the sole by a square-threaded screw which forces the sole into the desired curve, either convex or concave. The frog is riveted to the thin sole on both sides of the mouth. The tension on the sole should be released when the plane is not in use.

BLOCK PLANES (Fig. 235q)

These planes are for small work, such as forming through chamfers, and can be readily used with one hand. The cutting iron is 35 mm to 40 mm wide and is pitched from 20° to 25° with a special low angle pattern at 12°. The low angle of pitch makes for sweet cutting on end-grain work and provides sufficient support to the cutting edge for planing the edges of Formica

FIG. 235n   ROUTER PLANE.   WOOD

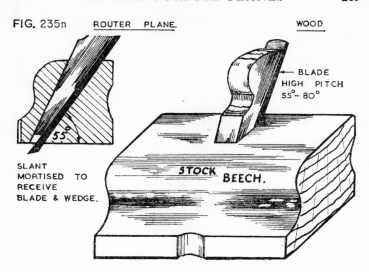

SLANT MORTISED TO RECEIVE BLADE & WEDGE.

55°

BLADE HIGH PITCH 55°- 80°

STOCK BEECH.

FIG. 235o   ROUTER PLANE   METAL

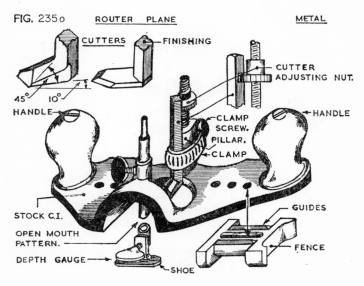

CUTTERS — FINISHING

45°   10°

HANDLE

CUTTER ADJUSTING NUT.

HANDLE

CLAMP SCREW.
PILLAR.
CLAMP

STOCK C.I.

OPEN MOUTH PATTERN.

DEPTH GAUGE —   SHOE

GUIDES

FENCE

and similar laminated plastics. Block planes with adjustable mouths are also available.

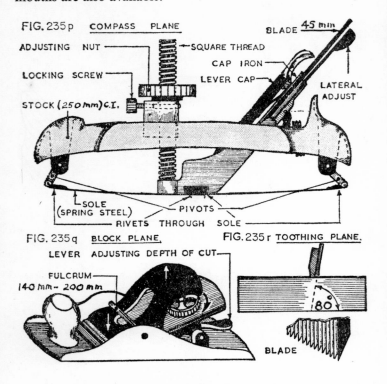

FIG. 235p   COMPASS   PLANE

BLADE 45 mm

ADJUSTING   NUT

SQUARE THREAD

CAP IRON

LOCKING   SCREW

LEVER CAP

LATERAL ADJUST

STOCK (250 mm) C.I.

SOLE (SPRING STEEL)

PIVOTS

RIVETS   THROUGH   SOLE

FIG. 235q   BLOCK PLANE.

FIG. 235 r   TOOTHING PLANE.

LEVER   ADJUSTING   DEPTH OF CUT

FULCRUM

140 mm - 200 mm

80

BLADE

TOOTHING PLANES (Fig. 235r)

Toothing planes are used to scratch and roughen the surfaces of groundwork prior to laying veneers, thus providing a "key" for the glue to hold the two surfaces together. They are also useful for roughing the tops of workbenches to provide a non-skid surface for planing. The stock, coffin shaped, and the wedge are similar in size and shape to those of the wooden smoothing plane (Fig. 153). The blade is grooved along the length of its back with between 80 and 120 grooves to 100 mm, providing the cutting edge with a series of fine teeth. The blade is sharpened in a similar manner to the cutting iron of a bench plane but it is not reversed on the stone to loosen the burr as this would damage the teeth. If anything, the slight "hook" gives added advantage to the scraping action. Toothing blades are also available for use with metal scraper planes (Fig. 164).

Chapter 20

MECHANICAL PRINCIPLES

SI units of measurement are basically a metric system. Reference to the preface will show the prefices which provide multiples and submultiples of units of the system. Although the decimetre and centimetre are not recommended for general use, they are still permitted for convenience in certain circumstances (see Preface).

For the following work in mechanics, gravitational units of force have been used in many cases to assist in an easier understanding of the subject matter. This is based on the CGS system—centimetre, gramme, second—while the SI system is based on the metre, kilogramme and second.

Mass. The mass of a body is the quantity of matter that it contains.

Weight. The weight of a body is the force that it exerts on anything freely supporting it due to the action of the force of gravity which attracts the body to the earth.

Force. Force is that which changes, or tends to change, a body's state of rest or of uniform motion in a straight line.

Gravitational units of force. It is more usual to use the word "force" rather than "weight". Thus the weight of a body of mass 4 kg would be 4 kilogrammes force and written 4 kgf instead of 4 kg wt (weight).

Absolute unit of force. The above gravitational units, useful for elementary work are, however, unsuitable for more accurate scientific work since the weight of a body depends upon its position with regard to the centre of the earth. At the equator a body will be further from the centre of the earth than it will be at the poles and therefore the gravitational pull will be less at the equator. There is also a centripetal force, except at the poles, necessary to keep a body moving in pace with the rotation of the earth about its axis. The effect of both of the above on the gravitational force is very small. Both are taken into account in the *absolute unit of force* derived from Newton's second law of motion which states that:—

The rate of change of momentum of a body is proportional to the applied force and takes place in the direction in which the force acts.

Example: Let a force of F units act upon a body of mass m kg for a time of t seconds and cause its velocity to change uniformly from u m/s to v m/s.

Rate of change of momentum $= \dfrac{mv - mu}{t}$ kg m/s²

But by Newton's second law,

$$F \propto \frac{mv - mu}{t}$$

$$\propto \frac{m(v - u)}{t}$$

but $\quad \dfrac{(v - u)}{t} = \dfrac{\text{change in velocity}}{\text{time}} = \dfrac{\text{acceleration } (a)}{(g \text{ for gravity})}$

$$= a \text{ m/s}^2$$

therefore $\quad F \propto ma$

or $\qquad\qquad F = \text{constant} \times ma.$

If $m = 1$ kg, $a = 1$ m/s² and the constant $= 1$, then F will equal 1 unit of force called the NEWTON (N) and therefore:

SI unit of force = Newton (N) and is that force which imparts an acceleration of 1 m/s² when it acts on a mass of 1 kg.

$$1 \text{ N} = 1 \text{ kg} \times 1 \text{ m/s}^2$$

Note:—An alternative method of writing 1 m/s² is 1 ms⁻².

CGS unit of force = Dyne (dyn) and is that force which imparts an acceleration of 1 cm/s² when it acts on a mass of 1 g.

$$1 \text{ dyn} = 1 \text{ g} \times 1 \text{ cm/s}^2$$

Both units are similarly defined but care must be taken not to intermingle units.

$$1 \text{ N} = 1 \text{ kg m/s}^2 \ (1 \text{ kg} \times 1 \text{ m/s}^2)$$
$$= 1000 \text{ g} \times 100 \text{ cm/s}^2$$
$$= 100\ 000 \text{ g cm/s}^2$$

Therefore $\quad 1 \text{ N} = 10^5 \text{ dyn.}$

Weight of a body expressed in newtons. For a body freely falling under gravity, then:—

$$F = mg \text{ newtons} \quad \text{(where } g = 9\cdot81 \text{ m/s}^2, \text{ the average value of } g.)$$

For accurate work, the actual value of g at the particular place of working must be taken.

If the body is at rest on the surface of the earth, this same force will apply and is known as weight.

Therefore in *SI units*   1 kgf = 9·81 N (approx.)

CGS units 1 gf = 981 dyn.

THE INCLINED PLANE (Fig. 236a)

If a load (L) is hauled up the sloping surface from A to C then the work done, apart from frictional losses is:—

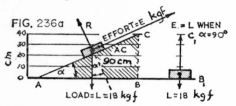

FIG. 236a

$L \times$ The vertical height that the load is raised,

i.e. $L \times$ BC = 18 kgf × 40 cm = 720 kg cm.

If E kgf is the effort required to pull the load from A to C then the work done = E.AC kg cm. (AC = 90 cm.)

Since energy cannot be lost, that is, the work done on a machine is equal to the work done by it (plus energy dissipated in friction, etc.), then the two above amounts of work must be the same, i.e.

$$L.\text{BC} = E.\text{AC} \text{ (neglecting friction)}$$

$$E = \frac{L.\text{BC}}{\text{AC}} \text{ or } L.\sin \alpha = 8 \text{ kgf.}$$

Velocity Ratio (V.R.) is the number of units through which the effort has to move in order to raise the load through one of the same units, i.e.

$$\frac{\text{Distance through which the effort } (E) \text{ moves}}{\text{Distance through which the load } (L) \text{ moves}} = \frac{90}{40} = 2\tfrac{1}{4}.$$

Mechanical Advantage (M.A.) is the number of times the load is greater than the effort, i.e.

$$\frac{\text{Load}}{\text{Effort}} = \frac{18}{8} = 2\tfrac{1}{4}.$$

Efficiency is equal to $\dfrac{\text{Work done by the machine}}{\text{Work done on the machine}} \times 100\%$

$$= \frac{\text{Load} \times \text{Distance load moves}}{\text{Effort} \times \text{Distance effort moves}} \times 100\%$$

$$= \frac{\text{M.A.}}{\text{V.R.}} \times 100\%.$$

Note that in a perfect machine V.R. would always be equal to M.A. but due to frictional losses, etc., M.A. is always less than V.R.

FRICTION (Fig. 236b)

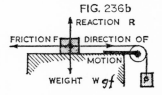

FIG. 236b

If a block of wood weight *W* gf is placed on a level table there will be an equal and opposite force exerted by the table upon the block. This force is known as the *reaction* (*R*). If the surfaces of both objects were perfectly smooth there would be nothing to prevent the block from sliding over the table. If a light push is given to the block a resistance will be felt which prevents it from moving. This resistance, known as friction, is always exactly equal and opposite to the force exerted on the body and ceases to exist as soon as the applied force is removed. Without friction walking would be impossible; a locomotive would not be able to pull its coaches; handles would not remain fixed to their chisel blades nor would nails hold in wood. As the applied force increases, so will the frictional force equally increase until a point is reached when the body or block is about to move. The resistance to motion at this instant is known as the *limiting friction*, that is, the maximum frictional force between the two bodies. If various weights are added to the block, and the frictional force (P) obtained that just causes the block to slide over the table, in each case it will be found that the magnitude of P is such that it always bears a constant ratio to the normal reaction R (the reaction at right angles to the sliding surface). The above constant ratio is called the *coefficient of friction* and is usually denoted by the Greek letter μ.

Thus if F is the friction and R the normal reaction,

then $$\mu = \frac{F}{R} \quad \text{or} \quad F = \mu R.$$

Should the applied force be greater than μR, then the block will begin to move.

Angle of friction (Fig. 236c). If the wood block is now placed on a smooth board and the board is raised until the block, with the help of a slight tap, just begins to slide down the board, then the angle θ is known as the angle of friction and its tangent may be obtained from the ratio h/l, or ($\tan \theta = h/l$).

FIG. 236c

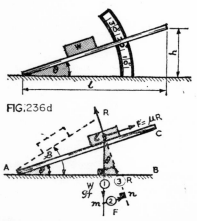

FIG. 236d

Let the block be on the point of sliding down the inclined plane AC (Fig. 236d). Three forces will be acting upon the block:—

1. The weight W, acting vertically downwards.

2. The limiting frictional force $F = \mu R$ (Fig. 236d), acting up the plane parallel to its surface and opposing the downward motion of the block.

3. The normal reaction R between the block and plane, acting at right angles to the plane in an upward direction.

The direction of all three forces and the magnitude of one, the weight W, are known, leaving only two unknown magnitudes. Thus the triangle of forces lmn can be constructed and thus the magnitude of forces F and R obtained.

Now $\angle BAC = \angle mln = \theta$ (similar triangles).
Therefore (1) $R = W \cos \theta$ and (2) $F = W \sin \theta$.
Dividing (2) by (1),

then
$$\frac{F}{R} = \tan \theta,$$

but
$$F = \mu R \quad \text{(Fig. 236d)}.$$

Therefore μ(Coefficient of friction) $= \tan \theta$.

Providing the sliding surfaces of two bodies are perfectly dry then the coefficient of friction μ depends entirely upon their composition (wood, metal, etc.), not on the extent of the area of the surfaces in contact nor on velocity. The coefficient of friction for wood on wood differs not only between species but also for wood of the same kind, owing to differences in grain, structure, degree of seasoning and whether polished. The coefficient may vary approximately between 0·2 and 0·5 with θ between 12° and 26°. Friction of metal on wood is less than for wood on wood, and metal on metal still lower, with figures for μ approximately between 0·15 and 0·3 and θ between 8° and 15°.

If a load is being pulled up an inclined plane it will be seen from the angle of friction that it is better if the inclination of the plane β is less than θ, thus allowing a rest to be taken without the load slipping.

Problem: To find the force P, acting at right angles to the normal reaction R, required to pull the weight W of 15 kgf, up the inclined plane AC (Fig. 236e(a)).

If β (20°) = the inclination of the plane AC to the horizontal and θ (10°) = the angle of friction, then the resultant reaction

Q will act in the direction shown, that is, opposing the movement of the block at an angle of $\beta + \theta$ to the vertical weight W.

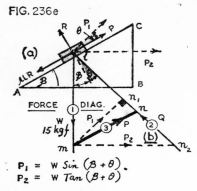

FIG. 236e

$$P_1 = W \sin (\beta + \theta).$$
$$P_2 = W \tan (\beta + \theta)$$

Construct the triangle of forces *lmn* (Fig. 236e(b)) to a scale of say 25 mm = 5 kgf. The measurement of *mn* to scale (approx. 11 kgf) will give the magnitude of the force required to pull the weight up the slope AC.

Note 1. The minimum force P_1, required to pull the block up the slope will be mn_1 in the direction at right angles to the resultant reaction Q. In other words:—

$$P_1 = W \sin (\beta + \theta)$$

Note 2. mn_2 (P_2) will represent, in magnitude and direction, the horizontal force required to pull the block up the slope AC, that is:—

$$P_2 = W \tan (\beta + \theta)$$

THE WEDGE

The wedge, which is virtually two inclined planes placed back to back, may be used to lift a load or to force two surfaces apart, either to hold them apart, or, in the case of the axe and a log of wood, to split the surfaces down the grain. Fig. 236f(a) shows the section of a steel wedge being driven into a log. Considering the right hand side of the figure, P is the force applied by a hammer in a vertical direction at the mid-point of AB, and

R is the normal reaction of the wood at the points of contact D and E, between wedge and wood. The wedge is moving down through the fibres of the log, therefore friction μR is acting upwards along CB. The resultant reaction Q, assuming the wedge to be at the point of being driven in, will act in the

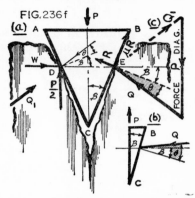

FIG. 236f

direction shown, opposing the downward motion. This action will be repeated for the other half of the wedge. If $\beta(\frac{1}{2}\angle ACB)$ is greater than θ, then a downward force will be necessary to prevent the wedge from being forced upwards.

If $W =$ the resistance of the wood fibres to separation and corresponds to the load, and $P/2$ represents the resistance to penetration of the wedge, including resistance due to friction when points D and E are about to move up the sloping surfaces CA and CB respectively. See the left hand side of Fig. 236f(a) and note the similarity to force P_2 in Fig. 236e.

If the wedge is now withdrawn, the resultant reaction Q (Fig. 236f(b)) will act on the opposite side of the normal reactance R as it must oppose the direction of movement. If $\beta(\frac{1}{2}\angle ACB)$ is less than the angle of friction, the resultant reaction will be downwards, thus tending to lock the wedge in place. Thus, to obtain maximum splitting power or holding power, the wedge should be as thin as is consistent with its required strength. In practice, a wedge should be about 12° so that β, at say 6°, is less than the angle of friction.

The splitting action of the wedge is seen in the axe, the adze with its blade at right angles to the haft, chisel and plane bevels and the cutters of centre bits. The holding power of the wedge is seen in the securing of chisel and screwdriver tangs, the wedge of the wooden jack plane and the wedges used to secure hammer heads to shafts.

THE SCREW THREAD

The screw thread is virtually an inclined plane wrapped around a cylinder (Fig. 215). Fig. 236g(a) shows the operative part of a screw jack. If E is the turning effort applied at the far

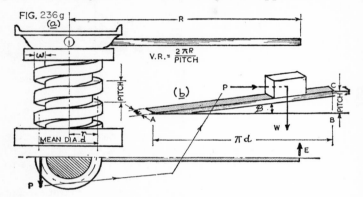

FIG. 236g (a)

V.R. = $\frac{2\pi R}{\text{PITCH}}$

end of the bar and P the force acting at the mean radius of the thread, then, taking moments about the longitudinal axis of the thread, $E.R = P.r$ or $E = P.r/R$. Fig. 236g(b) shows one complete turn of the thread, opened out to form the narrow inclined plane of width w. From Fig. 236e it will be seen that the force P_2 required to push the weight W up the inclined plane AC is equal to $W \tan(\beta + \theta)$ where θ is the angle of friction. If β is greater than θ, the load will lower itself.

MOMENTS

The moment, or turning effect, of a force about a given point is obtained by the product of that force and the perpendicular distance from the line of action of the force to the given point. Suppose the lamina in Fig. 236h to be pivoted about a fixed point O, *the fulcrum*, and two forces P and Q, acting in opposite directions, be applied at points A and B in the directions shown. The moment of force P about O, will be equal to $P.d = 15 \times 4 = 60$ gf cm acting *clockwise* (—). Similarly the

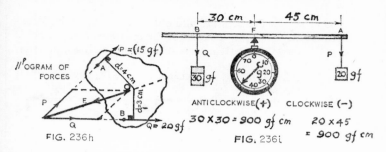

FIG. 236h

FIG. 236i

moment of Q about O will be equal to $20 \times 3 = 60$ gf cm acting in an *anti-clockwise* (+) direction. Since the two moments are equal but opposite, the lamina will not rotate in either direction but will remain at rest or in a state of equilibrium. The lamina cannot move in the general direction of force P and Q because of a resisting force at the fulcrum O. If the parallelogram of forces is constructed to any convenient scale as shown, it will be seen that this resisting force, known as *the equilibrant* (E), will pass through O and its magnitude may be determined by measuring its length from the scale.

Application of moments to the lever. The lever, which is a simple machine, is essentially a rigid bar which may be either straight or bent. It has a fixed point, *the fulcrum*, about which it may turn. If such a bar, neglecting weight, is balanced about its mid-point, *or fulcrum*, and weights are attached as shown in Fig. 236i, then a state of equilibrium or rest will exist. Therefore, a muscular action of 20 gf, called *the effort* (E), exerted at point A would permit a resistance or *load* (L) of 30 gf to be balanced or overcome at point B. The greater the distance of the effort from the fulcrum, compared with the load from the fulcrum, the greater is the *mechanical advantage*. In this case the mechanical advantage is:—

$$\text{Mechanical Advantage} = \frac{\text{Load}}{\text{Effort}} = \frac{30}{20} = 1\frac{1}{2}$$

K

LEVERS

Levers may be divided into three groups or classes depending on the relative positions of the load, effort and fulcrum (Fig. 236j).

Levers of the 1st Class. Load and effort are on opposite sides of the fulcrum. An example of this is the crowbar. It is usual to say that the crowbar exerts a certain force on the load, but the

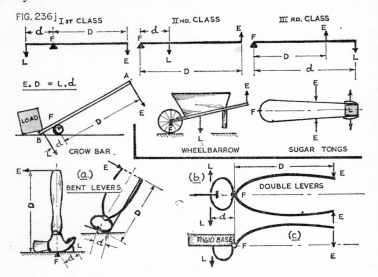

FIG. 236j

E.D = L.d

CROW BAR. WHEELBARROW SUGAR TONGS

(a.) BENT LEVERS. (b.) (c.) DOUBLE LEVERS — RIGID BASE

load also exerts an equal and opposite force on the crowbar, as shown. Two examples of bent levers in this class are seen in Fig. 236j(a). When the pincers first grip the nail, this is an example of a lever of the first class. When the pincers are bent over to lever out the nail, a second lever of the first class operates with its fulcrum moving towards the effort on the outside of the pincer head (at F in Fig. 236j(a)). The mechanical advantage thus decreases with the removal of the nail, often necessitating a second purchase on the nail.

Pincers and similar devices, which contain a second, identical straight or bent bar, are often referred to as double levers (Fig. 236j(b)). Note that although there are two forces E and two forces L, only one of each is operative as the second is an equal and opposite force preventing movement of the tool during use, since it is not fixed to any rigid base.

Other examples of levers of the first class are seen in the see-saw, pump handle, lever cap, bow saw, bench holdfast, scissors, pliers, wire cutters and forge tongs.

Levers of the 2nd Class (Fig. 236j). Load and effort are on the same side as the fulcrum with the load nearer to the fulcrum. Examples are seen in the wheelbarrow, nutcrackers and hinged doors.

Levers of the 3rd Class (Fig. 236j). Load and effort are on the same side of the fulcrum with the effort nearest to the fulcrum. There is always a mechanical disadvantage but this may be desirable for added convenience. Examples of this class of lever are seen in sugar tongs, coal tongs, treadle lathes, shovels, canoe paddles, safety valves of steam engines and the forearm when being bent (elbow $= F$, hand $= L$, contraction of muscles $= E$).

THE WHEEL AND AXLE

The wheel and axle (Fig. 236k) is a further example of the use of moments, whereby a heavy load is raised on a rope wound round a drum of small radius r, by an effort applied to the end of a handle tracing out a circular path of larger radius R. Taking moments about O, then $E.R = L.r$ or E (the effort required to raise the load L, neglecting friction) $= L.r/R$.

The principle of the wheel and axle applies to the brace and bit (Fig. 236k(a)), where the load L is the resistance offered to the spur as it traces out the circumference of the circle, radius r. A second mechanical principle is also involved, that of the wedge or inclined plane, whereby the downward force on the head causes the edge of the cutter, operating horizontally, to penetrate the fibres of the timber.

COUPLES (Fig. 236 l)

Two equal but opposite, parallel forces P, whose lines of action are not the same, form a couple. The perpendicular distance d, between the forces, is the arm of the couple. In other words the moment of the couple equals $P.d$. Assuming clockwise moments to be negative and anti-clockwise moments

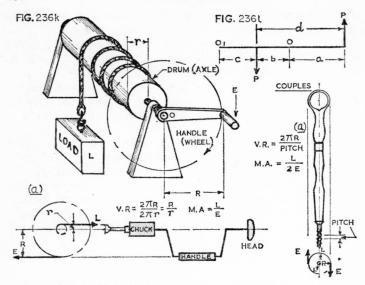

FIG. 236k

FIG. 236l

to be positive and taking moments about O, then the moment of the couple equals:—

$$+P.a + P.b \text{ (Anti-clockwise)} = P(a + b) = P.d$$

Taking moments about O_1, the moment of the couple equals:—

$$+P(d + c)\text{(Anti-clockwise)} - P.c\text{(Clockwise)}$$
$$= P(d + c - c) = P.d$$

Therefore the algebraic sum of the moments of the two forces, taken about any point in their plane is constant and is equal to the product of one of the forces and the arm of the couple. Examples of couples are seen in the capstan, bradawl, stock and die, twist gimlet and screwdriver (Fig. 236 l(a)). In this example the load L is the resistance to the advance of the screw thread in the hole.

CONVERSION OF POTENTIAL ENERGY TO KINETIC ENERGY

Work = force × distance moved in the direction of the force.

The SI unit of work is called the JOULE (J) and is the work done when 1 newton (N) moves through 1 metre (m) in the direction of the force.

If a weight (m) of 10 kg is raised to a height (h) of 2 m, then a force of 10×9.8 N has to be exerted through a distance of 2 m.

$$\begin{aligned} \text{Therefore, work done} &= mgh \\ &= 10 \times 9.8 \times 2 \text{ J} \\ &= 196 \text{ J.} \end{aligned}$$

If this weight was attached to a small machine by a length of string and allowed to return to its original position, it would do 196 J of work. An example of this is the weight which drives the mechanism of a grandfather clock. The capacity for doing work is known as *energy* and the energy possessed by a body due to its position is called *potential energy*. This means that when the above body has been raised to a height of $2\,m$ it will possess potential energy equal to 196 J. If the weight is allowed to fall freely under gravity it will accelerate at the uniform rate of 9.8 m/s², or "*g*".

Note 1. If the velocity (speed) attained at the end of the fall of height h is v m/s, then the average velocity will be $v/2$ m/s.

Note 2. For a body starting at rest (initial velocity $u = 0$ m/s) and accelerating under gravity at the rate of g m/s², then the velocity will increase by g m/s for each second that it is falling. Thus, after t seconds the velocity will have increased to gt m/s.

Therefore final velocity (v) = initial velocity (u) + increase in velocity after t seconds (gt).

i.e. $v = u + gt$

but $u = 0,$

therefore, $v = gt$ or $t = \dfrac{v}{g}.$

Note 3. Now distance (h) = velocity $\times$ time ($v.t$)

By combining 1 and 2 above we get:—

$$h = \frac{v}{2} \times \frac{v}{g} = \frac{v^2}{2g} \quad \text{or} \quad v^2 = 2gh.$$

When the weight reaches the ground, the stored up potential energy will have been converted to *kinetic energy* (energy possessed by matter in motion). The amount of kinetic energy gained, neglecting the small amount of work done in overcoming the friction between the weight and the air, will be equal to the potential energy lost, in other words:—

$$mg \times h \quad \text{or} \quad mg \cdot \frac{v^2}{2g} = \tfrac{1}{2}mv^2 \text{ J}$$

Consider the case of a mallet used in conjunction with a chisel to chop a mortice (Fig. 226). Let the weight of the mallet (m) be 1·5 kg and be raised to a height (h) of 60 cm (assume $g = 10$ m/s².

$$\begin{aligned}
\text{Potential energy} &= mgh \text{ Joules} \\
&= 1\text{·}5 \times 10 \times 0\text{·}6 \\
&= 9 \text{ J.}
\end{aligned}$$

$$\text{Kinetic energy} = \tfrac{1}{2} mv^2 \text{ joules}$$

from note 3,
$$\begin{aligned}
v^2 &= 2\,gh \\
&= 2 \times 10 \times 0\text{·}6 = 12
\end{aligned}$$

therefore   kinetic energy $= \tfrac{1}{2} \times 1\text{·}5 \times 12 = 9$ J.

It is this kinetic energy that will make the mallet continue its downward motion, overcoming the resistance offered by the wood to the chisel and driving the chisel blade into the wood until all energy has been exhausted. Since action and reaction are always equal and opposite, the resistance (R kg) offered to the chisel, assuming it to have been driven 1 cm (or 10^{-2} m) into the wood, may be found from:—

$$R\,g \times h = 9 \text{ J}$$

i.e.
$$R \times 10 \times 10^{-2} = 9 \text{ J}$$

therefore
$$R = 9 \times 10 = 90 \text{ kgf.}$$

PART IV

THE HISTORY OF PERIOD FURNITURE
(1100-1971)

Chapter 21

THE AGE OF THE CARPENTER
Medieval—Tudor—Jacobean

THE MEDIEVAL PERIOD (1100–1500)

IT was not until the period of the Norman Conquest that furniture, as we think of it today, came into use in Great Britain. It was very scarce even in the castles of the period and the majority of the British people, living as serfs under Norman rule, possessed little, if any, furniture at all. Under the feudal system the serfs lived either close to the outside of the castle walls or within the confines of the castle itself. This was not done for love of the Normans, but as a protective measure against the constant local warfare which existed. Such social conditions are not conducive to fostering the arts and much of the furniture of the day was strictly functional.

Craftsmen in metal, wood or stone were at the mercy of their local overlord and worked for him in exchange for food, clothing and lodgings. The time taken to complete a piece of work was considered of secondary importance to good craftsmanship. It took the combination of Oliver Cromwell and gunpowder, nearly five hundred years later, to undo the work of many medieval craftsmen. The craftsman/serf was sometimes made a freeman by his master, in which case he was allowed to leave the vicinity of the castle and offer his labour for hire. Because of the unsettled life of the period, however, he was often content to remain where he was.

The unsettled social conditions of the day, and the insecurity of life, made living conditions inside the castle rather primitive. When the prime need in one's surroundings is defence, there is little time for considering the beauty of furniture and furnishings. Far better that the table in the great hall should be capable of bearing the weight of a bowman as he fired through the slender lancet windows, than it should be an article of beauty. Window spaces in the castle were usually open, giving rise to draughty conditions, and the floor was of trodden earth strewn with rushes which were changed periodically. This floor covering was liberally sprinkled with discarded bones, from food thrown down by the inhabitants of the castle.

During this period the Church of Rome was the dominant influence on the moral life of the people. The Gothic Church offered some of the few examples of aesthetic beauty and it is not surprising that the decorative details seen in Gothic architecture should be seen in the furniture of the day. Often this decoration, in the church, was carried out in stone. The craftsman in wood cheerfully translated the same decorative motif into wood, regardless of the fitness of the decoration for the material. We must remember, however, that this was "The Age of the Carpenter" when there were no specialist furniture makers. Thus it was only natural that the craftsman should use the ideas he had seen while working in a church, on the furniture he made for the castle.

The furniture in the castle, often very heavy, was made almost entirely from oak, as were the doors and structural timbers. This was, indeed, the birth of the "Age of Oak".

Tables were at first made from very thick, flat boards which rested on trestles. When not in use in the great hall, where life in the castle centred, these tables were often dismantled and placed at the side of the hall. A rather more permanent form of table, which developed from the trestle table, had solid ends with a stretcher across the bottom. This stretcher, tenoned through the table ends, was held by means of a wedge passing through a hole in the end of the tenon. This was known as a tusk tenon (Fig. 237a). As social conditions became more settled, the table gradually took on a more permanent form as a long refectory table with massive Gothic pedestals and a top in the region of 50 mm thick. This item of furniture could obviously not be moved about in times of emergency.

Chairs were extremely scarce; in the whole of the castle there would probably be only two, placed on a raised dais at the end of the hall. Only important members of the family sat on chairs. Guests and others in the castle sat on long benches. (It was from this scarcity that the dignified office of "Chairman" was named.) During the early part of the medieval period, the benches in the great hall were fixed along the walls and served a second use as platforms for the defence of the castle. Later they were made movable and used along both sides of the long refectory tables. The bench supports were

FIG. 237a MEDIEVAL   TABLE

FIG. 237b MEDIEVAL "x" CHAIR

often carved in simple Gothic forms, similar to the table in Fig. 237a.

The chair on the dais in the great hall often had a tall back with a canopy overhead. The purpose of this was to prevent

soot from the open fire in the centre of the hall from falling
on the people seated below. (The great hall had no chimney
and the smoke and soot settled on the massive roof timbers.)
This chair was similar in form to the box chair shown in
Fig. 245, had square arm rests and most probably developed
from the chest construction. (The chest was no doubt used for
seating purposes until someone first thought of raising the
back of the chest to give a more comfortable posture.)

One style of chair is often depicted on tapestries of the
medieval period. This is the X chair, similar to the modern
camp stool but on a grander scale, with a tapestry seat and
back rest (Fig. 237b). This chair folded up, so that when the
lord of the castle was travelling he took his chair with him.
This would increase his prestige in the eyes of those who were
not important enough, or could not afford, to own a chair of
their own.

Chests. The earliest known examples of wooden chests in
Great Britain consisted of a hollowed-out log (Fig. 238). As
techniques improved, boards were sawn in a saw-pit and rough-
hewn with the axe or adze. These boards were nailed or pegged
at the corners (Fig. 238) and the lids held by iron strap hinges.
Few of these chests have survived to the present day, for three
reasons. Firstly, they stood on damp floors, which would both
cause movement of the timber and initiate decay. Secondly, the
boards were rigidly fixed together with no movement allowance
and they would split. Thirdly, the combination of oak, an
acidic timber, and iron nails, would cause rotting at the corners.

The first development from the planked chest, was to tenon
the back and front into vertical stiles which were gradually
lengthened to become legs; thus raising the chest from the
damp floor. The back and front were pegged into solid ends
which still suffered from splits, since there was no movement
allowance (Fig. 238). By the middle of the 15th century, the
idea of the framed-up construction had developed, although at
first only the back and front were framed with loose panels.
This was a major development in furniture construction and,
by the middle of the 16th century, the fully framed-up chest
with lengthened stiles for legs was a common piece of furniture
(Fig. 248).

The panels of the chest in the 15th century were often carved

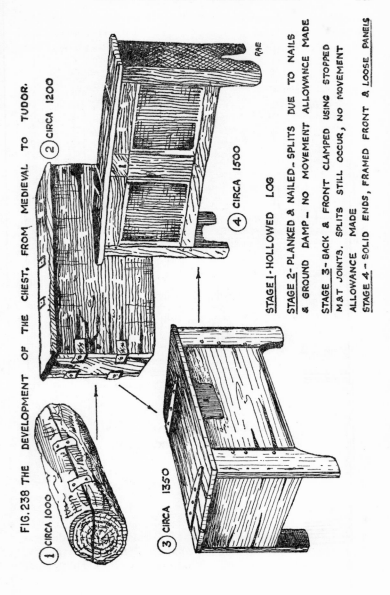

FIG. 238 THE DEVELOPMENT OF THE CHEST, FROM MEDIEVAL TO TUDOR.

① CIRCA 1000

② CIRCA 1200

③ CIRCA 1350

④ CIRCA 1500

STAGE 1 - HOLLOWED LOG

STAGE 2 - PLANKED & NAILED - SPLITS DUE TO NAILS & GROUND DAMP - NO MOVEMENT ALLOWANCE MADE

STAGE 3 - BACK & FRONT CLAMPED USING STOPPED M & T JOINTS. SPLITS STILL OCCUR, NO MOVEMENT ALLOWANCE MADE

STAGE 4 - SOLID ENDS, FRAMED FRONT & LOOSE PANELS

RAE

to depict the folds of drapery or linen. This was known as the linen-fold panel (Fig. 249) and is believed to have originated from either the folds of wall tapestry or the folds of the linen

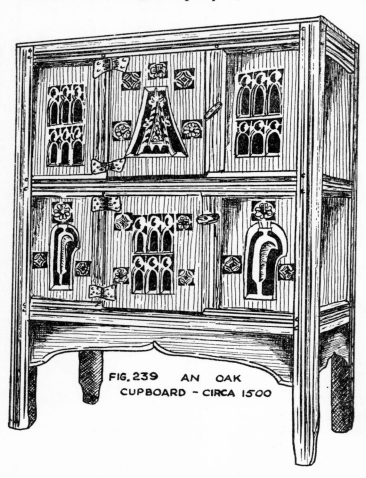

FIG. 239   AN   OAK
CUPBOARD – CIRCA 1500

which the chest often contained. The influence of Gothic decoration is seen in the use of Romayne panels (Fig. 240) and tracery, similar to that seen in church windows (Fig. 239). The greater use of decoration reflects the more settled social life of the late medieval period. A decorative motif was replacing sheer utility and thus giving scope to the ideas of the individual craftsman.

The chest was used to hold clothing and valuables and was often made sufficiently small to be easily transportable. One class of chest was, in fact, known as a "mule chest". Inside the top of the chest there would sometimes be a narrow tray which held valuables or sweet-scented herbs. This tray was known as a "till" and gave the name to the money drawers used below

FIG. 240   ROMAYNE   PANEL

the counters in shops. The very name counter was derived from the long flat top of the chest, which was used as the board across which the merchants bargained and counted. Sometimes the chest was strengthened and decorated with iron strapwork and locks, making an early form of strong box. Old churches in this country sometimes still use these as alms chests.

Another piece of medieval furniture which developed from the chest was the hutch or food cupboard (Fig. 239). This article of furniture was to be found in the "solar", the only bedroom in the castle and fortified manor house, and often used as a withdrawing room by the lady of the manor. The hutch would contain snacks of food for the lord and his lady, thus explaining the fretted panels and doors which would provide ventilation for the contents. (Note the Gothic style of the fretting on Fig. 239.) The hutch, in construction, amounts to no more than a chest on top of a chest, with a door at the front. The stiles are lengthened to provide legs. With the decline of the fortified manor house, the hutch gradually disappeared as an article of furniture. In the manor house of the 15th and 16th centuries, where a large number of smaller rooms replaced the great hall, the court cupboard and buffet were used in place of the hutch.

THE TUDOR PERIOD (1500–1600)

The Tudor Period gave rise to more settled social and economic life than had been experienced in this country before. With a more settled social life the people were able to think of greater comfort in their homes, since defence was no longer of primary consideration. The uncomfortable fortified manor house, draughty and austere, had been gradually replaced over a period of three centuries by the manor house. In the manor house life no longer centred on the great hall. Bedrooms, living- and drawing-rooms gave far greater privacy to the inhabitants but also gave a very much increased demand for furniture. This increase was met by the carpenter, still not a specialist in furniture making and still working in oak, the most abundant timber in England in those days. This was, indeed, still "The Age of the Carpenter" and "The Age of Oak".

The carpenter, in his constructional processes, developed the framed-up constructions of the late medieval period and for his decorative detail turned to the Gothic church with its beautifully carved furniture. With the dissolution of the monasteries by Henry VIII much of this beautiful work was destroyed. Much, however, was saved by being given away and no doubt served as a pattern for reproduction by local craftsmen. The carpenter was also given further scope for experiment by the invention of the screw-cutting lathe in 1550. This enabled much more efficient turnery to be accomplished than was ever possible before. Like most new processes, however, it tended to be overdone with the result that, in our eyes, much of the turnery of the day looks ostentatious. The quality of the workmanship, however, cannot be questioned, especially when the poor quality of the metal in the tools and the tools themselves are borne in mind.

During the Tudor period there was a large increase in the wealth of both privileged persons and merchants. This increase in wealth led to a desire to display the wealth in some more tangible form than mere bags of money, so that the houses, clothing, furniture and furnishings took on a lavish appearance. The sons of the wealthy, travelling in Europe as part of their education, came under the influence of the Italian Renaissance to a far greater degree than if they had remained in England, where only some of the effects of the Renaissance had been felt. Not only were they influenced by the continental revival of Greek and Roman forms, decorative detail, use of colour and gilt, but they also brought back continental craftsmen to perform similar work in England. The work of these foreign craftsmen was no doubt examined, and in many cases copied, by the carpenters of this country. The foreign influence is seen in such decorative detail as acanthus carving, Gothic tracery, vine carving, inlay work and parquetry.

Doors with solid panels set in morticed and tenoned frames were in common use, the joints often being dowelled. Heavy strapwork hinges in wrought iron (Fig. 266) were used on the outsides of doors. This strapwork often took on intricate curved forms and was held in place by clenched iron nails. Some examples of clapboard doors were still to be seen (Fig. 241), but on the whole the framed-up and panelled door was far more common, especially inside the new manor houses. The framed-up door, often moulded and decorated, was made to blend into the oak-panelled rooms of the day. In early panelled rooms, often covered from floor to ceiling, the stiles and rails were very heavy indeed, sometimes made from timber with a 100 mm × 75 mm section. This was partly due to the limitations of the workmen and the tools they used, but to some extent they wished to capture the feeling of strength given by the stone they had long been used to. By Tudor times, the panels and frames had been reduced to more pleasing proportions, more in keeping with the smaller sized rooms of the day.

The increasing skill of the craftsmen may be seen by following the development of the frame and panel (Fig. 242). The moulding on stiles and rails was at first merely butted, but gradually the mitre used by the stone mason was incorporated

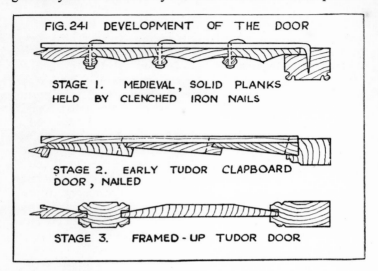

FIG. 241 DEVELOPMENT OF THE DOOR

STAGE 1. MEDIEVAL, SOLID PLANKS HELD BY CLENCHED IRON NAILS

STAGE 2. EARLY TUDOR CLAPBOARD DOOR, NAILED

STAGE 3. FRAMED-UP TUDOR DOOR

FIG. 242 DEVELOPMENT OF THE CARPENTERS MITRE

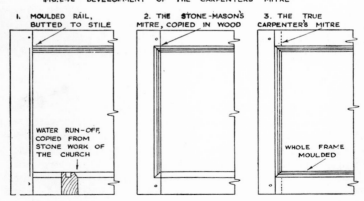

1. MOULDED RAIL, BUTTED TO STILE — WATER RUN-OFF, COPIED FROM STONE WORK OF THE CHURCH

2. THE STONE-MASON'S MITRE, COPIED IN WOOD

3. THE TRUE CARPENTER'S MITRE — WHOLE FRAME MOULDED

to give a better blend between stile and rail. The mason's mitre is an unsuitable construction in wood owing to the awkward tool operations involved. Note also how the carpenter, although

moulding the stiles and underside of the rails, left the top edge
of the rails with only a chamfer or bevel. This was again copied
from the stone mason, who was mainly interested in providing
a good water run-off from the bottom of the stone windows.
Gradually the true carpenter's mitre developed, in which the
mouldings were run right along the stiles and rails and the joint
shoulders cut to match. This, of course, gave a much more
pleasing appearance by unifying the whole frame.

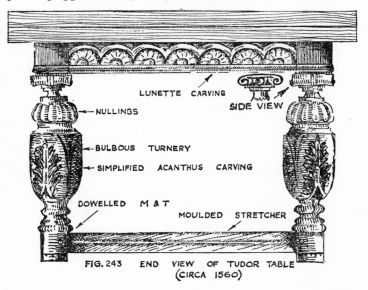

LUNETTE CARVING

SIDE VIEW

NULLINGS

BULBOUS TURNERY

SIMPLIFIED ACANTHUS CARVING

DOWELLED M & T

MOULDED STRETCHER

FIG. 243   END VIEW OF TUDOR TABLE
(CIRCA 1560)

Tables and chairs became much more common than hereto-
fore. The family, now taking meals away from the servants in
the dining-room, required a table which was small enough for
normal daily use but which could be made larger for use when
guests were invited. This led to the adoption of the draw-leaf
table which could be doubled in length when required (Fig. 243).
(The draw-leaf table probably came to this country by way of
Holland.)

The trestle type of construction was thus superseded by the
table often seen today, where the four table legs are placed in
four corners of a top frame and stretchers added below to give

greater rigidity. In the Tudor table, the stretchers were very low down on the leg, sometimes actually resting on the floor. A similar table construction, but where the stretchers were

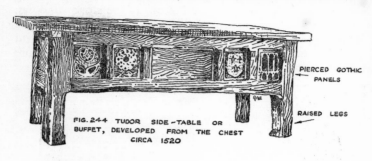

FIG. 244 TUDOR SIDE-TABLE OR BUFFET, DEVELOPED FROM THE CHEST CIRCA 1520

PIERCED GOTHIC PANELS

RAISED LEGS

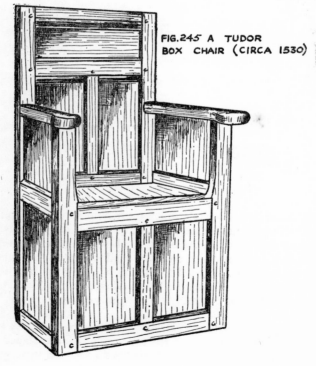

FIG. 245 A TUDOR BOX CHAIR (CIRCA 1530)

sometimes omitted, is seen in the side-table or buffet (Fig. 244). This construction may have developed from the medieval hutch and is the forerunner of the modern sideboard.

The legs, rails and stretchers of tables, court cupboards, buffets and stools were usually very heavily decorated with various forms of carving, much of Renaissance character. (See list at end of Tudor Period.)

Chairs became a common feature of the house by this time, thought obviously being given to greater comfort. The early form of box chair (Fig. 245) had developed from that seen in the Gothic church. Windows in houses were now far more common, since small pieces of glass could be made, thereby reducing draughts. This fact, coupled with smaller rooms and closer fitting doors, was probably the reason for the removal of the box chair panels, leaving four independent legs with connecting bottom rails or stretchers (Fig. 246). Gradually the stretchers were raised and no longer used as foot-rests (Fig. 247). In some cases, the front legs were "thrown" on a lathe, but this was not general in the early part of the period. As the stretchers were raised, so the bottom of the leg was shaped to form a foot.

Chair backs were straight, sometimes given a slight back rake, often solid and made no allowance for the curvature of the human spine. The back would sometimes be decorated with elaborate carving, or inlay work in the form of parquetry. (Geometric and formal patterns in veneers of holly, bog oak, cherry, etc.) Sometimes the chair back was extended in width at the top with carved brackets or "ear-pieces". In order to reduce the possibility of the chair tipping backwards, a small block was sometimes added to the bottom of the rear legs (Fig. 247).

Another form of chair which evolved during the period arose from the social conditions of the day. This was a light form of chair with a straight back for use in the withdrawing room, to which the ladies literally withdrew. The chairs were called, rather appropriately, "gossiping chairs". During the time of Queen Elizabeth I, largely owing to the queen's influence, there was a fashion for enormous spread skirts called farthingales. To allow the ladies to sit down, the chair arms had to be removed. This type of chair was known as a "farthingale chair".

Chests of the Tudor period were of framed-up construction
(Fig. 248) with various kinds of decorative panelling. One very

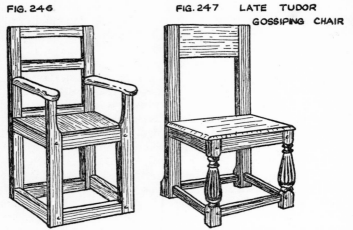

FIG. 246

FIG. 247   LATE TUDOR
GOSSIPING CHAIR

DEVELOPMENT OF THE CHAIR DURING THE
TUDOR PERIOD — FROM THE BOX CHAIR (FIG. 245)
TO THE GOSSIPING CHAIR.

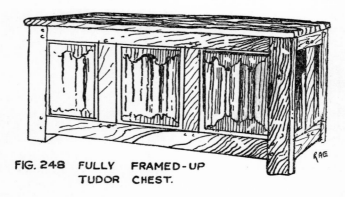

FIG. 248   FULLY   FRAMED-UP
TUDOR CHEST.

popular panel was the linen-fold panel described earlier (Fig.
249), but the carved portrait panel (Fig. 240) of the late medieval

period was still being made. Panels of inlay work in holly, boxwood, pear, bog oak, cherry and ebony appeared in this country, for the first time so far as is known from evidence available. The marriage of Mary to Philip of Spain was responsible for the introduction of inlays incorporating bone, ivory and mother of pearl. (The technique of inlaying was not a new one. An exquisitely inlaid box was recovered from the tomb of Tutankhamen who died 3,300 years ago.)

Under the Renaissance influence, artists and architects studied Greek and Roman methods of building and decoration and then introduced these forms into their own work. The semi-circular arch appeared in many buildings, and as lunette carving on rails of tables, chests and court cupboards. This style was extremely popular in Italy, and appeared in the work of the noted Italian architect Palladio (1518–1580).

During this period the chest of drawers developed further from the basic chest construction. In a chest it is difficult to get at those items which inevitably fall to the bottom of the chest. At some time in the past an enterprising craftsman must have sat down and pondered this problem in fitness for purpose. Eventually he arrived at the solution; make the bottom part of the chest removable. The "till" of the medieval chest may have given rise to the idea of a drawer but the drawer was put at the bottom of the chest, not in the top where the "till" was placed. These early drawers had thick sides which were grooved to run on side bearers. The sides, however, were nailed on to the back and front of the drawer. This would no doubt cause splitting and rust and by the end of the Tudor period one large dovetail was used to joint the drawer sides to the drawer front.

The increased usefulness of the chest with drawer caused it to become very popular and gradually the idea developed until the whole of the front of the chest became filled with drawers. This article of furniture took the logical name of "chest of drawers".

The hutch of the medieval period no longer served a useful purpose and gradually changed its form. It was replaced by the court cupboard, a heightened chest construction with doors at the front. The court cupboard was usually very heavily carved in various ways typical of the period.

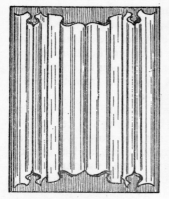

FIG. 249 LINENFOLD
        PANEL

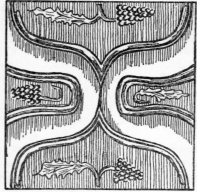

FIG. 250 PARCHEMIN PANEL
        WITH VINE MOTIF

FIG. 251   ACANTHUS   LEAF

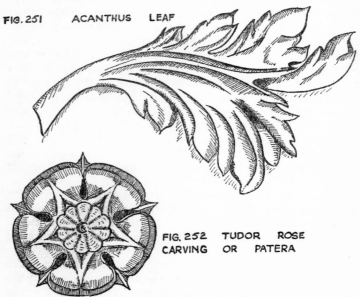

FIG. 252   TUDOR   ROSE
CARVING   OR   PATERA

Main features of Tudor furniture:—

1. The wide use of oak.
2. Massive, bulbous turnery, sometimes called "Melon Turnery" (Fig. 243).
3. Gothic tracery (Figs. 239 and 244).
4. Acanthus leaf decoration (Figs. 243 and 251).
5. Lunette carving on rails (Fig. 243).
6. Vine motif carving (Fig. 250).
7. Tudor rosette carving (Fig. 252).
8. Linen-fold panels (Fig. 249) and Parchemin panels (Fig. 250).
9. Nullings on turnery (Fig. 243).
10. Inlay work in the second half of the 16th century, in the form of parquetry.
11. Deep gouge cuts and flutings, elaborate carving.
12. All mouldings cut in the solid wood.
13. Sturdy, heavy furniture.
14. The work of the carpenter/craftsmen.

THE JACOBEAN PERIOD (1600–1688)

To understand the Jacobean period fully, it must be realized that historically there were three separate and distinct social and economic eras involved:—

(1) The first era was the reign of James I (1603–1625) and Charles I (1625–1649). During this time the full influence of the Renaissance was felt in this country, 200 years after its birth in Italy. The combination of "imported" Flemish craftsmen and late Renaissance ornament helped to create the ornate Jacobean style in which the "barley-sugar" turnery of legs, rails and stretchers are most distinctive.

Social life, however, seethed with unrest, owing to the unwise granting of monopolies and discontent in the ranks of the workers. This contributed, with other factors, to the outbreak of civil war and the establishment of the Commonwealth.

(2) The Commonwealth (1649–1660), under the leadership of Cromwell, re-established trade and largely suppressed the aristocracy. Under the rule of Cromwell, life became staid, severe and simple. This influence is seen in both the clothing of the day and the furniture.

(3) The Restoration of Charles II (1660–1685) ended the severity imposed by the Commonwealth and the restraint shown in life, dress, customs and furniture disappeared. Furniture in particular underwent great changes, as the ornate style of the early Jacobean period was revived.

The introduction of a new furniture timber, walnut, was partly due to shortage of oak which had been wastefully used for many years. The fact that walnut had been in use for many years in Holland, where Charles II had lived in exile, may have aided its introduction.

This new material was found to glue easily and because of

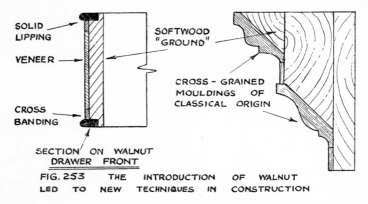

SOLID LIPPING

VENEER

CROSS BANDING

SOFTWOOD "GROUND"

CROSS - GRAINED MOULDINGS OF CLASSICAL ORIGIN

SECTION ON WALNUT DRAWER FRONT

FIG. 253   THE   INTRODUCTION   OF   WALNUT
LED   TO   NEW   TECHNIQUES   IN   CONSTRUCTION

its close, even grain could be carved more readily and cut into very thin sheets or veneers. These veneers could then be glued on to a cheaper and more plentiful groundwork timber (Fig. 253). This form of construction, relying on the beauty of the grain for decoration, was originally Venetian but was extensively practised in Holland prior to its introduction to this country. The close grain of walnut also allows it to be carved across the grain. This led to the use of built-up cross-grained mouldings (Fig. 253).

Panels were filled with geometric patterns of veneers and other materials to exploit this new technique. Later on, pictures of birds, leaves and flowers were formed in the same way, completely covering the doors of the late 17th-century cabinets. This technique was known as marquetry.

The introduction of tea, during the Restoration, had a marked effect on the furniture of the day. It was a very expensive drink, called "bohea" in those days, and was kept inside small locked boxes which were often ornately veneered. The key to the box was kept by the lady of the house who gave the bohea to the cook in measured quantities. The social custom of bohea parties led to an increase in the quantity of furniture, since more chairs were needed. Small tables for occasional use also appeared, with side flaps which could be lowered when not in use.

During the late Jacobean period, lacquered furniture first appeared in this country. This was again linked to the introduction of tea and the trade with eastern Asia. Lacquered furniture was constructed in China and it is quite possible that the first example of this style came into the country from the traders returning to England with tea and spices. Furniture is a bulky object to transport and since the demand could not be met by importing, the craftsmen of both England and Europe rose to meet the occasion. Although not of equal quality to the Chinese lacquering, many beautiful articles were made.

A further fillip to the craftsman in wood came through Charles II's interest in clock mechanisms. These clocks, with expensive mechanisms, needed protection from dust and damage. They were therefore enclosed in a box or cabinet, often very ornate with veneers and inlay. The "grandfather" clock was a very popular pattern.

It was during the late Jacobean period that specialization in furniture construction began, as distinct from the general work of the carpenter. This can be attributed to the various factors already mentioned; the introduction of walnut and lacquering, the increase in demand for furniture and the desire for higher quality. The ordinary carpenter could not hope to cope with this situation and the end of the Jacobean period marks the beginning of "The Age of the Cabinet Maker". The principal timber used was still oak, but walnut gradually came into increasing use as the ability of the cabinet maker improved.

Tables. With the increased number of smaller houses, the value of a smaller table, which would occupy little space when not in use, was realized. This led to the gate-leg table which first appeared in the reign of James I (Fig. 254). At first, only a single gate was made but this was later extended to form the double gate-leg table. The idea was copied for the smaller occasional tables used at tea parties. The tops were usually

FIG. 254   GATE — LEG   TABLE   (CIRCA 1640)

FIG. 255   JACOBEAN   DRAW - LEAF   TABLE

round or oval and had the drop leaf supported by a gate pivoted into the top rail of the table and the stretcher. Sometimes a wooden pin hinge would be used.

The dining-table in larger houses followed the same lines as in Tudor days, but the stretchers were raised clear of the floor in most cases. Some kept the low stretcher which was used as a foot-rest (Fig. 255), and the turnery, although still heavy

FIG. 256 LEGS OF THE JACOBEAN PERIOD

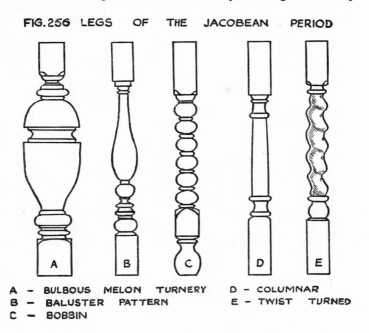

A — BULBOUS MELON TURNERY
B — BALUSTER PATTERN
C — BOBBIN
D — COLUMNAR
E — TWIST TURNED

and bulbous, took on a more simple form, free from heavy carving (Fig. 256A).

Chairs. Some attribute the introduction of upholstery on chairs to the influence of James I, who had a bodily deformity which he hid with padded clothing. Others state that it is due to a desire for comfort which came about quite naturally. Whatever the reason may be, it was during the early Jacobean period that luxuriously upholstered chairs with deep cushions and heavy fringes first appeared.

During the Commonwealth era this luxury ceased and chairs became simple in design and severe in their comfort. The only forms of decoration used were the simple turnery of the baluster leg (Fig. 256B) or bobbin turnery (Fig. 256C), the seat and back being covered with hide held with brass studs (Fig. 257). The farthingale chair (Fig. 258) was still in use during the early part of the 17th century.

With the return of the monarchy under Charles II, restraint in design and decoration disappeared. The introduction of

FIG. 257 BOBBIN TURNERY
ON JACOBEAN CHAIR (CIRCA 1650)

FIG. 258 FARTHINGALE
CHAIR (CIRCA 1620)

walnut, easily carved with and across the grain, led to graceful chairs with tall backs. The back and seat were often filled with laced cane work (rattan cane came from India—further evidence of the effects of trade on fashion in furniture). The front stretcher of the chair was well above floor height and was often elaborately carved (Fig. 259). The ladder back became popular and the legs and backs were often decorated with "barley-sugar" or twist turnery (Fig. 256E).

It was during the Restoration that the splat or splad back first appeared (Fig. 259). The back still remained straight but was given a slight rake backwards as a concession to the comfort of the sitter. The legs were very slightly splayed to increase the stability of the chair, as shown in Fig. 269. The day bed

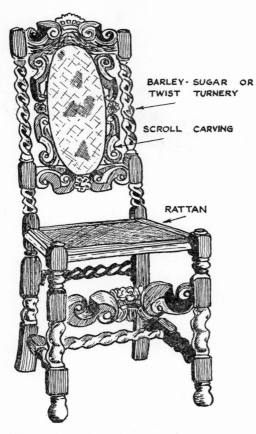

BARLEY- SUGAR   OR
TWIST   TURNERY

SCROLL   CARVING

RATTAN

FIG. 259   RESTORATION   WALNUT CHAIR
WITH   RATTAN   SEAT AND BACK (CIRCA 1660)

(Fig. 260) developed from the chair and was the forerunner of the settee.

Chests continued to be made in the fully panelled form and carried decorative carving on rails, muntins and stiles. This carving followed the forms typical of the period, such as

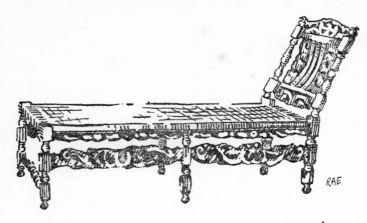

FIG. 260　WALNUT　DAY　BED　(CIRCA 1670)

FIG. 261　APPLIED　ORNAMENT　OF
THE　JACOBEAN　PERIOD

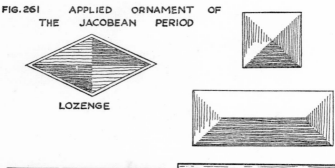

LOZENGE

FIG. 262　APPLIED　MOULDINGS　ON　DRAWER　FRONTS

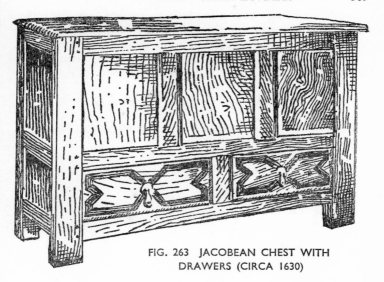

FIG. 263 JACOBEAN CHEST WITH
DRAWERS (CIRCA 1630)

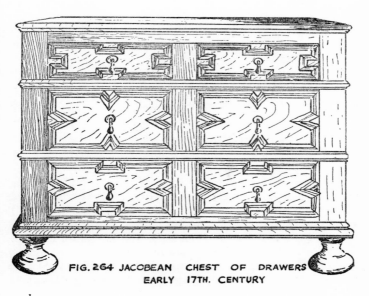

FIG. 264 JACOBEAN CHEST OF DRAWERS
EARLY 17TH. CENTURY

L

acanthus leaf, scrolls and the lozenge pattern (Fig. 261). One distinctive feature of Jacobean carving is that it was often cut separately and then applied to the chest with pins and glue. This was also done with mouldings which were built-up into many forms of mitred, geometric patterns (Fig. 262).

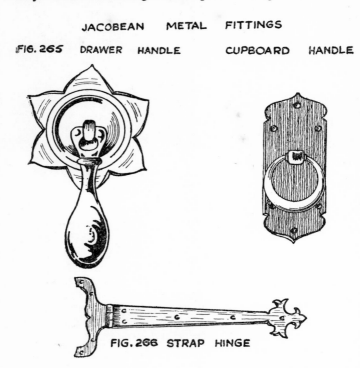

JACOBEAN   METAL   FITTINGS

FIG. 265   DRAWER   HANDLE   CUPBOARD   HANDLE

FIG. 266 STRAP HINGE

As mentioned previously, drawers were included in the chest, at first only at the bottom (Fig. 263). Gradually, the whole front of the chest became filled with drawers (Fig. 264). The drawers were fitted with locks, and "pear-drop" handles became a popular feature (Fig. 265). The hinges on ordinary chests, often a decorative feature in themselves, were usually made from wrought iron in various patterns (Fig. 266). The drawer fronts were decorated with applied mouldings (Fig. 262).

Main features of Jacobean furniture:—

Early Jacobean
1. Gate-leg and tea tables (Fig. 254).
2. Upholstered seats with fringes.
3. Simpler turnery than the Tudor period; less bulbous, without carving and fluting (Fig. 256A).
4. The baluster leg (Fig. 256B).
5. Decorative upholstery with large-headed studs.
6. Farthingale chairs (Fig. 258).
7. Chairs with open backs, padded at the top to give greater comfort.

Commonwealth
1. Bobbin turnery (Figs. 257, 256c).
2. Hide seats, sometimes upholstered (Fig. 257).
3. Restraint in decoration.
4. Ball feet (Fig. 264).

Late Jacobean (Carolean)
1. "Barley-sugar" turnery (Figs. 259, 256E).
2. Rattan cane seats and backs (Fig. 259).
3. The day bed (Fig. 260).
4. Applied mouldings, mitred to form geometric patterns (Fig. 262).
5. Applied ornament, lozenges, squares, rectangles and balusters (Fig. 261).
6. Walnut cross-grain mouldings (Fig. 253).
7. Veneers in walnut.
8. Splat back chairs, pierced and heavily carved, often using the scroll motif (Fig. 259).
9. Elaborate front stretchers on chairs, carved with scroll and floral motifs.
10. Ornate grandfather-clock cases, often veneered with walnut on pine or oak.
11. Ladder-back chairs (rows of horizontal slats across chair back).

Chapter 22

THE AGE OF THE CABINET MAKER

WILLIAM AND MARY PERIOD (1688–1702)

LIKE the Restoration period this was a time of transition with new ideas, new designs and new decoration in furniture. This may have been partly due to the influence of William

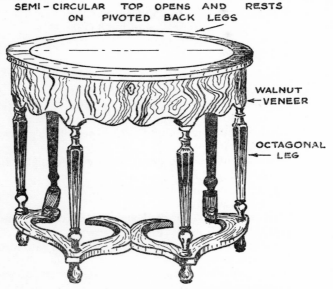

SEMI - CIRCULAR TOP OPENS AND RESTS ON PIVOTED BACK LEGS

WALNUT ← VENEER

OCTAGONAL ← LEG

FIG. 267 WILLIAM AND MARY GAMING TABLE

of Orange, who came from Holland to the throne of England in 1688, bringing continental ideas with him. Historically, this was a period of graceful living and fostering of the arts. Periods of ease and leisure often lead to the cultivation of hobbies, creative work and collecting. One direct result of this was the collection of rare china, so that china display cabinets were needed; books became more plentiful and bookcases were demanded from the cabinet makers.

The most important factor influencing furniture during this period was the rise of the cabinet maker, a specialist in the

FIG. 268 LEGS OF THE WILLIAM & MARY PERIOD

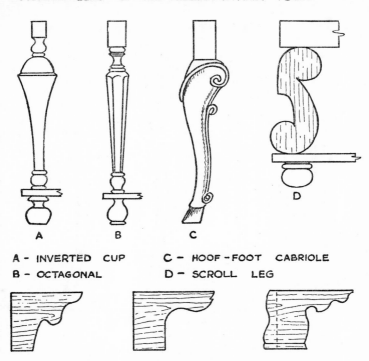

A - INVERTED CUP   C - HOOF-FOOT CABRIOLE
B - OCTAGONAL   D - SCROLL LEG

BRACKET FEET OF THE WALNUT AGE

making of chairs, cabinets, chests and tables. Some cabinet makers even specialized in making one class of furniture only, such as chairs, and by doing so became very highly skilled indeed. The master cabinet maker would employ journeymen, skilled workers in their own rights but not owning a furniture shop, and apprentices who had to serve their time—from five to

seven years—before being admitted to the guild as a journeyman. The cabinet makers and journeymen were capable of
making almost all articles of furniture and could successfully
master all of the stages of their construction. There was, in
these early days, no breakdown of labour whereby each man
performed a small repetitive operation day after day. This fact
can be seen in the quality of work produced in the late 17th

FIG. 269   THE   DEVELOPMENT   OF   THE   CHAIR   BACK

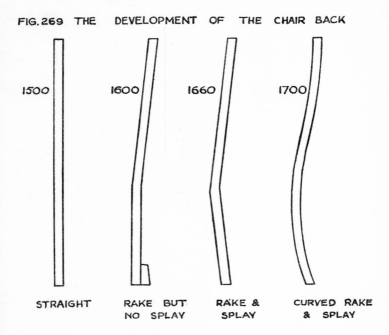

1500   1600   1660   1700

STRAIGHT   RAKE BUT   RAKE &   CURVED RAKE
              NO SPLAY   SPLAY   & SPLAY

century which reflects the pride and skill of the early cabinet
makers.

The use of walnut was extended to cover all forms of furniture. This was, indeed, the beginning of "The Age of Walnut"
as well as "The Age of the Cabinet Maker". Veneered cabinets
and tables were made which exploited the beauty of walnut
grain in both herringbone and burr. Matched veneers were used
to balance one side of a door against another and applied
decoration largely disappeared. Many fine examples are seen

where the sole decoration lies in careful use of veneers and the good proportions of the article.

Tables were made in a wide variety of shapes and sizes to

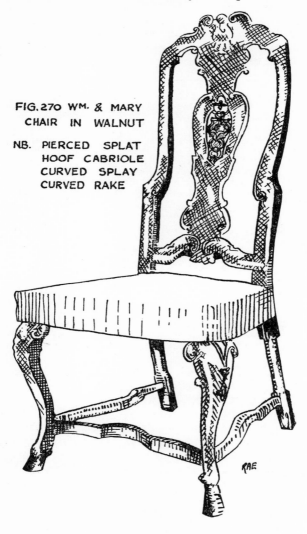

FIG. 270 WM. & MARY
CHAIR IN WALNUT

NB. PIERCED SPLAT
HOOF CABRIOLE
CURVED SPLAY
CURVED RAKE

RAE

meet the new mode of living. Interest in card playing led to the development of card and gaming tables which were usually made with hinged tops and pivoted legs (Fig. 267). Small bureaux and writing tables reflected the social life of the times and display tables for china and *objets d'art* were popular.

Legs were shaped by both turnery and hand carving, one of the most popular being the inverted cup leg with simple turned slopes and bobbins. Such legs often terminated in the ball foot

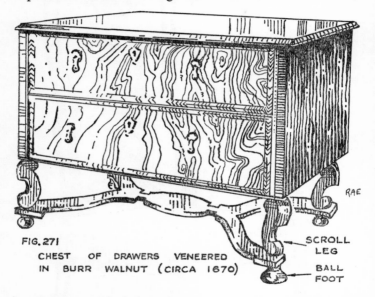

FIG. 271
CHEST   OF   DRAWERS   VENEERED
IN   BURR   WALNUT   (CIRCA   1670)

SCROLL LEG

BALL FOOT

RAE

or turnip foot (Fig. 268A). Octagonal legs (Figs. 268B and 267) were also popular and were connected by stretchers which were gracefully curved in the plan view (Fig. 267).

Chairs underwent great changes during this period, mainly owing to the increase in skill shown by specialist chair makers. For the first time chairs are seen to have a curved rake in the back and the leg, thus giving greater comfort and greater stability (Fig. 269). Splat backs, often pierced and carved, were popular and the back of the chair was tall. The beginning of the cabriole leg was seen, often with a hoof foot and horns at the top of the leg (Fig. 270).

This period marks a most important stage in the development of the chair in its traditional form. The chair legs were still linked by stretchers but they were lighter and more delicate in appearance. Inverted cup turnery, ball feet and turnip feet also appeared on chair legs.

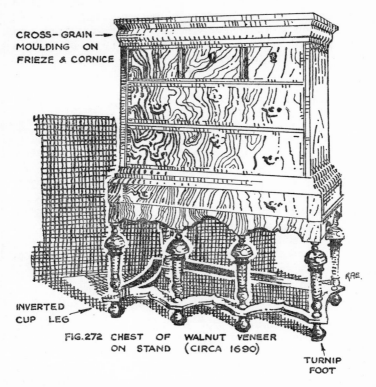

CROSS – GRAIN → MOULDING ON FRIEZE & CORNICE

INVERTED CUP LEG →

FIG. 272 CHEST OF WALNUT VENEER
ON STAND (CIRCA 1690)

↑ TURNIP FOOT

Chests of the traditional pattern had been largely replaced by the chest of drawers. Surface treatment was fairly simple and relied mainly on exploiting the beauty of veneers, especially in walnut (Fig. 271). On small chests of drawers the scroll leg was a popular feature, and although rather weak construction-ally, was strengthened with curved stretchers.

The height of the chest of drawers was considerably increased and sometimes the chest unit was mounted on a small table construction, since the scroll leg would give inadequate support (Fig. 272). Gradually the height of the chest unit rose almost to the ceiling, giving rise to a new article of furniture known as a tallboy. The chest was then extended to ground level and to give sufficient support the table construction was replaced with bracket feet (Fig. 268). The tallboy was usually a veneered construction with matching veneers on the drawer fronts and cross-grained cornices, but examples are seen of tallboys lacquered in red, gold and black.

Main features of the period:—

1. Inverted cup turnery (Figs. 268A, 272).
2. Octagonal legs (Figs. 267, 268B).
3. Hoof foot cabriole leg (Figs. 268C and 270).
4. Scroll legs (Figs. 268D, 271).
5. Bracket feet (Fig. 268).
6. Ball feet (Fig. 271) and turnip feet (Fig. 272).
7. Flat stretchers, curved in the plan view (Figs. 267, 271, 272).
8. Veneers exploiting the beauty of burr walnut (Fig. 271).
9. Graceful, delicate lines; "dignified" furniture.
10. Restraint in both carving and applied decoration.
11. Influence of the architect on cabinet friezes and cornices (Figs. 272, 253).

QUEEN ANNE PERIOD (1702–1714)

England continued to profit from both trade and territorial expansion, new materials were introduced into the country and leisure became a normal feature of the life of the well to do. Long fast ships plied between England and China, bringing back not only tea but also silks and lacquered furniture. This style of furniture was much favoured and lacquered chairs and cabinets became very popular. Commercial development and prosperity both helped in the rise of the rich merchant class and created greater demand for furniture and furnishings.

With the spread in education came a demand for more writing furniture such as the bureau, secretaire and writing table with drawers. There was an increase in the quantity of literature and there was leisure available in which to read and cultivate the arts. Bookcases became an everyday article in the homes of the leisured classes.

An English cabinet style, distinct in its own right, was rapidly developing. Intricate carving and imposed decoration was largely discarded and furniture took on graceful, curved lines.

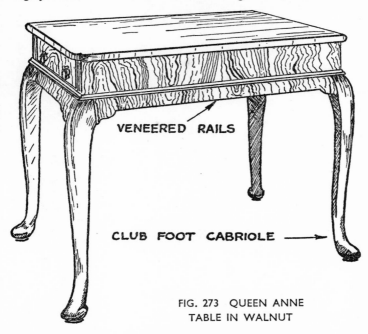

VENEERED RAILS

CLUB FOOT CABRIOLE ——→

FIG. 273   QUEEN ANNE
TABLE IN WALNUT

The cabriole leg became very popular in both chair and table constructions. Upholstering fabrics, in fine needlepoints, reflected the leisured way of life.

Walnut was the principal timber used for furniture construction, but a new timber, mahogany, was being imported. Mahogany first came to England as a ballast timber on the triangular slave route, but it was taxed at first and was only used for building purposes. Many old houses in south-western England have their main timbers and doors made from mahogany because of the tax imposed on mahogany as a furniture timber.

Tables required for writing, cards and display of china increased in quantity. Walnut veneers were extensively used for table tops and rails, but the most notable feature was the complete omission of the stretcher rails and the use of the club-foot cabriole leg (Fig. 273). This construction calls for very good

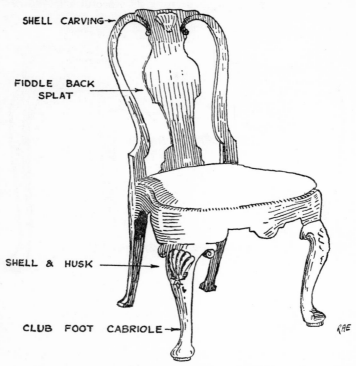

SHELL CARVING

FIDDLE BACK SPLAT

SHELL & HUSK

CLUB FOOT CABRIOLE

RAE

FIG. 274 QUEEN ANNE WALNUT CHAIR

joints between the leg and top rail, if the table is to be strong and rigid. The top rail was usually made wider than in the past to give a stronger mortice and tenon joint.

Very few examples have been found of large dining-tables in this style. This is probably due to the difficulties encountered with shrinkage and subsequent splitting in large sheets of veneered timber.

Chairs became more comfortable and strength in construction had so developed that, as on tables, the stretchers were dispensed with. The cabriole leg, with its graceful, curved line was extensively used, often ending in a club foot (Fig. 274). Some examples of the flattened hoof foot were to be seen as well as early examples of the ball and claw foot (Fig. 275). Delicate shell and husk carving on the knee of the cabriole leg was a popular form of decoration (Fig. 274).

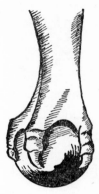

FIG. 275   BALL AND CLAW FOOT

The chair back took on a curved form to counterbalance the curve of the cabriole leg. The splat, or splad, was often of urn or fiddle shape (Fig. 274). It is often said that the chair makers of the Queen Anne period set a standard of beauty, delicacy and sound construction that has never been surpassed since. This may or may not be true, but at the very least it can be said that they achieved a very high standard in both fitness for purpose and pleasure to the eye.

The chest. It became common practice to raise the chest construction on a table or to place chest on top of chest, resulting in the tallboy (Fig. 276). As in the previous period, bracket feet were used to support this heavy article of furniture. The drawers, with matching veneers and cross-bandings, were sometimes hidden behind doors veneered with exotic burr walnut.

The multiple dovetail joint was in common use and the skill of the cabinet maker is clearly seen in the beautiful, well-built furniture of the day.

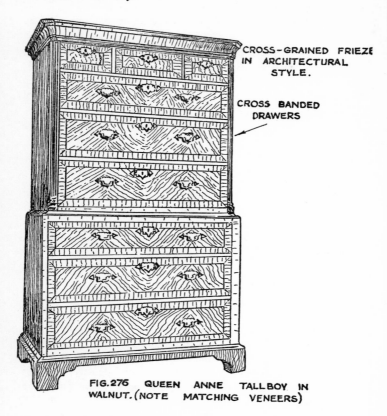

CROSS-GRAINED FRIEZE
IN ARCHITECTURAL
STYLE.

CROSS BANDED
DRAWERS

FIG. 276   QUEEN ANNE   TALLBOY IN
WALNUT. (NOTE   MATCHING   VENEERS)

Main features of the period:—

1. Graceful cabriole legs with no stretchers (Fig. 273).
2. Club feet (Fig. 274), hoof feet, ball and claw feet (Fig. 275).
3. Bracket feet on tallboys (Fig. 276).
4. Decoration in proportions and delicate curves; carving and applied decoration largely omitted (Fig. 273).
5. Fine fabrics, brocades and needlepoint.

6. Veneers exploiting beauty of grain, matched veneers and cross-bandings (Fig. 276).
7. Shell and husk carving on cabriole knees (Fig. 274).
8. Curved chair backs.
9. Urn-shaped and fiddle-back splats (Fig. 274).

Chapter 23

THE AGE OF THE DESIGNER

Georgian—Chippendale—Adam—Hepplewhite—
Sheraton—Empire

THE GEORGIAN PERIOD (1714–1804)

HISTORICALLY this was a period of much elegance, socially and domestically. Trade was making England a very rich country and, as always, wealth meant leisure and the ability to travel.

In France the sovereigns were no longer content with medieval castles and built luxurious palaces furnished in the most lavish style by the cabinet makers of France and the surrounding countries. This source of ideas had a great influence on English designers, particularly the Adam brothers.

The influence of the architect is seen in many things during the early part of the Georgian Period, not only in buildings but also furniture, gardens and even clocks. In the first half of the 18th century this influence mainly came from the work of Wren and Inigo Jones, who were themselves influenced by the classical revival. The second half of the century saw the building of many fine country houses for the use of the rising commercial and industrial leaders.

The life of the cabinet maker and his workers began to undergo a subtle change during the second half of the 18th century. The master cabinet maker, for reasons to be seen, gradually became divorced from the workshop. The poorly paid worker began to lose the satisfaction of making and completing all forms of furniture and concentrated on one form of article to the exclusion of all others. This was the real beginning of sub-division of labour which today condemns many people to monotonous repetitive work; killing the joy of creating with the hands.

The master cabinet maker, to meet demand and save time, published a catalogue of designs and ideas for furniture. This was not a catalogue in the same sense that a catalogue is used

324

today, but a book of suggestions from which the customer would decide on his particular piece of furniture and then commission the cabinet maker to make the article. (Chippendale, Hepplewhite and Sheraton tend to be more famous than they deserve because of their catalogues. There were many equally fine craftsmen whose names are unknown.)

Printing was fairly cheap and this aided the distribution of the "catalogues", which were much in demand. It must be remembered that this was the first time in history that designers and craftsmen had written about furniture and the books sold throughout the country. Many catalogues found their way to the hands of other cabinet makers who not only used the ideas of the well-known designers but also made copies of their furniture. This makes it very difficult to decide whether some work attributed to, say, Chippendale, ever saw the inside of his workshops. All that can be said, in many cases, is that the furniture is in the style of Chippendale or Hepplewhite.

With the increase in business brought about by the catalogues, many of the master cabinet makers had to delegate their authority in the workshop to their senior journeymen so that they themselves were free for designing and business purposes. It is a fact that Chippendale eventually became so much a business man and so little a craftsman that even his designs were made by his employees. This state of affairs often leads to serious results; the article made becomes of small importance and the money it can bring assumes paramount importance.

Craftsmen still worked in oak and walnut but in 1733 the tax on mahogany was repealed. This reduced the price of mahogany and increased the demand for it. The Georgian period was not only "The Age of the Designer", it was also the beginning of "The Age of Mahogany". Mahogany is red in colour with a pronounced stripe owing to interlocking grain, and is not suitable for the same decorative and constructive treatment as walnut. The art of veneering was still carried on, using both walnut and mahogany, but gradually new decorative media evolved. This was partly due to the strength of the mahogany interlocked grain and the stability of the timber, which permitted more fretting, more delicate treatment and the use of thinner pieces of wood in construction.

Thomas Chippendale (working from 1754 to 1792)

Chippendale, born in 1718, is probably the best known of the designers. In 1754 he went to London and became well known as soon as he published the first of his catalogues, *The Gentleman and Cabinet Maker's Director*. This brought him to the notice of wealthy people and soon he was acting as the managing director of his own concern, rather than working as a cabinet maker.

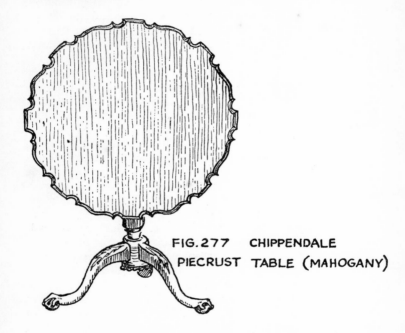

FIG. 277   CHIPPENDALE
PIECRUST TABLE (MAHOGANY)

Chippendale's work is distinguished for its excellence of craftsmanship, strength of construction and pleasant appearance. At first he followed any fashion that arose, using mahogany almost exclusively, and at one time specialized in furniture in the Chinese style. This class of work is now known as "Chinese Chippendale". It was in chair construction that Chippendale excelled himself; his ribbon or riband back chairs have never been surpassed for comfort, strength and

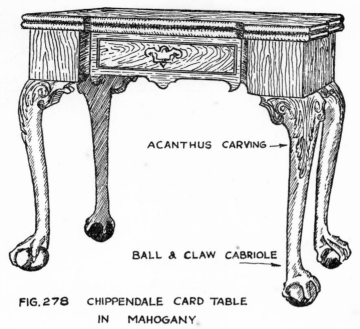

ACANTHUS CARVING →

BALL & CLAW CABRIOLE →

FIG. 278   CHIPPENDALE CARD TABLE
IN   MAHOGANY

FIG. 279 CHIPPENDALE RIBBON
OR RIBAND BACK

FIG. 280   CHINESE   FRET
(CHIPPENDALE)

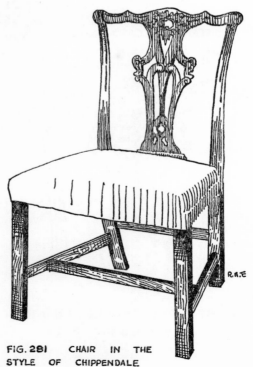

FIG. 281   CHAIR   IN   THE
STYLE   OF   CHIPPENDALE

appearance. The use of mahogany made the intricate carving, piercing and fretting possible, by virtue of its interlocking grain.

Some of Chippendale's work tends to be rather heavy in appearance, but in the large rooms of the Georgian period this would not be so noticeable. Other features of his work include:—

1. Ball and claw feet (Fig. 277).
2. Acanthus carving on cabriole knees (Fig. 278).
3. Riband back chairs (Fig. 279).
4. Delicate, fine carving in solid timber.
5. Little use of inlay.
6. Chinese frets (Fig. 280).
7. Both straight legs of moulded section (Fig. 281) and cabrioles.

Robert Adam (working from 1754 to 1792)

Adam was a very well-known Scottish architect who entered the sphere of cabinet making through his interest in the work of Chippendale. He had studied in Italy and had been influenced by the classical forms and decorative detail of the Greek and Roman civilizations. This is reflected in the many fine country houses designed by him.

Adam believed that the whole of the house, gardens, interior decoration, furnishings and furniture should be under the control of the architect. This is quite obvious from the close harmony seen in original Adam work. He engaged both Chippendale and Hepplewhite to carry out some of his cabinet work and thereby influenced their designs. Some Hepplewhite wheel back chairs are almost identical with those of Adam, making it very difficult to identify the original designer.

The designs of Robert Adam are noted for:—

1. Wheel back and shield back chairs (Fig. 282).
2. Urn finials (Fig. 283), a classical motif.
3. Classical decorative detail, such as:—
    (a) Scrolls.
    (b) Flutes and reeds on turned legs (Figs. 282, 285).
    (c) Wreath and garland.
    (d) Draped cloth (carved in wood) (Fig. 283).
    (e) Swags of husks (Fig. 283).
    (f) Wheat ears (Fig. 284).

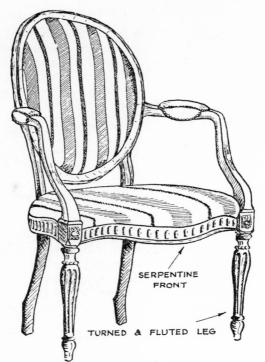

SERPENTINE
FRONT

TURNED & FLUTED LEG

FIG. 282 ADAM WHEELBACK CHAIR

FIG. 283

ADAM DECORATION

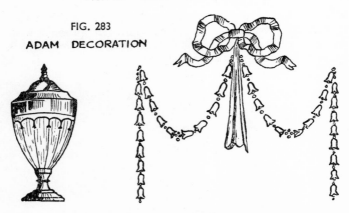

VASE OR URN   SWAG OF HUSKS

4. Use of inlay and veneers.
5. Gesso work, that is, plaster moulded or carved on a wooden background, then painted or gilded (Fig. 285).
6. Use of lacquer.
7. Fairly light carving.

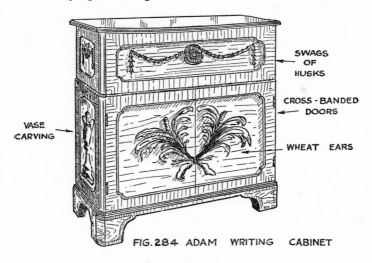

VASE CARVING

SWAGS OF HUSKS

CROSS - BANDED DOORS

WHEAT EARS

FIG. 284 ADAM WRITING CABINET

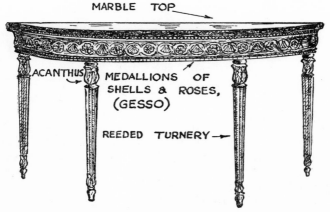

MARBLE TOP

ACANTHUS

MEDALLIONS OF SHELLS & ROSES, (GESSO)

REEDED TURNERY

FIG. 285 GILT SIDE TABLE (ADAM)

George Hepplewhite (working from 1760 to 1786)

Hepplewhite's work was greatly influenced by the designs of Robert Adam, but tended to be rather more restrained in its decorative detail. In this way his work is closer to Chippendale but has a more delicate appearance.

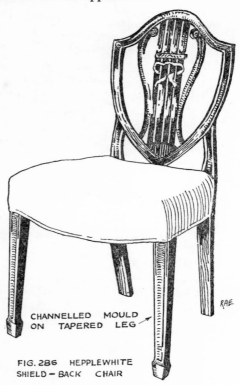

CHANNELLED MOULD
ON TAPERED LEG →

FIG. 286 HEPPLEWHITE
SHIELD — BACK CHAIR

Some of the finest examples of Georgian chairs are to be seen in Hepplewhite shield-backs, which combine strength with delicate lines. A very common feature of these chairs was the gentle taper of the leg, ending in a spade foot (Fig. 286).

Sideboards made by Hepplewhite were usually veneered in mahogany and often inlaid with satinwood imported from America. These sideboards often had bow or serpentine fronts

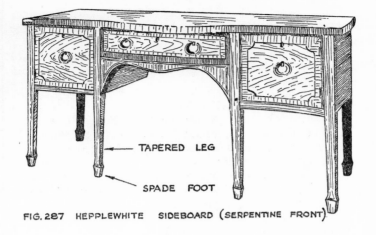

FIG. 287 HEPPLEWHITE SIDEBOARD (SERPENTINE FRONT)

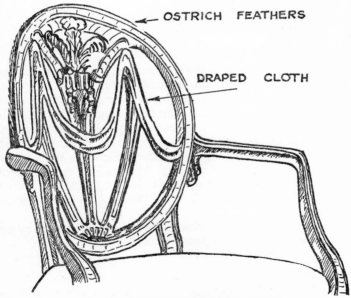

FIG. 288 HEPPLEWHITE WHEEL-BACK

(Fig. 287), which makes a far more difficult construction since doors and drawer fronts had to be jointed and shaped to the curves.

Hepplewhite's main book of designs was not published until two years after his death, but gives many examples of the main features of his work:—

1. Shield-back chairs (Fig. 286).
2. Wheel-back chairs (Adam influence—Fig. 288).
3. Tapered chair legs, moulded in section (Fig. 286).
4. Turned legs, fluted or reeded (Figs. 282, 285).
5. Spade feet (Figs. 286, 287).
6. Serpentine and bow-fronted sideboards (Fig. 287).
7. Use of veneer and inlays of rosewood, ebony, satinwood.
8. Painted and gilded furniture.
9. Carved decoration:—
    (a) Vases and festoons (Fig. 283).
    (b) Draped cloth (Fig. 288).
    (c) Swags of husks.
    (d) Ostrich feathers (Fig. 288).
    (e) Wheat ears (Fig. 284).

Thomas Sheraton (working 1790 to 1806)

Sheraton left Stockton-on-Tees and settled in London at the age of 40. Although he worked in Stockton as a journeyman cabinet maker there is no evidence that he made furniture while in London. This may well account for the nature of some of his late designs, which tend towards novelty and bizarre fashion. He applied himself mainly to designing furniture and publishing books on design and through these publications was able to influence the fashion of the day. Many of his early designs reflect the gracious life of the late Georgian period and his use of classical decorative motif revived the fashion set by Robert Adam.

Although his work was much admired and his designs extensively copied, he died in penniless obscurity.

Sheraton's work is noted for:—

1. Very delicate lines and "spidery" construction.
2. The use of string inlays and bandings on veneered constructions (Fig. 291).

FIG. 289   SHERATON   CARD   TABLE   IN
INLAID   MAHOGANY

FIG. 290 SHERATON   CHAIR   IN   MAHOGANY

FIG. 291 SHERATON WRITING BUREAU IN BURR ELM VENEER WITH SATINWOOD CROSS BANDINGS AND PARQUETRY. NOTE ALSO LEG INLAY.

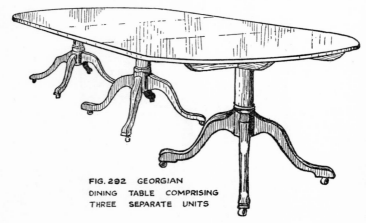

FIG. 292 GEORGIAN DINING TABLE COMPRISING THREE SEPARATE UNITS

3. Restrained delicate ornament, little carving.
4. Low chair backs (Fig. 290).
5. Straight tapered legs with spade feet (Fig. 289).
6. Fluted or reeded chair legs and arm supports (Fig. 290).
7. Pedestal and tapered leg sideboards with bow and serpentine fronts (almost identical to Fig. 287).
8. Parquetry and use of exotic veneers (Fig. 291).

The Georgian table

The dining-table was often made in separate, push-together units (Fig. 292). When not required for seating large numbers, the various units were sometimes pushed to the walls and used for display of china and glassware.

The "piecrust" table was made by various designers. The name was derived from the scalloped edge given to the table top. The top, sometimes veneered and treated as a background for parquetry, was hinged to fall forward as shown in Fig. 277.

THE EMPIRE OR REGENCY PERIOD (1804–1840)

This period marks the end of the Golden Age in the story of furniture; very gradually the quality of design and construction declined as the minds of men turned from aesthetics to social position and money.

The main theme in the fashion of the period came through the life of one man, Napoleon Bonaparte. In 1804 he returned the splendour of the court to France, after the drabness of the post-revolution years. The influence of his Egyptian campaign and the subsequent re-vitalization of classical forms was to be seen in the dress and furniture of the day.

Gradually, by the middle of the century, new forms of power and new machines brought an end to the last remnants of Georgian elegance and the march of the machines had begun.

Tables. The principal timber in use was still mahogany. Tables of all types were made, including the "piecrust" with exotic matching veneers such as zebrano and macassar ebony inlays.

A new form of table evolved during the period was the "pembroke" table (Fig. 293). This table had drop sides, usually with a rule joint edge, supported by a wooden bracket with an interlocking hinge known as a knuckle joint. The table end-frame or legs often appeared with the lyre motif and carried inlaid brass ornament on the ends and feet (Fig. 293).

It was during the Georgian and Empire periods that the single pedestal table with a round or elliptical top first appeared. In order to give a sufficiently strong joint the centre pedestal was often made very heavy and solid. In spite of this, the centre pedestal table was basically a poor construction and the joint between the top and pedestal seldom held for very long. It

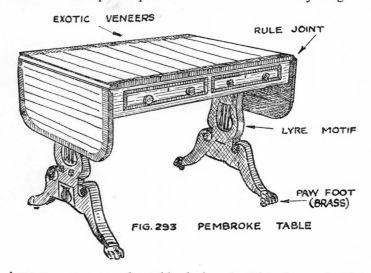

EXOTIC VENEERS

RULE JOINT

LYRE MOTIF

PAW FOOT (BRASS)

FIG. 293   PEMBROKE TABLE

became a very popular table during the Victorian period in spite of this disadvantage, possibly because it was ideal for the comfort of the sitters who were not inconvenienced by the positioning of the single leg (see Fig. 295—Victorian).

The chair. The chair back, following the Sheraton influence, stayed low and was given a comfortable rake which terminated at the top in a roll or scroll (Fig. 294). The legs often curved inwards and ended in paw feet, an idea obtained from Ancient Egypt. The scroll form was also brought into the curve of the arm rest, sometimes to an exaggerated degree (Fig. 294).

The decorative motifs of the sphinx, lyre and floral garland show the influence of the classical forms of the past.

Main features of the period:—

1. Paw feet (Fig. 294).
2. Flutings, elaborate scrolls, wreath, urn and garland decoration.
3. Use of gilt and gesso.

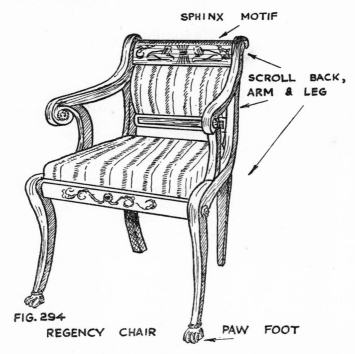

SPHINX MOTIF

SCROLL BACK, ARM & LEG

FIG. 294
REGENCY CHAIR   PAW FOOT

4. The lyre and sphinx motif (Figs. 293 and 294).
5. Lion head mounts on chair and settee arms.
6. Marble-topped tables.
7. Use of exotic veneers (Fig. 293).
8. Scroll chair backs, legs and arm-rests (Fig. 294).
9. Use of striped chair upholstery (Fig. 294).

Chapter 24

THE AGE OF THE MACHINE

Victorian—20th Century—Utility—Contemporary

THE VICTORIAN PERIOD (1840–1914)

IN the past the only forms of power available for easing the labour of man were wind and water. During the 18th century the steam engine was invented and the areas around the coal mines became centres of industry and commerce. With the vast increase in production and the invention of more and more machines, a change came about in the lives of people in England, brought about mainly by the machines and the rise of capitalism. Human values became of little importance; money and machines were of prime value.

A new search for wealth began among the manufacturers as it had done in the past with the nobility. "Mineral rushes" began, despoiling the countryside and perhaps helping in the migration of country people to the towns. (But they were also tempted by the wages offered.)

Another remarkable happening was the rise in population:—

In England and Wales 1801— 9,000,000
1821—12,000,000
1891—29,000,000

This caused further overcrowding in the already crowded towns and cities and people became habituated to slums, filth and squalor. Thus, although the machines gave material wealth, as a country we became spiritually poorer.

The expensive machines in use caused the owners to demand maximum money in return and thus the machines, and the workers, were kept working for 24 hours a day. The homes of these workers had no running water, no baths and usually no sanitation. People washed rarely and disease was prevalent. Children of 4 and 5 years of age, girls and boys and women worked for 16 hours a day in the coal mines, often naked, some

340

never seeing daylight, but living and dying in the mines. For those in factories, Sunday was the only day of leisure, but there was little for them to do except lounge on the streets. Life became nasty, brutal and unpleasant, as shown in the stories of Charles Dickens.

During this Industrial Revolution the country dwellers left the villages and drifted to the towns in search of high wages, and thus another link was broken between the country squires and "gentry", and the craftsmen. Gradually village life fell into decay.

The rise of the railways in the 19th century made movement easier and aided the growth of large industrial centres. This further despoiled the countryside and the colour in life was replaced by dirt and blackness.

Life for the craftsmen became revolutionized and variety of occupation became severely limited as specialization increased. A man no longer did all aspects of the job himself but only one small part of it, while someone else did another part. This imposed restrictions on the craftsmen and they rapidly forgot many of the crafts of bygone days. In the event of unemployment they were then unable to find other work, and poverty, often starvation, resulted. The worst aspect of this from the human side was that the man had become of minor importance compared with the machine. The craftsman had to discipline himself to the machine, for the machine was adapted to produce money, not to ease the labours of man.

The full blast of the Industrial Revolution was felt after the Great Exhibition in 1851 when the need for technical education arose. The machines needed the attention of highly skilled technicians who could maintain them to give maximum output.

In this welter of machines few of the old craftsmen survived to produce beautiful articles for reasons other than monetary gain. A few clockmakers and cabinet makers still had their apprentices and journeymen but they were a small minority. These few remaining craftsmen made articles for the new "aristocracy", the wealthy manufacturers. These manufacturers, unaccustomed to the wealth they had gathered together, desired to show it off to their fellow men. Thus furniture, and practically all articles for the home, were embellished with useless, and often vulgar, ornament. A period of ostentation arose

M

with useless bric-à-brac and it became customary to crowd as many articles of furniture and ornaments into a room as was possible.

Because of these influences the spirit seemed to disappear from furniture designing, although the quality of workmanship was often high. Although the workmanship was good, and the polish and finish may well have been excellent, the effect as a whole was drab, cumbersome and heavy. Servants, of course, were easily obtainable to keep these articles, with tassels,

FIG. 295 VICTORIAN TABLE

fringes and elaborate mouldings, clean. (Perhaps this is one reason why we now prefer simplicity in our decorative schemes.)

Tables. Round mahogany tables, sometimes up to 1·5 m in diameter, were very common, supported by a massive, solid, single pedestal, often turned on the lathe with separate feet jointed in with mortice and tenon joints (Fig. 295).

Screw extending tables were popular and there was a large miscellany of side tables to house the numerous *objets d'art* or bric-à-brac with which the Victorians loved to surround themselves.

Chairs. Armchairs were noted for their horsehair stuffing which, as is typical of the period, was carried out to excess.

Fringes and tassels were added as a form of "decoration", making the whole effect ugly and ungainly. Armchairs were even made from such materials as papier maché, usually in the most vulgar taste.

"Parlour" chairs were usually made from mahogany (or beech stained to look like mahogany) with the inevitable horse-hair stuffing and glazed upholstery. They were sturdy and well made but lacking completely in elegance or beauty (Fig. 296).

FIG. 296   VICTORIAN   CHAIR

Perhaps the only noteworthy feature among Victorian chairs was the large production of Windsor chairs, a cheap article of furniture turned out for use in small homes and villages (Fig. 297). The centre of this industry was High Wycombe, where the beech forests gave an ample supply of timber. In the South of England the Windsor chair was made with turned spindles for legs, backs and stretchers, using such native woods as yew or ash for the frames; beech or ash for the spindles and elm for the seats. The joints were made by fitting the turned ends of the members into round holes made with the brace and bit.

Sometimes an attempt was made to copy some mode of the

day and one example is seen in the fretted splat-back or "Wheel-back Windsor" chair (Fig. 297). Another example was the Windsor armchair with front legs in cabriole form. In the North of England the back spindles were often arranged in rows or tiers and became known as "spindle-back" chairs.

In the early forms of Windsor chair a top-rail was jointed to the top of the back rest, until it was found that beech could be

FIG. 297   WHEEL - BACK   WINDSOR   CHAIR

bent into shape when steamed. Thus the whole of the back frame was made from one bent piece of timber, and this type of chair became known as the "hoop-back" chair. (This was the forerunner of the Austrian bent-wood chair.)

On the whole Windsor chairs have a graceful form, are rigid and lasting. It is worth noting that they were originally the work of the village carpenters and not the cabinet-makers.

The revolt against the machine. During the Victorian era, a voice was raised against the domination of the machine, the bad design and the low state into which humanity had sunk. This came from William Morris (working 1858–1896), who refused to be controlled by machines and returned to hand craftsmanship. In his workshops every form of craft was carried out entirely by hand. Furniture was made, fabrics were hand-woven, dyed and printed by hand; even the dyes were made on the spot from ancient recipes. Nothing was omitted, even wall-paper being hand-printed and paper for publishing books made by hand.

In design, Morris advocated a return to the Romantic Period and much of his furniture shows a marked resemblance to Tudor and Medieval designs. To return to the past was no answer to the march of the machines, but much good did come from the ideals of Morris and the band of friends and craftsmen he gathered around him.

His influence on such craftsmen as Gimson and the Barnsleys was profound and their work carried on the tradition of good hand-made furniture, distinguished by:—

1. Solid wood constructions.
2. Fitness for purpose.
3. Functional decoration, which depended on:—
   (a) Beauty of the wood itself.
   (b) Use of the chamfer and simply functional mouldings.
   (c) No dishonesty with staining and imitations.
   (d) Simplicity.

These details are still to be seen in the furniture produced in the Cotswold Workshop of Edward Barnsley.

THE 20TH CENTURY

Early in the 20th century, some furniture manufacturers, including Gordon Russell and Ambrose Heal, made intelligent and successful attempts to make the machine produce beautiful items of furniture consistent with the ideals of William Morris (Fig. 298). Many beautiful articles, well made, soundly con-structed and pleasant in appearance were produced and in a way seemed to blend the hand-made furniture and machine-made furniture into one (Fig. 299). This can never be entirely achieved, however, especially with the materials used today which, by virtue of their plastic nature, give rise to new forms and constructions.

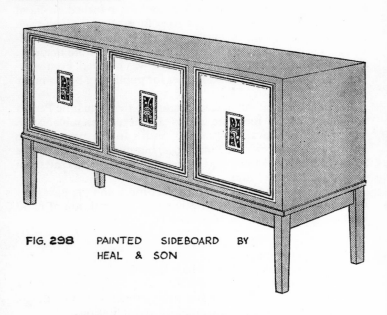

FIG. 298   PAINTED   SIDEBOARD   BY
HEAL & SON

BETWEEN THE WORLD WARS

In the 1920's came the release from the restrictions of war which resulted in the period known as the "Mad Twenties". It resulted in frivolity and carefree abandon typified by the "gay young things". This social attitude was reflected in the furniture and furnishings of the day and the cubism and surrealism of the artists and the artistic was applied to all forms of furniture. The craftsman and the true designer were lost in this welter of "artistic" fervour and the advent of new materials made matters even worse, since little attempt was made to use the new materials in the manner for which they were best fitted.

The more common furniture between the wars was made from plywood and laminated wood on an underframe of beech or oak. The plywood was given a veneer, often walnut or figured oak, and then given a high polish with shellac or cellulose.

Mouldings of all descriptions were pressed from steamed wood and applied lavishly, as were many forms of cheap carving. The whole effect was usually over-ornate and shoddy workmanship was common.

FIG. 299   CHAIR BY GORDON RUSSELL LTD   1928

Another feature of the period was the imitation and reproduction of "Period Furniture" from the good examples of the past. The most exploited were Tudor and Jacobean, even to the extent of supplying artificial wear, bruises and even wormholes!

With the outbreak of war in 1939 all production of furniture ceased and the machines were converted to war production for the defence of Great Britain.

UTILITY FURNITURE

In 1946, with the end of the war, came a huge demand for furniture from people married during the war and settling down for the first time. Timber was almost unobtainable and a council was set up to advise on designs for simple furniture which could be produced quickly and cheaply, using the minimum

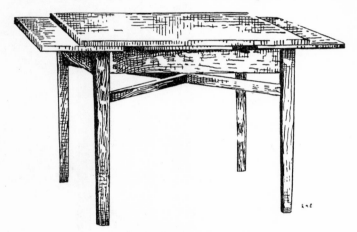

FIG. 300   UTILITY TABLE   1946

amount of wood. (Mr. Gordon Russell served on this committee.)

The council produced several designs, entailing the use of home-grown or Commonwealth timbers, and their designs are noted for:—

1. Simplicity (Fig. 300).
2. Lack of applied decoration (Fig. 301).
3. Sound use of materials.
4. Good proportions (Fig. 302).

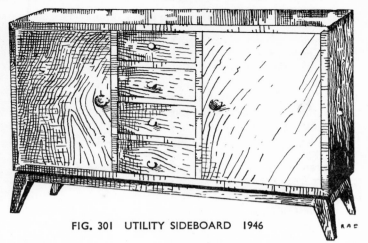

FIG. 301   UTILITY SIDEBOARD   1946

FIG. 302   UTILITY   CHAIR   1946

The main timbers were English oak, Australian walnut and African mahogany.

Unfortunately the great shortage of sound timber led to the use of poor quality wood, unseasoned and often with the sapwood left in. Thus the furniture, although of good design, could not last long. Worms attacked the sapwood, doors and drawers twisted out of shape and were impossible to close. Thus utility furniture, admirable in every other way, fell into disrepute and was rejected by the majority of people.

The return of normal timber supplies released the manufacturers from the control of the government and utility furniture gradually disappeared. Instead, the manufacturers returned to 1939 and once again we saw, in the majority of shops, poor quality furniture with ornate veneers highly decorated with plastics, unsuitable carving and elaborate brass and oxidized handles.

CONTEMPORARY FURNITURE

In this rather depressing survey of modern furniture a ray of hope was to be seen. Certain concerns have studied the nature and limitations of the laminated woods used today and by employing craftsmen/designers who know the limitations and possibilities of the materials and machines, have produced a range of designs termed "contemporary" (Fig. 303). As a result of economic difficulties, Commonwealth timbers such as Australian walnut, African mahogany and sapele are often used, in the form of veneers on laminated softwoods and hardwoods (Fig. 304).

Conventional framed-up constructions are often ignored, for very good reasons, since shrinkage and warpage can be ignored when using laminated wood. Often a table top has the legs screwed directly to it with no top rails or stretchers, the legs being given an attractive outward splay, which also gives greater stability. Some table tops are surfaced with melamine, a synthetic resin product, on which the grain of wood has been photographed so realistically as to defy all but close examination. Cigarettes can be stubbed on this material and no mark is left.

The chair has undergone similar changes although retaining,

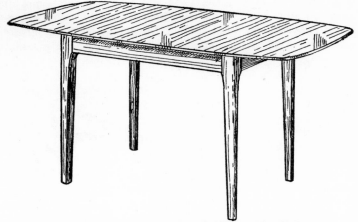

FIG. 303 SIMPLICITY AND GOOD PROPORTION IN
A DINING TABLE BY GORDON RUSSELL LTD.

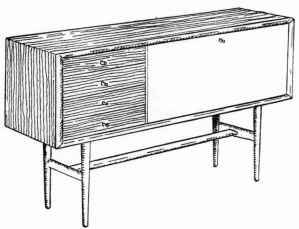

FIG. 304 SIDEBOARD BY HEAL & SON IN
CONTRASTING VENEERS OF TEAK AND
BEECH

as it must, its main form. Legs and sides are sometimes of moulded aluminium, sometimes bent laminated wood, sometimes conventional solid timber. Most contemporary chairs also have a splayed leg giving greater stability with pleasant appearance (Fig. 305).

FIG. 305   DINING TABLE AND CHAIR BY HEAL & SON.
SIMPLE SHAPES , BEAUTY OF GRAIN , GOOD PROPORTION
& FITNESS FOR PURPOSE

From 1960 the influence of Scandinavian designers continued to simplify the lines of English furniture (Fig. 305a), exploiting the beauty of natural wood colour and texture with the golden tones of teak or the exotic hues of rosewood veneers. The long, low lines of modern furniture can be directly attributed to the influence of Scandinavian designers who were among the first to study ergonomics and its relationship to the design of furniture for the mass markets of home, office and industry. "Contract" furniture designed by such experts as Robin Day may have many thousands of pounds spent on prototype models which are thoroughly investigated and tested at every stage of manufacture. The basic raw materials are tested for strength and suitability, the forms and shapes used are related to the human frame, and how the human frame relates to the particular article of furniture has, at last, become a prime criterion of good design. The Council of Industrial Design has played no small part in this return to basic consideration of what constitutes good design.

FIG. 305a SCANDINAVIAN CHAIR IN TEAK

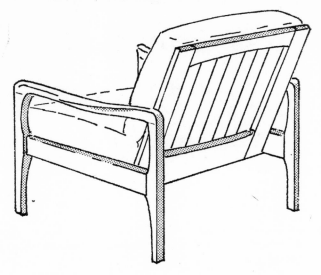

THE EFFECT OF NEW MATERIALS ON DESIGN

Tube steel, bent and welded, is painted or plated and gives a clean, hygienic surface. This may well be suitable for use in hospitals and public places but the material is cold to the touch and fails to give the feeling of warm comfort which is necessary in the home. The use of tube steel furniture in a kitchen has some justification, from the point of view of hygiene. Note how the construction and shape of the chair (Fig. 306) is in keeping with the nature of the material and how it can be worked.

Built-up materials: Plywood has been factory-produced since 1880 and, in common with the other built-up timbers, is easily bent and moulded under steam and pressure. This opened a new field for wood as a constructional medium and has considerably affected the traditional framed-up and carcase con-

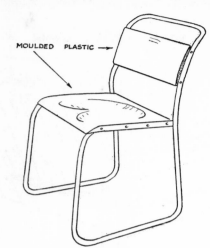

MOULDED PLASTIC →

FIG. 306 TUBE STEEL CHAIR

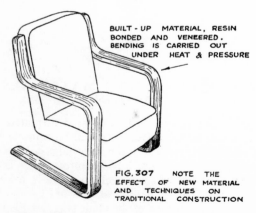

BUILT - UP MATERIAL, RESIN BONDED AND VENEERED. BENDING IS CARRIED OUT UNDER HEAT & PRESSURE

FIG. 307 NOTE THE EFFECT OF NEW MATERIAL AND TECHNIQUES ON TRADITIONAL CONSTRUCTION

structions (Fig. 307). These materials lead to new ideas on design which are quite distinct from work done in the past; for example, the top, front and bottom of a radio or television cabinet can be moulded from one piece of plywood. This results in saving in labour costs, by cutting out jointing and assembly work, and gives an example of how the machine and new materials can work together to produce an article which is pleasant in appearance.

Moulded aluminium: Like bent steel, aluminium is cold to the

FIG. 308   CONTEMPORARY   CHAIR   WITH
"T" SECTION   MOULDED   ALUMINIUM   LEGS

touch but hygienic. It has a softer texture than steel and great strength. Delicate lines are possible, often very pleasant in appearance (Fig. 308).

Plastics: Easily moulded, strong, clean and hygienic. As a decorative feature, plastic items can be over-ornate. The use of heat-resisting plastics such as Formica, etc., are of great value in the kitchen for table tops and other working surfaces. The aesthetic objections to photographed woodgrains incorporated in melamine plastic have now been overcome by the production of "Belfort" melamine which has real wood veneer in the upper layer. In this way, the beauty of real wood and the protection of melamine have come together in a most suitable combination.

The use of glass reinforced plastic (G.R.P.) (Fig. 309) has revolutionized some aspects of furniture design and given rise

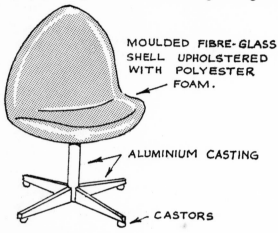

MOULDED FIBRE-GLASS SHELL UPHOLSTERED WITH POLYESTER FOAM.

ALUMINIUM CASTING

CASTORS

FIG. 309 THE "EGG" CHAIR

to completely new shapes in furniture. The strength and lightness ratio of G.R.P. shells is very great and coupled with the fact that they may be moulded to match the human form, give rise to most comfortable chairs which are also clean, hygienic and strong.

Upholstery. The traditional method of upholstering, using jute or canvas webbing and curly horsehair, has almost entirely disappeared today. This is partly due to the slow and laborious hand techniques required when using the traditional methods. The process of change has, however, been considerably accelerated by the invention and development of foams in rubber, polyester and polyether. These materials may be obtained in moulded or sheet form and the value of polyester and polyether is particularly great since they are chemically inert and retain their "spring". Foams with varying degrees of density or resilience may be obtained according to requirements for chair back or seat or cushion. Traditional upholsterer's webbing has been superseded by laminated rubber plies such as those made by Pirelli Ltd which, with special clips and holding devices, provide a far stronger and more durable way of suspending the upholstering medium.

CONVERSION FACTORS

To Convert	Into	Multiply by
Inches	Millimetres	25·4
Millimetres	Inches	·03937
Yards	Metres	·9144
Metres	Yards	1·0936
Miles	Kilometres	1·609
Kilometres	Miles	·621
Square Inches	Square Cm	6·45
Square Cm	Square Inches	·155
Square Yards	Square Metres	·836
Square Metres	Square Yards	1·196
Square Miles	Square Kilometres	2·59
Square Kilometres	Square Miles	·386
Cubic Inches	Cubic Centimetres	16·39
Cubic Centimetres	Cubic Inches	·061
Cubic Yards	Cubic Metres	·76
Cubic Metres	Cubic Yards	1·308
Oz (Avoir)	Grammes	28·35
Grammes	Oz (Avoir)	·0353
Lb (Avoir)	Kilogrammes	·4536
Kilogrammes	Lb (Avoir)	2·2046
Cwt	Kilogrammes	50·8
Kilogrammes	Cwt	·01968
Tons	Kilogrammes	1016·
Kilogrammes	Tons	·000984
Gallons	Litres	4·546
Litres	Gallons	·22
Tons per Square Inch	Kilogrammes per Square mm.	1·575
Kilogrammes per Square mm	Tons per Square Inch	·635
Square Metres	Acres	·000247
Acres	Square Metres	4046·9
Square Yards	Acres	·000206
Acres	Square Yards	4840·
Horse Power	Watts	746·
Watts	Horse Power	·00134
Gal of Water	Pounds	10·
Pounds of Water	Gallons	·1
Cubic Feet of Water	Gallons	6·23
Gal of Water	Cubic Feet	·16

Inches	Millimetres	Inches	Millimetres
$\frac{1}{64}$	·397	$2\frac{1}{2}$	63·500
$\frac{1}{32}$	·794	$2\frac{5}{8}$	66·675
$\frac{3}{64}$	1·191	$2\frac{3}{4}$	69·850
$\frac{1}{16}$	1·588	$2\frac{7}{8}$	73·025
$\frac{1}{8}$	3·175	3	76·200
$\frac{3}{16}$	4·762	$3\frac{1}{8}$	79·375
$\frac{1}{4}$	6·350	$3\frac{1}{4}$	82·550
$\frac{5}{16}$	7·938	$3\frac{3}{8}$	85·725
$\frac{3}{8}$	9·525	$3\frac{1}{2}$	88·900
$\frac{7}{16}$	11·112	$3\frac{5}{8}$	92·075
$\frac{1}{2}$	12·700	$3\frac{3}{4}$	95·250
$\frac{9}{16}$	14·288	$3\frac{7}{8}$	98·425
$\frac{5}{8}$	15·875	4	101·600
$\frac{11}{16}$	17·462	5	127·0
$\frac{3}{4}$	19·050	6	152·4
$\frac{13}{16}$	20·638	7	177·8
$\frac{7}{8}$	22·225	8	203·2
$\frac{15}{16}$	23·812	9	228·6
1	25·400	10	254·0
$1\frac{1}{8}$	28·575	11	279·4
$1\frac{1}{4}$	31·750	12	304·8
$1\frac{3}{8}$	34·925	13	330·2
$1\frac{1}{2}$	38·100	14	355·6
$1\frac{5}{8}$	41·275	15	381·0
$1\frac{3}{4}$	44·450	16	406·4
$1\frac{7}{8}$	47·625	17	431·8
2	50·800	18	457·2
$2\frac{1}{8}$	53·975	19	482·6
$2\frac{1}{4}$	57·150	20	508·0
$2\frac{3}{8}$	60·325	21	533·4

INDEX